D1047643

The Nature of Human Aggression

THE NATURE OF
HUMAN AGGRESSION

Ashley Montagu

Oxford University Press
Oxford London New York

OXFORD UNIVERSITY PRESS
Oxford   London   Glasgow
New York   Toronto   Melbourne   Wellington
Ibadan   Nairobi   Dar es Salaam   Cape Town
Kuala Lumpur   Singapore   Jakarta   Hong Kong   Tokyo
Delhi   Bombay   Calcutta   Madras   Karachi

Library of Congress Cataloging in Publication Data
Montagu, Ashley, 1905-
The nature of human aggression / Ashley Montagu.
New York : Oxford University Press, 1976.
ix, 381 p. : ill. ; 22 cm.
Includes bibliographical references and index.
ISBN 0-19-501822-2
ISBN 0-19-502373-0 pbk.

1. Aggressiveness (Psychology)   I. Title.
BF575.A3M62   155.2′32   75-32360
MARC

Printed in the United States of America

To the Memory of Hadley Cantril

Acknowledgments

The subject of the origin, development, and nature of human nature is a complicated and highly controversial one. Its study presents many difficulties and draws upon many disciplines. Political prejudices, private suppositions, and ideological commitments often play an important role in influencing the views that people will take of human nature and the differences between human beings. Hence, it is necessary for all of us who think and write, and those of us who read and think, on the subject to be aware of those biasing influences, and do all that we can to avoid the distorting effects of such partialities. The errors, let us always remember, we are called upon to chronicle and correct in others are only equaled by those we may commit ourselves. To help me in the task of keeping such errors to a minimum I have greatly benefited from the generosity of friends who have read critically either parts or the whole of the manuscript, and who have made many suggestions for its improvement. I am most grateful to each of them, and for their friendly services I thank Professor Richard D. Alexander of the Department of Zoology, University of Michigan, Mrs. José M. R. Delgado and Professor José M. R.

Delgado, formerly of the Neurobiological Laboratory, Yale University and now of the Universidad Autonoma Facultad de Medicina, Madrid; Professor Annette Ehrlich of the Department of Psychology, California State University, Los Angeles; Dr. Gilbert Gottlieb of the Psychology Laboratory, Dorothea Dix Hospital, Raleigh, North Carolina; Dr. Julian Jaynes, Department of Psychology, Princeton University; Dr. Paul D. MacLean, Chief of the Laboratory of Brain Evolution, National Institute of Mental Health, Bethesda, Maryland; Professor Floyd Matson of the Department of American Studies, University of Hawaii, Honolulu; Dr. Martin A. Nettleship, Humansville, Missouri; Dr. Michael Potegal, New York State Psychiatric Institute; Professor Phillip Tobias of the Medical School, University of the Witwatersrand; and Professor Elliot S. Valenstein of the Department of Psychology and Neuroscience, University of Michigan.

It should, of course, be added—in the time-honored but very necessary disclaimer—that I alone am responsible for the views expressed in this book, views with which those who read the manuscript may well disagree.

Finally, I should like to thank my friend Suzanne Fremon for her help with the manuscript, and my editor at the Oxford University Press, Mr. William Halpin, for his general benevolence. I am also grateful to Dr. Philip Gordon for reading the galleys, and to Charmion Semple for making the index and picking up some errors that had escaped everyone else.

To Ms. Jean Williams and Ms. Louise Schaeffer of the Biology Library at Princeton University I owe a special debt of gratitude for their bibliographic assistance.

Princeton, New Jersey   Ashley Montagu
September 1975

Contents

"The fateful question [of] the human species seems to me to be whether and to what extent the cultural process developed in it will succeed in mastering the derangements of communal life caused by . . . aggression and self-destruction. In this connection, perhaps, the phase through which we are at this moment passing deserves special interest. Men have brought their powers of subduing the forces of nature to such a pitch that by using them they could now very easily exterminate one another to the last man. They know this—hence arises a great part of their current unrest, their dejection, their mood of apprehension."

Sigmund Freud, *Civilization and Its Discontents,* 1930

"Know then thyself, presume not God to scan,
The proper study of mankind is man.
Placed on this isthmus of a middle state,
A being darkly wise, and rudely great:
With too much knowledge for the sceptic side,
With too much weakness for the stoic's pride,
He hangs between; in doubt to act or rest;
In doubt to deem himself a god, or beast;
In doubt his mind or body to prefer;
Born but to die, and reas'ning but to err;
Alike in ignorance, his reason such,
Whether he thinks too little or too much;
Chaos of thought and passion, all confused;
Still by himself abused, or disabused;
Created half to rise, and half to fall;
Great lord of all things, yet a prey to all;
Sole judge of truth, in endless error hurled;
The glory, jest, and riddle of the world!"

Alexander Pope, *An Essay on Man,* Epistle ii, 1. I

The Nature of Human Aggression

1
A Controversy

Purpose of This Book

A major purpose of this book is to examine in detail the facts and the arguments, and in the end to refute the conclusions, presented to an enormous public in recent years by a group of popular writers who state that human beings are inescapably killers—that because of their animal heritage, they are genetically and instinctively aggressive, and cannot be otherwise.

A further purpose of this book is to provide and support an alternative view of aggression. It is not enough, in a matter as important as this, simply to say, "They are wrong," or even to point out in detail the mistakes, the misinterpretations, the prejudices, and the carelessness with facts and language that combine in these works to produce the final fallacy. It is also essential to present and to give evidence for the different view:

that no specific human behavior is genetically determined;

that human beings are capable of any kind of behavior, including aggressive behavior, and also including kindness, cruelty, sensitiveness, selfishness, nobility,
cowardice, playfulness; aggressive behavior is but one
in a long list, and any explanation of human behavior
must explain all behavior, not just one kind;

and that the kind of behavior a human being displays
in any circumstance is determined not by his genes,
although of course there is some genetic contribution,
but largely by the experience he has undergone during
his life in interaction with those genes.

This is the view of human nature and human aggression
that will be set forth in this book, and supported by the
necessary evidence. It has two advantages over the proposition that Man Is a Killer: it is more rational, and it more
nearly fits the facts as we know them.

Observing the evidences of aggression all about us, not
alone in others but also in ourselves, the readiest explanation at hand is that we are born that way. The popularity of
the writings of those who tell us that man is instinctively
aggressive, that he inherits his aggressivity from his prehistoric and animal ancestors, derives from the fact that most of
us want an authoritative explanation of man's "beastliness"
that enables us to relate it to ourselves and to the behavior
of others. There could hardly be a better reason for seeking
such an explanation. However, in a matter as complex as
this, truth is not advanced when only one interpretation of
the evidence is presented. The reader has a right to alternative points of view, for only in this way will he be able to
evaluate the often conflicting interpretations. Contrary to
the conventional wisdom, facts do not speak for themselves,
but are at the mercy of whoever chooses to juggle them. The
reader will come to this book wanting to know how he can

best interpret the facts relating to the origin and nature of human aggression. This book is designed to assist the reader toward that end. It is, indeed, on the basis of the facts that have become available in recent years that the critique of the view of the "innate aggressionists" has been mounted—a critique, it so happens, which leads to a rather more constructive and optimistic view of man's possibilities than those envisaged by the innate killer view of the human species.

No one can question the need to understand the aggressiveness in human beings. Among all the problems of twentieth-century humankind, this is surely one of the most urgent. And it weighs more heavily on our spirits than others, because we know that unless we learn to understand and to cope with our aggressiveness, we may not be here long enough to solve the rest.

War comes first to mind when we think about violence. As institutionalized, rationalized, state-sanctioned horror, war is the ultimate large-scale violence. It is always with us, somewhere among the human family, bringing untimely death, separation, pain, suffering, and grief, depleting our resources, and ravaging our planet.

Even during times of official peace, violence surrounds us: students are shot at and killed by uniformed guardians of the peace; policemen are killed by armed robbers; construction workers and peace marchers battle in the streets; political leaders are assassinated; men and women working for their civil rights are beaten and killed; city dwellers riot and burn their own cities; terrorists kill for political causes; murderers and rapists walk the dark streets; prison guards abuse their charges; and even inside the walls of family dwellings, battered children die of unexplained injuries.

Assault by human beings on their fellows is nothing new,

of course. We have records attesting to violence between people that are as old as any records on earth. One of the earliest acts in one of our major mythologies is the murder of a brother. Age by age, century by century, down to the current version in this morning's newspaper, human achievement has almost always been accompanied by human violence.

Then why bother to ask "why?" We have survived thus far, we may tell ourselves. In fact, better than that: we have come a long distance as a species. Can we not simply continue as before, living out our own lives and protecting ourselves individually as best we can? Why bother?

There are two reasons. One is that as a species we want to understand. One of the qualities of human beings in general is our urge to understand—call it curiosity, or an inquiring mind, or a thirst for knowledge, or whatever—combined with a willingness to go to considerable trouble to understand even when it is not yet clear how understanding will be of any practical use. People climb Mt. Everest, we are told, "because it's there." Other people study microbiology because it provides an interesting view of life. Others build engines to perform unnecessary functions because they want to see if it can be done.

The other reason for trying to understand our aggressiveness is that the time has come when we must. Finally, after some five or six million years of human existence on this planet, human violence threatens to take the reins from human cooperativeness and inventiveness and to drive us into extinction. Until now, we have balanced out fairly well as a species, and in fact we have continued to grow and develop. But now, with our human ingenuity working full blast, we have devised ways to wipe out ourselves with a speed and a thoroughness unknown to us before. If we want this pleasant planet to be inhabited by any of our descendants, we have no choice but to arrive at some better under-standing of our natures. Or at least to keep on trying.

There is no lack of trying, of course. Solutions to our problems have always rained down upon us as thickly as the problems themselves. In thousands of books, in lectures, on film, on television, in social conversations, in magazines and newspapers, we examine ourselves endlessly for clues. And we come to many different conclusions.

Some deplore our flight from God, and preach to the rest that faith will bring peace to each of us and to the world. Others see violence as an expression of individual psycho-logical inadequacies. Still others blame it on the growth of permissiveness, the decline of classical education, the im-position of the graduated income tax, the breakdown of class distinctions, the inequities of the social system, and so on and on and on.

Some, whose ideas and conclusions are to be examined and refuted in this book, have informed us that aggressive-ness is an instinct that we have inherited from our remote prehuman ancestors. It is deeply embedded in our genes and it is therefore, they say, ineradicable. Humans are violent creatures in their most fundamental nature. They are nat-urally killers.

These writers also tell us that it was through the inven-tion of weapons—tools for killing—that pre-human creatures became human. Weapons and humanity are thus in their accounts inseparably linked from the beginnings of both.

They tell us, too, that humankind's aggressiveness is pow-ered by a spontaneous force, a kind of energy that builds up inexorably within each of us and that must be periodically discharged.

They tell us that along with being aggressive we are also territorial, characterized by an instinct of territorial defense, inherited from our animal ancestors, and stronger and more

compelling than sex as a motivating force. Hence: war between nations, *West Side Story* gang battles, and individual
cruelties and murders.

This book takes up these points one by one, and examines
them.

The people who write these books take their evidence
from the science of animal behavior, called ethology, and
some of the writers are among the world's foremost ethologists. In many cases, their studies are careful and detailed
and constitute major additions to our knowledge of the way
their subjects behave. For the most part there is no quarrel
with the quality of that work, or with its importance. There
is strong disagreement, however, with the easy analogies
these writers have made between genes and the behavior of
fish on the one hand, and human beings on the other.

The most important writers who have taken this position
of innate aggressiveness during the past decade have been
Konrad Lorenz, Robert Ardrey, Raymond Dart, Desmond
Morris, Anthony Storr, and Niko Tinbergen. Their books,
addressed to the general public—as distinct from books writ-
ten by some of them for fellow scientists—are well known:
Lorenz's *On Aggression;* Ardrey's *African Genesis, The
Territorial Imperative,* and *The Social Contract;* Dart's *Ad-
ventures with the Missing Link* and other writings; Morris's
The Naked Ape and *The Human Zoo;* and Storr's *Human
Aggression* and *Human Destructiveness;* finally, there is
Tinbergen's Oxford Inaugural Address, "On War and Peace
in Animals and Man."

Opposing Viewpoints

Another view of human nature and human aggression—what
might be called the opposite view—and the one that is described here, reads the evidence very differently from the

writers of all these popular works. While not in the least denying a genetic component to human aggression or that prehistoric humans were capable of aggression, it will be shown in the following pages that both the genetic determinance of aggression and its prehistoric practice have been greatly exaggerated, that human beings have lived rather more altruistically and peaceably over the greater part of their evolutionary history than these writers would have us believe. Even now, when large-scale violence threatens to put an end to our world, most humans in fact are not violent at all, and there are whole societies on earth at this moment in which violence is minimal or nonexistent.

This observation supports the contention—the recognition —that human beings are capable of the full range of behavior, and that they are no more certain to kill than to succor. We know they do both. The challenge for us as a society, then, is not so much to find a single, simplified explanation of why a man kills another man, but why, under similar provocations, one man kills, another succors, and another passes by on the other side of the street. It is the contention of this book that the explanation lies not in supposed human instincts, which would tend to drive all men and women always in one direction, but principally in the experiences of their entire lives, which vary widely from one person to another.

This is not for a moment to deny that there is a genetic contribution to almost every form of behavior. But it is to deny that specific behavior in human beings is determined genetically. Potentialities are genetic in origin. A talent for music, for example, seems to be inherited. The ability to play the piano, a specific form of human behavior, is not; it is learned. It is often difficult, of course, to separate the two strands; sometimes, in our present state of knowledge, it is impossible. But that should not blind us to the fact that two strands are present. A musical child in a musical family has an excellent statistical chance of growing up to be an accomplished musician. But how much of that musical behavior is due to the talent for music inherited from two musical parents, how much comes from a family attitude that "music provides the only reasonable basis for life," how much from a desire to excel among people who believe in excellence, and how much to entirely other causes—a temperamental quality, a desire to please a parent—is impossible to say. What is certain in this situation is that no amount of inherited musical talent will make a musician unless it is combined with many years of several different kinds of experiences. And in this situation as in most others where the two factors are mixed, the cultural factor is clearly more important than the genetic. That is, the inheritance provides only the potentiality; it is the decades of daily experiences that determine the specific outcome. We will see evidence later that aggressiveness or aggressive behavior, like piano playing, is largely a result of approval and active help, and that peaceful behavior, too, comes about because it is rewarded. In the end it comes down to which kind of behavior is the more highly valued.

As in individuals, so in societies. Cultures differ from each other—Eskimos from suburban Americans, for example—not because of different genes but because of differences in social histories. The Eskimo culture is a comparatively peaceful culture, characterized by friendliness and mutual aid, as of course it must be to survive in the rigorous climate of the Arctic Circle. Our own culture is warlike, characterized by profound belief in the development of the individual and by intense competition between individuals, groups, and nations. But all of us, Eskimos and Americans, are human beings, members of the same species, and as such subject to whatever drives are common to our species. It seems clear that the differences between the two groups, which are profound and important, cannot possibly be explained by an appeal to determinate innate mechanisms, but must be the result of the differences between the values of the two cultures.

These two opposing views of human aggression—that aggressive behavior is innate, and that making every allowance for genetic influences it is largely learned—constitutes more than an academic debate carried on in polite language in the pages of a scientific journal. And they are certainly more than a faddy question to be gummed into obscurity on television talk shows. The subject is neither a dry-as-dust science nor a popularity contest. The two views define not only two ways of looking at human beings—important enough in itself—but also two ways of being human. And that has implications for us as individuals, as societies, and as survivors.

The solutions to all our problems depend on which view we finally settle on. If human beings are inescapably murderous, our solutions should accommodate our killer tendencies; on the other hand, if human behavior is largely learned, our solutions should be based on this capability.

In detail, the differences show themselves in attitudes and practices in schools, in family life, in courts of law, in prisons, in social services of all kinds, in efforts to cope with population vs. resources, in national arms races, in every area of human endeavor. If we are killers by nature, we are wasting precious time, with the minute hand approaching midnight, in teaching people to think independently, in rehabilitating criminals, in compensating people for unlucky beginnings, in trying to improve the physical and mental health of all human beings. We should instead be devising ways of discharging our aggressive drives—Lorenz suggests sports as a good way—and at the same time building up our individual defenses against the inevitable holocaust.

The Limitations of Our Knowledge

The fact is that we do not know, scientifically and unquestionably in detail, why human beings behave as they do. Some people—Lorenz and Ardrey among them—claim to know, and these people, of course, speak with the loudest voices. The rest of us recognize that until much more work has been done, we cannot know the causes of human aggression in the sense that we know, for example, the cause of malaria. We are at about the same point in the study of human violence that we are in the study of the common cold or that we were in 1899 in the study of the atom.

In the meantime, we know a few things about it. The major fact we know is that the subject is too complex—as perhaps the study of the common cold is too complex—to treat as a single phenomenon. What precisely do we mean by "aggression" and "aggressive behavior"? It is easy enough to lump together a great many human actions under the general heading of "aggression," but in fact, in order to study and to understand this kind of human behavior, it is necessary to do quite the opposite: to try to separate the different threads that make up the behavior that we conveniently call aggressive. When we do that, we find ourselves pausing in some unexpected places, and being forced to think again, from the beginning, about some aspects of human activities.

War, for example: on a personal level, how aggressive is a modern warrior, anyway? Think of a pilot, flying 30,000 feet up over enemy territory toward an unknown destination where the plane will drop its bombs: is this man exhibiting aggressive behavior? He is deliberately planning to harm, perhaps kill, other human beings; yet his feelings fail to match his actions. He is not filled with a hatred to match the destruction his bombs will wreak. And the infantryman in the jungles of Southeast Asia, who claimed when asked that he didn't really know why he was there: is this aggressiveness? Perhaps, perhaps not, but his bullets are just as lethal as though he were firing them in the heat of anger. Perhaps the official hostility of the government that sent him there toward the hapless and helpless victims somehow covers the agents of that government.

This is not to claim that war, even modern depersonalized war, is a peaceable pursuit. But it is to call attention to the complexity of the subject, and to suggest that before we talk about what causes aggression we should know what it is we are discussing. We may find, after we think about it, that "aggressive behavior" includes some actions we had not included previously, and excludes some we had automatically placed in that category.

Erich Fromm, in his book *The Anatomy of Human Destructiveness,* recognizes two types of aggression. One, he describes as biologically adaptive and life-serving, and it is this kind of aggression, he claims, that is phylogenetically programmed and is common to animals and humans. An example of this, according to Fromm, is the impulse to attack or flee when vital interests are threatened. The other type, malignant aggression, i.e., destructiveness and cruelty, is biologically nonadaptive and malignant. This type of aggression is seen most notably in the behavior of such men as Hitler, Goebbels, Himmler, and others like them, and it is common only to humans, and arises out of the conditions of human existence.

As we shall see, the facts do not support such a theory of aggression. There are many forms of aggression, and these are briefly described in what follows.

Forms of Aggression

In animals a variety of forms of aggression have been recognized. Each form of aggression is classified on the basis of the stimulus situation that will evoke it.

1. *Predatory aggression:* Evoked by the presence of a natural object of prey.
2. *Antipredatory aggression:* Evoked by the presence of a predator.
3. *Territorial aggression:* Defense of an area against an intruder.
4. *Dominance aggression:* Evoked by a challenge to the animal's rank or desire for an object.
5. *Maternal aggression:* Evoked by the proximity of some threatening agent to the young of the particular female.
6. *Weaning aggression:* Evoked by the increased independence of the young, when the parents will threaten or even gently attack their offspring.
7. *Parental disciplinary aggression:* Evoked by a variety of stimuli such as unwelcome suckling, rough or overextended play, wandering, and the like.
8. *Sexual aggression:* Evoked by females for the purpose of mating or the establishment of a prolonged union.
9. *Sex-related aggression:* Evoked by the same stimuli which produce sexual behavior.
10. *Inter-male aggression:* Evoked by the presence of a male competitor of the same species.
11. *Fear-induced aggression:* Evoked by confinement or cornering and inability to escape or the presence of some threatening agent.

12. *Irritable aggression:* Evoked by the presence of any attack-able organism or object.

13. *Instrumental aggression:* Any changes in the environment as a consequence of the above types of aggression which increases the probability that aggressive behavior will occur in similar situations.

As Professor Kenneth E. Moyer, upon whose classification of aggression the listing above is in part based, emphasizes, these types of aggression are not mutually exclusive. His position, however, is that there are different neural and en-docrine bases for each of them. Obviously, not all these forms apply equally to humans and to nonhuman animals. But it is worth contemplating this work with animals in order to make clearer to ourselves the basic fact that to speak of "aggressive behavior" as if it were a single phenomenon is to be guilty of a misleading oversimplification.

"There is no single kind of behavior which can be called aggressive," writes Roger N. Johnson, professor of zoology at Ramapo College, in his book *Aggression in Man and Animals,* "nor is there any single process which represents 'aggression.' Perhaps this is the most important thing that can be said about defining aggression, for it suggests that aggression may be understood and analysed at many levels."

Heredity and Environment

Another fact we know is this: human behavioral traits are not determined exclusively by heredity or exclusively by environment. The concept of either/or, nature/nurture is a fallacy, and it has been responsible for more misleading statements in this area than any other, including the statements of Lorenz and Ardrey as they apply to human beings. The fact is that the development of virtually every human behavioral trait is the result of the interaction between genetic and environmental factors. Not only does this apply to our musician, combining his inherited talent, his personality traits, and the influences of his parents, teachers, friends, critics, and audiences to make him or her a performer; the same fact applies to all the rest of us, too, who combine all these factors, and perhaps others, in all our behavior.

There are, obviously, some *physical* traits in human beings that are not quite as amenable to the influences of the environment: these are, for example, basic color of skin and hair, hair form, nose shape, control of respiration, auditory and visual acuity, and the like.

Genes also determine the potential limits of the development of any trait in any given environment. Size, longevity, intelligence, and constitutional strength are examples of this kind of limitation set by genes. It is not likely, for instance, that a child of two long lines of forebears all under five and a half feet tall would grow to be over six and a half feet. But here we are faced with still another consideration: perhaps those forebears were five and a half feet tall not because of their own genetic makeup but because of malnutrition. What then? If a pregnant woman in this family were to be given a nutritious diet from the very beginning of her pregnancy, and her child were given nutritious food throughout childhood and adolescence, it might easily grow to be within an inch or two of six feet. We have seen something like this happen with whole generations of Americans who because of improved nutrition and child care have grown appreciably taller in each generation than their parents. In short, even in connection with such a strictly physical attribute as height, the genes for which are clearly inherited, we cannot know in any individual case what is genetically and what environmentally determined.

This is also true for intelligence. Theoretically, any individual inherits his basic intellectual capacity. That is, his genes determine the outside limits of the development of his intellect in any given environment. But we cannot know what these limits are. In fact, many students of child development have concluded that since it is impossible to determine what the limits are in most individuals the only practical course is to work through the environment, and to proceed as if in most cases of failure to learn, the block is not so much innate ability as the effect on the person of previous experiences of all kinds.

The simplest example of this, one familiar to most people, is the widespread conviction that "I can't do mathematics," "I never could learn French," or "Mechanics is beyond me," or "I can't understand all that stuff." These inabilities to learn are almost never the result of intellectual deficiency; they are demonstrably the result of many other forces, all of them environmental. Poor teaching, lack of interest, the assumption by society that girls are not good at math, or that mechanics is somehow demeaning, or that intellectual endeavor of any kind is suspect: these are a few of the many factors that bear on learning. The least likely explanation of any failure to learn is that the person is innately incapable.

Another example, with much broader social implications, is the question that revolves around "intelligence" testing in schools, and the conclusions to which some people come that black students are less "intelligent" than white students, and that therefore there are basic "racial" differences in intelligence. This is such a complex question, involving as it does the definition of intelligence, an evaluation of the tests that purport to measure intelligence, and the weight placed by different people on the different contributing factors, that the whole matter requires more extended treatment than it has been possible to give in this book. It is relevant here be-

cause these tests provide strong evidence of a direct reflection of social and cultural factors, and it has been shown
that individual scores can be raised by improved environment. Again we see that failure to learn is more likely to be
cultural than genetic.

Even people who are mentally retarded or who suffer
other kinds of brain damage are often the victims not of
deficient inheritance but of forces originating outside themselves that have acted on their brain cells. This kind of damage occurs frequently during the prenatal period. A pregnant woman whose nutrition is inadequate runs a serious
risk of damaging the brain cells of her child; its intellectual
capacity may well be less than it might have been had she
supplied its developing brain with sufficient nourishment.
We all know that a shutting-off of oxygen to the brain of an
adult for a brief period will cause irreversible brain damage;
to the brain of the developing fetus the process is identical,
and since the oxygen is carried to the cells through the
bloodstream of the child's mother, the oxygen content of her
blood is the crucial factor. If she is a heavy smoker, for example, or if she takes drugs of any kind, the oxygen content
will be lowered and the child's development will be affected.

The other side of this coin has been observed, too, by
countless teachers and child-care workers, including parents:
given a favorable environment, any child's intelligence,
measured by any yardstick, will increase. It is this observation that keeps good teachers coming back year after year.

All this adds up to a single point: genes never exist in a
vacuum; they exist always in an environment of some kind.
Even at the moment of conception, when chromosomes
come together and combine all the genetic material a person
will ever have, the ovum, fertilized that instant, is resting in
a specific organ within the body of a specific human being
who is herself the result of years of environmental influ-

ences. She is well nourished or she is poorly nourished. Her
organs are well formed and well functioning and adequate
to the job, or they are not. Her blood contains enough oxygen for the proper development of the fetus, or it does not,
or sometimes the blood is properly oxygenated in the individual development of the fetus and at other times not.
We know from volumes of studies of hundreds of thousands
of human beings that the prenatal environment constitutes
an influential factor in an individual's general physical
health and mental capacity. No matter what the genetic
endowment, our condition is *always* affected one way or another, for the better or for the worse, by the quality of our
experiences before birth.

And this is just the beginning. Through birth itself and
into independent life, a human being's whole response to
the world is largely determined by experience. And not only
physical and mental responses, but personality traits, behavior, and attitudes, are the result much more of environmental factors than of inheritance.

Where the line between them lies, we do not know: and
that is perhaps the most tantalizing aspect of all. What precisely *was* the genetic contribution of those short parents to
their son's height? That is a difficult enough question to answer, but it deals with straightforward matters—mostly gro-
ceries, nutrition. Other aspects of a person are more difficult
to localize. "He has his father's charm," we say. He did inherit his father's eyes, and the muscles of the face that produce the attractive smile are much like his father's. But the
manner? The manner is really what we mean when we speak
of charm, and the boy's charming manner came from many
sources: watching his father and imitating him; seeing the
effect of his father's manner on other people; seeing the effect of other kinds of manner on other people; seeing the
effect of his own manner on people; chance remarks over-

heard; how much he cares what other people think of him, which in turn comes from another whole set of experiences. We do know this much: if someone had smacked him, or laughed at him, the first few times he tried his father's "charm," the chances are excellent that no one would ever say "He has his father's charm." That so-called inherited quality would never have appeared again.

This same principle applies to any kind of behavior, of course, including aggressive behavior. Many students and observers of children have concluded that aggressive behavior is learned. That is, a child whose aggressive behavior is rewarded—by winning, for example, or by approval from adults, or by enhanced status of any kind—is likely to be a more aggressive child than one whose aggressive behavior is discouraged by constant losing or by disapproval.

The familial transmission of aggression or nonaggression has been the subject of many studies. Thus, Drs. Sheldon and Eleanor Glueck of Harvard University found that the incidence of aggressive behavior in the home was much higher for delinquent than for nondelinquent boys. Drs. Silver, Dublin, and Lourie, in their longitudinal study of child abuse over three generations, found that children who were abused by their parents tended to become abusers of their own children.

Most aggressive children in slum districts usually learn their aggressive behavior from their peers in the streets and from extrafamilial sources. In middle-class families, Bandura, and Bandura and Walters, found that one or both parents of aggressive boys encouraged their sons to be aggressive toward peers, teachers, and other adults outside the family. Nonaggressive boys came from families in which the parents encouraged their sons to be firm in defending their principles, but deprecated physical aggression as a means of settling disputes. Again, children often draw on parental aggression toward themselves as the model for their own behavior toward others. Hoffman found that mothers who employed verbal and physical aggression to enforce their children's compliance with their demands, most frequently produced children who used similar aggressive behavior toward their peers.

Where aggressive behavior is strongly discouraged, as among the Hutterites and the Amish, the Hopi and Zuñi Indians, it is practically unknown.

Whether we study aggression within our own society, in its different social classes, ethnic and religious groups, or cross-culturally in different societies, the story is everywhere the same: aggressive and nonaggressive behavior are mainly learned.

This hardly comes as a surprise. It bears out what anyone with any experience with human beings would guess about human behavior. And it certainly bears out what common sense would dictate. But guessing and citing common sense are not the same thing as finding out, and the many scientific studies that have been made on the subject of aggression in children give unequivocal support to the contention that whatever aggression exists within children's natures, overt aggressive behavior is mainly if not entirely learned.

In other words, that while there may exist substrates in the brain which may be activated to function in aggressive behavior, the major part if not all of human aggression is learned, much of that learning being achieved in interaction with whatever genetic potentials for aggression may exist.

It begins to be clear, then, that the subject of human violence, its causes and cures, is by its nature extremely complex, and any simple answer is automatically suspect. Much of the rest of this book is devoted to an examination of the oversimplifications and false analogies on which the innate aggressionists base their contentions, and to the presentation of a more synthetic and considerably more interesting and scientifically valid alternative.

But first, in order to lay the groundwork for an understanding of the whole controversy, it may be useful to try to understand the reasons for the wide support of the idea of innate aggression, in spite of scientific evidence and much general knowledge to the contrary, and the consequences, past, present, and future, of such support. It is not the first time in recent history that popular acclaim has been given to a misinterpretation of valid scientific ideas, and we would do well to think back to that development before we repeat it in all its disastrous details.

2
Man as a Killer: An Acceptable Idea

The Congenial Idea

On a subject as complex and as little understood as the causes of human violence, we may expect people to believe not the few facts that are available to scholars, because most people do not even know what those facts are, but whatever proposition happens to fit best with what they already believe.

Consider: once upon a time all right-minded people believed that all matter was made up of four basic elements—earth, fire, air, water—and that nothing more basic than this existed. This was an entirely satisfactory explanation of things: it was enunciated by respected authorities and accepted by leaders in other areas of life; it was simple; it corresponded with what a person could see around him, and it seemed to account for everything, more or less, in his own rather limited world.

Thus it is not surprising that many people accept as truth today the statement that human violence is a built-in human quality, and that man kills his fellow man because of his inheritance from his killer ancestors. This, too, has been enunciated by authorities with reputations and honor, and supported by other articulate people. It is simple; it corresponds with what we can see around us, and it accounts for much that disturbs us deeply in our own world. Most important of all, the concept of Man as Killer fits in with what we already believe, and have believed for many centuries.

The Authorities

First, the scholars with reputations and honors: the scientists and the writers who have brought us the message that we are incurably violent are able, imaginative workers, without exception. Two of them are Nobel laureates. One is a first-class science writer. All are serious in their pursuit of an explanation of human aggression.

Konrad Lorenz, perhaps the best-known member of the group, is one of the founders of the modern science of animal behavior, ethology. Until recently director of the Department of Behavior Physiology at the Max Planck Institute in Bavaria, in 1973 he shared the Nobel Prize with Niko Tinbergen, professor of animal behavior at the University of Oxford, for their work in ethology. Lorenz has studied with meticulous care the behavior of birds and especially geese, and has reported on his observations in detail. In his own field, he is clearly a world figure.

When he leaves his own world of nonhuman animals and addresses the even more complex subject of human behavior, in which he is not, in fact, an expert at all, Lorenz writes with the same certainty, clarity, and persuasiveness. "There is evidence," he states, "that the first inventors of pebble tools, the African Australopithecines, promptly used their new weapon to kill not only game but fellow members of their species as well." When he says this, his readers, of course, believe him. They do not know—how could they know?—that the evidence to which he refers is open to considerable question.

Robert Ardrey, a playwright turned science writer, is the most widely read of the group, partly because of his layman's enthusiasm for the subject of animal behavior, and partly because he can express this enthusiasm in lively, persuasive language. He reports engagingly on his personal observations, his own discoveries, and his delighted involvement in the world of science. He is an excellent writer and an interesting man.

Raymond Dart, emeritus professor of anatomy at the University of Witwatersrand, Johannesburg, South Africa, is Ardrey's acknowledged source of inspiration. In an article entitled "The Predatory Transition from Ape to Man," published in 1953, Dart argued that our animal ancestors were carnivorous, predatory, and cannibalistic. "The blood-bespattered, slaughter-gutted archives of human history," he wrote, "from the earliest Egyptian and Sumerian records to the most recent atrocities of the Second World War, accord with early universal cannibalism, with animal and human sacrificial practices or their substitutes in formalized religions, and with the world-wide scalping, head-hunting, body-mutilating and necrophiliac practices of mankind in proclaiming this common bloodlust differentiator, this predacious habit, this mark of Cain that separates man dietetically from his anthropoidal relatives and allies him rather with the deadliest of Carnivora."

When Ardrey popularized Dart's work, incidentally, he was able to express these ideas more simply: "The human being in the most fundamental aspects of his soul and body is nature's last if temporary word on the subject of the armed predator," he wrote. "And human history must be read in those terms." Elsewhere, Ardrey expressed Dart's beliefs as "the simple thesis that Man had emerged from the anthropoid background for one reason only: because he was a killer."

But Raymond Dart, for all his purple prose, was and is a scientist, the man who, in 1924, first described the newly discovered *Australopithecus africanus,* the humanlike primate of the high African veldt. It was this discovery, and the developments stemming from it, that established the origin of the earliest humanlike creatures in Africa rather than in Asia, a discovery of major importance. Therefore, when Dart talks about "bloodlust" the general reader may blink and wonder how Professor Dart knows about *that,* but on the whole the general reader tends to believe the "expert." An expert in one subject is likely to be believed when dealing with another.

Desmond Morris, a gifted ethologist, is another widely read writer whose books *The Naked Ape* and *The Human Zoo* also support the notion of innate human aggression, as do the writings of his teacher, Niko Tinbergen. Anthony Storr, a psychiatrist, lends the weight of his medical authority to the idea of innate aggression in man. But among anthropologists Lionel Tiger and Robin Fox stand virtually alone in support of the doctrine of innate aggression.

Other scholars and well-known names back this group of scientists and writers. Margaret Mead, the noted social anthropologist, discusses Lorenz's ideas on aggression with complete approval. Roger Masters, who teaches political science at Yale, hoped that Ardrey's *Territorial Imperative* would be widely read, "especially in Washington, D.C." The late Marston Bates, professor of zoology at the University of Michigan, wrote that Lorenz's views as expressed in *On Aggression* had left him completely convinced of their truth "for man as for animals." Sherwood L. Washburn and David A. Hamburg, the former professor of anthropology at the University of California at Berkeley, and the latter professor of psychiatry at Stanford University, declare themselves "in general agreement" with Lorenz's views. Dr. Howard E. Evans, professor of zoology at Colorado State University, highly approves of Lorenz's and Ardrey's views, and concludes that "if man is basically aggressive then the continued mouthing of platitudes about brotherly love is clearly no solution."

The Arts

These commentators are all respected authorities in their fields, and their views are accorded the attention they deserve in the scientific community. It is small wonder that their opinions, even outside their areas of specialization, also carry conviction among laymen.

The idea of Man-as-Killer has found support, too, among novelists and film makers, people whose appeal is emotional rather than rational, and who are therefore considerably more influential than the scholars. William Golding's novel *Lord of the Flies,* a brilliant and terrifying story, has been read by countless young people on college campuses and in high school English classes. It concerns a group of English schoolboys cast away on a small island, and their struggle for leadership. Ralph, Piggy, and Simon, representing order, intelligence, and religion, are persecuted and crushed by the mob led by Jack, representing sadism, superstition, and lust for power. It is a strong and deeply depressing book. Golding has been quoted as saying that his purpose in writing it was "to trace the defects of society back to the defects of human nature." Whatever his purpose, his effect has been to persuade many thousands of students that human beings are intrinsically evil.

Golding is no scientist, and so he may perhaps be excused for not realizing that such behavior may be an expression not so much of human nature as of the background and education of the small group with which he is familiar, namely, British schoolboys. Not all children under similar circumstances behave as his fictional characters did. A similar episode, with quite another outcome, is reported to have occurred some years ago in Melanesia. I give it here for what it may be considered to be worth.

In 1967 Dr. Alphonse van Schoote, a Belgian physician, while traveling among the islands, learned of a Melanesian group, perhaps an extended family, that had embarked upon what was evidently a routine voyage between islands. At some point they deposited six or seven children, ranging in age from two to twelve, on an atoll, planning to return shortly to pick them up, but a storm ensued which kept them away, not briefly but for some months. When the children were finally "rescued," it turned out that they had got along famously: they knew how to dig for water, evidently copious underground in the form of brackish water wells; they lived mainly on fish; they had no difficulty fashioning shelters, and in general they flourished, without any fighting or falling out or issues of leadership.

This account was given Mr. Bob Krauss, of the *Honolulu Advertiser,* by Dr. van Schoote when he was on a journalistic assignment in the Pacific. It points to the relativity of human nature rather than to its fixity. Native children readily adapt to the kind of situation in which these children found themselves; such conditions scarcely pose a challenge. One can, however, *imagine* English schoolboys, rendered "nasty" by traditions of infant depravity and the virtues of caning, making a sordid mess of such a situation. But it is *imagination,* of course, bred on Dickens and the exploits of Dr. Arnold of Rugby and all that, which makes it *obvious* that such wicked creatures should devour each other. "Boys!"

said Mr. Jagger on meeting Pip. "I've seen a good many boys in my time, and I find them a bad lot!"

It is much more likely that conditioning rather than "the defects of human nature" were responsible for the anarchy among Golding's boys. Unfortunately, not many people have heard about those Melanesian children.

Anthony Burgess's novel *A Clockwork Orange* is another book in this genre, made into a chillingly violent—and popular—movie by Stanley Kubrick, celebrating rape, violence, sexual sadism, brutality, and "the eternal savagery of man." Mr. Kubrick said, in an interview, "I'm interested in the brutal and violent nature of man because it's a true picture of him." On another occasion Kubrick wrote, "I am convinced it is more optimistic to accept Ardrey's view that we are born risen apes, not fallen angels, and the apes were armed killers besides." Later he said, "Man isn't a noble savage; he's an ignoble savage. He is irrational, brutal, weak, silly, unable to be objective about anything where his own interests are involved—that about sums it up. . . . Any attempt to create social institutions on a false view of the nature of man is probably doomed to failure."

The star of *A Clockwork Orange*, Malcolm McDowell, agreed with his director. In a letter to the *New York Times,* McDowell wrote: "People are basically bad, corrupt. I always sense that man has not progressed one inch, morally, since the Greeks. Liberals, they hate *Clockwork* because they're dreamers, and it shows them the realities, shows 'em not tomorrow but *now. Cringe,* don't they, when faced with the bloody truth."

Another film director who subscribes enthusiastically to Ardrey's view of Man-as-Killer is Sam Peckinpah, director of *The Wild Bunch* and *Straw Dogs.* This latter movie revels in multiple killing by a variety of hideous methods, double rape, and other refinements of calculated violence. "The myth of the noble savage is bull," declared Peckinpah as he handed out copies of Ardrey's books. "People are born to survive. They have instincts that go back millions of years. Unfortunately some of these instincts are based on violence in every human being. If it is not channeled and understood, it will break out in war or in madness." Mr. Peckinpah, one of the more talented of American film directors, is no scientist, and so perhaps he, too, like William Golding—and like Stanley Kubrick and Malcolm McDowell, for that matter—cannot be expected to weigh the evidence critically, or to recognize the lack of it, in the books he admires so much. And when he states, inaccurately, that all men are violent, or that men are "just a few steps up from the apes in the evolutionary scale," people believe him, and why not? They admire his movie-making, and they, like him, have only the sketchiest understanding of what constitutes valid scientific evidence, and they, like most of us, tend to confuse their own personal opinions with solid fact. It is a common failing to mistake our prejudices for the laws of nature.

These novelists and dramatists provide us, incidentally, with an example of another phenomenon common enough when we discuss a subject no one knows much about, and one that all serious searchers after truth need to guard themselves against constantly, the tendency to circular thinking: One starts with a conviction; one proceeds to illustrate that conviction in dramatic terms; the illustration is then taken as proof of the original conviction. William Golding, for instance, "in tracing the defects of society back to the defects of human nature," was really not "tracing" anything. He was clearly beginning with his conviction that both society and human nature are filled to overflowing with cruelty, sadism, and murder. He wrote a brilliant book to illustrate it. To many people, however, *Lord of the Flies* is not so much an illustration of Golding's profound pessimism as it is searing proof that human beings—even children!—are basically evil. In the face of his terrible story, it is in truth difficult to remember that such facts as we have on such a situation do not in the least support his conclusions.

No wonder, then, that a vast number of people today accept the statements, made by scholars with reputations and by novelists and dramatists with the ability to terrify, and especially when the statements are made by both at once, that human beings in the "right environments" are inescapably and inevitably killers.

The Comforting Rationalization

There are other reasons for this wholehearted acceptance— no single reason could possibly account for the wide range of believers. There is the fact that any simple explanation is appealing just for the very reason that it is simple. There is nothing more beguiling. People who in their own areas of special knowledge would not for a moment be conned into accepting an explanation that evidence and personal observation rejected are nevertheless vulnerable to this seduction in other areas of life.

Also, the particular oversimplification we are discussing has a great deal to recommend it. It is exhilarating, for one thing. People who themselves lead peaceable lives—and this is most people, when you come to think about it—can be titillated by the flat statement that they are, in fact, killers. Why should this be? Perhaps the answer lies somewhere in the general assumption in our society that it is somehow better to be hostile than to be friendly. In any case, some people appear to derive a certain therapeutic value from being told that they are naturally violent. In their imaginations, at least, if not in reality, they can act out the roles that they believe are the most valued. A Walter Mitty can indulge his dreams of glory—browbeating his boss, throwing a quick left to the jaw of the surly salesman, horsewhipping the man who insults his dignity—without actually violating the codes of behavior that he believes in and knows are right for him.

Man-as-Killer is drama, too. Lorenz and Ardrey entertain us as a good thriller entertains. Much scientific work is so detailed that it is boring beyond description to the layman, but an account of a dove—a dove!—pecking its companion to death combines all the pleasurable feelings of horror, surprise, and shock. Everyone who has ever read that description in *On Aggression* remembers it. And unless they know some facts which contradict Lorenz's conclusions, they accept it as an example of the natural killer in all of us, men and women as well as doves.

Man-as-Killer is a more comfortable state of mind than the alternative view. If we really believe that we behave as we do because we were born that way and we can't help it, well then, we can't help it, can we? And every time we betray a friend, or fail ourselves, or hurt somebody, or cheat or lie, in order to get ahead, we can blame it on human nature. "I'm only human," we say, shrugging, by which we mean, "I'm naturally bad" or "I'm naturally weak."

"To err is human, to forgive divine." This is a particularly interesting version of this cop-out. The fact is, of course, that both erring and forgiving are performed by the same human creature, but for my own reasons I want to avoid taking responsibility for either act. The erring comes from my inescapable base nature, the forgiving from God. *I* am just a bystander.

On the other hand, to believe that I am responsible for my actions is to live an uncomfortable life. It means that I must think about what I do, and hold up the alternatives to some standard, and make judgments, and choose, and then take the consequences. How many of us enjoy that process? Not many, and their number decreases substantially when an easy way out is shown to us by a group of noted scientists, who are, as everbody knows, brighter than anybody else.

"Original Sin"

The most important reason of all, however, why people accept so readily the indictment of themselves as killers is that it supports and is supported by what they already believe. For Man-as-Killer is no more than the present-day secular version of an idea that has had a fierce grip on the Western imagination for many centuries: the doctrine of original sin.

When Lorenz and Ardrey state flatly that there is in every man the instinct to kill other men, and that it is locked into his genes in the same way that the color of his hair is locked in, they are telling us again, in different words, the age-old religious story that men are conceived in sin, born in sin, live all their days and finally die in sin. And when Golding and Burgess and Kubrick and Peckinpah show us ourselves as sadistic, brutal, savage, and murderous, they are joining the long line of story-tellers that goes back to the beginnings of civilization, if not somewhat earlier, when the more articulate members of a group entertained their fellows—and warned them, and frightened them, and thrilled them—with tales of human weakness and evil. It is significant that such stories are not told by foodgathering-hunting peoples.

The doctrine of original sin has been one of the most powerful and influential principles of Hebrew-Christian belief. It has had formidable support throughout the Western world, not only from the most effective organization in that world, the Church, and from many of the most brilliant minds in Western history, but also seemingly from history itself, which sometimes appears to be nothing but an account of wars, bloodshed, plunder, treachery, murder, and elaborate methods devised by clever people to rob other people of their possessions.

Actually the idea of Man-as-Evil antedates even Judaism and Christianity. Many early peoples, for example, needing to explain the existence of evil in their worlds and in themselves, hit upon the idea of the Fall. Man was once innocent and good, and the world was once a garden, a paradise but he was tempted, he succumbed, and he fell; he was never again to regain that early innocence. The Old Testament incorporates the concept of man's depravity. "Behold, I was shapen in iniquity; and in sin did my mother conceive me" is from Psalms 51:5.

The tradition was reinforced and elaborated in the West with the spread of Christianity, which brought together the teachings of the Old and the New Testaments and the pessimism of the Greeks. The Christian version of the doctrine of depravity can be attributed mainly to Paul of Tarsus—there is no such idea, needless to say, in the teachings of Jesus—for it was Paul who preached that man is carnal and sinful. "In his flesh dwelleth no good thing," declared St. Paul. "Sin dwelleth in him."

St. Paul's teachings were systematically elaborated by the developing Church, and soon became accepted doctrine throughout the Christian world. They held undisputed sway through the long centuries of the Middle Ages. The doctrine was embroidered upon, in due course, by numerous earnest churchmen who tended to put their emphasis, almost always, on more rather than less sin. The question of sin became a debate on precisely *how* sinful, or *when* sin first made its appearance in human life, or what, if anything, could wash it away, but never whether humankind was naturally sinful; that was assumed.

Jansenism, for instance, the seventeenth-century Christian cult, held that the individual becomes progressively more evil with age. Calvinism maintained that all that humans will and do is sin, that all human works outside the Christian faith are sins, and that even the good works of Christians are intrinsically evil though not entered in the divine account books as sins because of the grace of Christ. The theology of the Puritans was essentially Calvinist, holding among other things that the proof of the inherently evil nature of humans lay in their apparently unlimited capacity for enjoyment. Thomas Macaulay, the English historian succinctly described this position when he wrote in his *History of England,* "The Puritans hated bearbaiting, not because it gave pain to the bear, but because it gave pleasure to the spectators."

Jonathan Edwards, the American theologian of the eighteenth century, regarded as the most brilliant mind of pre-Revolutionary America, was a particularly violent exponent of the doctrine of total depravity. In 1741 he delivered a famous sermon, entitled "Sinners in the Hands of an Angry God," in which he expressed his and Puritanism's contempt for sinful humanity. The only escape from the consequences of that sin, Edwards preached, was divine grace.

With the exception of the brief interlude in the eighteenth century known as the Enlightenment, when not only light but fresh air was let into the inquiry into what is meant by human nature, the concept of original sin and natural depravity has held sway. For example, children were considered to be "naturally depraved creatures" by Hannah More, the English bluestocking, who died in 1833; and as recently as 1922, children were being spoken of by

Dr. Edward Glover, the doyen of English psychoanalysts, in these engaging terms: "The perfectly normal infant is almost completely egocentric, greedy, dirty, violent in temper, destructive in habit, profoundly sexual in purpose, aggrandizing in attitude, devoid of all but the most primitive reality sense, without conscience of moral feeling, whose attitude to society (as represented by the family) is opportunist, inconsiderate, domineering and sadistic. In fact, judged by adult social standards, the normal baby is for all practical purposes a born criminal." Dr. Glover's lecture was reprinted in a book of his collected pieces in 1970.

At the present time, one of the largest and most ardent popular movements in Western society continues to be the various evangelical sects scattered across this country and western Europe. In spite of some drifting away from organized religion in general, and in spite of a small-scale movement toward Eastern religions among some young people, there is still a strong—and some say a growing—adherence to "old-time religion." This is characterized by the belief that humankind is naturally sinful and will remain so throughout eternity unless it is saved through the intervention of God or his personal emissary, Jesus Christ. The Bible is the source of inspiration to these believers; it is accepted literally, and it contains all that is necessary for guidance through this life and for life after death. One has only to talk with a follower of one of these sects, or to see, for example, a mass meeting on television of one of Billy Graham's Crusades, to recognize the force of this faith in humankind's inherent depravity.

The Influence of Freud and Darwin

Two other developments during the past century have contributed unexpectedly to the ready acceptance of evil as a natural characteristic of humans. One of these is in the field of psychology and psychoanalysis, under the leadership of Sigmund Freud; the other is in biology, following Charles Darwin.

These two giants, in making their magnificent contributions to human understanding, also quite naturally contributed to human confusion. Freud, the founder of psychoanalysis, demonstrated to the prudish world in which he lived the paramount importance of sex as a motivating force among human beings. He was savagely attacked by the Church for this position, and he was widely criticized by the medical profession and even by some of his early followers, but he unlocked and opened another door to the inner workings of human beings. What people saw through that doorway was more often disturbing than reassuring, and one of the major results of having looked was renewed conviction that evil was an integral part of human nature.

Freud himself contributed further to this in the form of his so-called death instinct. And as late as 1930 he wrote, in even deeper pessimism: "Men are not gentle friendly creatures wishing for love. . . . A powerful measure of desire for aggression has to be reckoned as a part of their instinctual endowment. . . . *Homo homini lupus:* who has the courage to dispute it in the face of all the evidence in his own life and in history? This aggressive cruelty usually lies in wait for some provocation, or else it steps into the service of some other purpose, the aim of which might well have been achieved by milder measures. In circumstances that favor it, when those forces in the mind which ordinarily inhibit it cease to operate, it also manifests itself spontaneously and reveals men as savage beasts to whom the thought of sparing their own kind is alien. Anyone who calls to mind the atrocities of the early migrations, of the invasions by the Huns or by the so-called Mongols under Genghis Khan and

Tamerlane, of the sack of Jerusalem by the pious Crusaders, even indeed of the horrors of the last world war, will have to bow his head before the truth of this view of man."

When Freud tells us to bow our heads humbly before something, many of us who are not susceptible to the evangelical calls to salvation find ourselves agreeing with this "truth." The fact is, of course, that psychoanalytic doctrine is only a little more scientific than is religious doctrine; to a large extent, like religion, it is a philosophy, and has its base in moral judgments about human nature. Perhaps for that reason, Freud's influence on human thinking over the past fifty years has been immense, and many people who reject the notion of themselves as Freudians have incorporated many of his concepts into their own ways of thinking.

Likewise, when Darwin implied in 1859, in *The Origin of Species,* and in 1871 stated, in *The Descent of Man,* that man had evolved from nonhuman animals, and described how that might have happened, he was suggesting such a new concept that most people were unable to absorb it. As a matter of fact, many people still misunderstand those concepts. But at the time it seemed that Darwin was adding the power of science to the power of religion in characterizing man as a violent, bestial creature. The Church attacked him, too, as much later it attacked Freud—and in some places is still attacking Darwin—but his influence with the general public was, and remains, enormous. If you could not quite believe that the human species is steeped in sin through its inheritance from Adam and Eve and the Fall, then surely you could accept that we are killers through our heritage from our animal ancestors.

Darwin himself did not carry his ideas so far; he never intended that they should be used as they were, misinterpreted and extended into areas where they had no relevance and indeed caused much damage. Nevertheless, he did use the

phrase "the warfare of nature," and inadvertently contributed to the force of the belief that man is warlike by virtue
of his natural state and animal heritage.

Thus, the present-day animal behaviorists—Lorenz, Tinbergen, Morris, and others—whose message is "We are all
killers," are speaking by and large to people who already
have the message. If we are not taught it in church, we have
absorbed it through the atmosphere that contains bits and
pieces of Freudianism and Darwinism. It is nothing new to
us to be told that as human beings we have in our souls—or
our emotions, or our instincts, or our automatic responses—
a built-in evil; there has been an awareness of it for more
than two thousand years, since the unknown Psalmist sang,
"Behold, I was born in iniquity; and in sin did my mother
conceive me." And if our intellects reject that statement,
the psychologists and the biologists—or their popularizers,
more often than not—are waiting to tell us the same thing in
other words.

It has always been difficult to speak against what people
already "know." The early scientists who tried to demonstrate that earth, air, fire, and water were in fact not the
basic materials of our world spent many generations in the
attempt. A small group of scientists of the last century who
tried to argue that animals do not, in fact, live by the so-
called law of the jungle were entirely unable to make their
voices heard. And the social and political consequences of
that failure were so great that it is worth a brief account, to
call our attention to the similar dangers that face us today.

3
Social Darwinism: A Case History
and a Cautionary Note

Darwin and Social Darwinism

When Charles Darwin broke in upon the sin-soaked Victorian society of England with his revolutionary concept of evolution, he inadvertently provided for the people of that time and place a scientific sanction for two entirely false ideas: that the animal world is characterized by a ferocious struggle for existence; and that human society, because it is directly descended from that animal world, is characterized by struggle, hostility, unbridled competition, and aggressiveness.

Darwin had no such intention, of course. The interpretation of Darwinism that purported to "prove" such characterizations was not his. Nevertheless, many of his followers used his ideas in inappropriate ways, in areas where they had little applicability, and thereby supported and encouraged some of the most repressive social ideas Western society has ever known. And one of the main reasons it is important today is that this particular bit of history may be repeating itself now.

Darwin's theories were based on the fact that offspring of living creatures can vary from their parents in important ways, by sudden development of traits not inherited. These changes are today called mutations. Darwin postulated that changes that best suit the conditions under which a species lives will be most likely to survive to appear again in the next generation. The most successful variations, therefore, will be transmitted down through the generations and the species will gradually, over the course of many generations, evolve through this process of "natural selection" into a species with somewhat different characteristics. Darwin explained in this way his belief that humans had evolved from nonhuman animals.

For example, as the climate gradually became colder during the advent of a glacial period the survival of a thinly furred species would be gravely threatened. The occasion of a mutation governing additional hair on the body would provide those animals so endowed with a thicker growth of body hair. Such animals would be more likely to reproduce than the less hairy animals. They would probably be stronger than their fellows, and they would probably live longer. Some of their offspring would inherit the thicker hair, and these in turn would manage better in the increasingly cold climate than their thinner-haired brothers and sisters, and would transmit their thick-hair-carrying genes to still another generation. And so it would happen that slowly—slowly over a number of generations—an entire species could change, in response to a change in its environment, from sparsely furred to thickly furred.

This process is hardly characterized by savage struggle for survival between members of the same species. Conflict is not involved in such a struggle for survival. It is a "struggle for existence," as Darwin termed it, only in the sense that every organism strives to maintain itself, and does so willy-nilly in relation to other organisms. Darwin himself stated that he used the term "in a large and metaphorical sense including dependence of one being on another, and including (which is more important) not only the life of the individual but success in leaving progeny."

By "competition," which is usually employed as a synonym for "the struggle for existence," is generally meant the process of striving against others to achieve the same goal. But within this meaning the term is used in many different senses, from peaceful endeavor to lethal struggle. In the emphasis on "struggle" it has been too often overlooked that cooperation also constitutes a form of competition, that those individuals or groups who are the most cooperative are likely to enjoy the greatest survival benefits. This aspect of competition or "the struggle for existence" has been insufficiently emphasized.

Thanks to Darwin's most devoted followers, his ideas were misstated and misinterpreted to the point where they were far from his original intention. Perhaps the major influence in this regard was Thomas Henry Huxley, English biologist, teacher, publicist, and Darwin-popularizer, who published in 1888 an article entitled "The Struggle for Existence: A Programme." In this article he described animal behavior in the state of nature in these words: "From the point of view of the moralist, the animal world is on about the same level as a gladiators' show. The creatures are fairly well treated, and set to fight—whereby the strongest, the swiftest, and the cunningest live to fight another day. The spectator has no need to turn his thumbs down, as no quarter is given."

This is a very one-sided picture of the evolutionary process. But it is a dramatic picture: a couple of large animals circling each other warily, perhaps on an improbable sand clearing in the midst of a jungle, and perhaps surrounded

by grandstands filled with—what? other animals? human beings? gods?—in any case, some kind of eager audience, waiting to see the animals leap at each other's throats. Shrieks
fill the air, blood soaks into the ground, one of the animals
begins to weaken, whereupon the other doubles its efforts
and finally finishes the victim. The victor!

The connection between this gory scene and the process
Darwin was setting forth is a tenuous one: it is difficult to
see just how Huxley's gladiators' show would result in the
evolutionary development of human from nonhuman animals. Also, to many people it is much less interesting than
Darwin's concept. Nevertheless, it was unquestionably more
dramatic and easier to understand, and therefore more
popular.

Cooperation or Mutual Aid: An Unrecognized Idea

Not everyone was so one-sided and absolutist as Huxley, of
course. The French philosopher and economic historian Alfred Espinas, the Russian zoologist Karl Kessler, and Prince
Petr Kropotkin, the Russian geographer and humanist, all
addressed themselves to the question of animal behavior
during the period between 1878 and 1902, and all came to
the conclusion that cooperation rather than conflict was the
principal factor operative in the process of evolution among
animals. Alfred Espinas, French philosopher, economist and
historian, published in 1878 a remarkable book, *Des Sociétés animales,* in which he drew attention to the universal cooperativeness rather than conflict that characterized
the social life of animals. Kessler, who was professor of zoology and dean of the University of St. Petersburg, delivered a
lecture in 1880 entitled "On the Law of Mutual Aid," in
which he endeavored to show that besides "the law of mutual struggle" there is in nature "a law of mutual aid,"

which, "for the success of the struggle for life, and especially for the progressive evolution of the species, is far more important than the law of mutual contest." Kessler's lecture, which he read in 1880 at a Russian congress of naturalists, was the principal inspiration of Kropotkin's thinking on the subject. The following year Kessler died.

Kropotkin as a young man had spent several years in Siberia and Manchuria, where he had busied himself in the study of animal life under natural conditions. His observations then as well as later convinced him that Huxley had given "a very incorrect representation of the facts of Nature, as one sees them in the bush and in the forest." He published a series of articles over the years from 1890 to 1896 in reply to Huxley's gladiatorial view of evolution. It was these articles that were published as a book in 1902 under the title *Mutual Aid: A Factor of Evolution*. In the introduction to this Kropotkin wrote that although he was eagerly looking for it during his observations in eastern Siberia and northern Manchuria, he failed to find "that bitter struggle for the means of existence, *among animals belonging to the same species,* which was considered by most Darwinists (though not always by Darwin himself) as the dominant characteristic of the struggle for life, and the main factor of evolution." Without denying the importance of the struggle for existence, and natural selection in the evolution of living forms, Kropotkin endeavored to show that mutual aid has been, in his words, "the chief factor of evolution."

While such claims may be too strong, the fact remains that to this day cooperation as a factor in the competitive "struggle for existence," and especially in the evolution of social relationships, has been undeservedly slighted. In Kropotkin's time views such as his were simply disregarded.

There is a striking and depressing similarity between that period and our own with regard to general acceptance of unreliable "scientific" conclusions. Darwin himself described a revolutionary concept not easily understood in a world that had for centuries accepted blindly the assumptions and accounts of the Christian religion; many of his supporters and popularizers took his words, stretched them to cover all sorts of unjustifiable ideas, and presented them to the world in a classic example of misinterpretation.

Today, in a parallel development, the interesting and valuable work of imaginative scientists in the field of animal behavior has been stretched—sometimes by the scientists themselves and sometimes by others—to cover interpretations that are not justified by the original work. Konrad Lorenz, Niko Tinbergen, Desmond Morris, and others, are all valued members of the scientific community, and so long as they confine their conclusions to the work they have actually done, they contribute greatly to knowledge about the behavior of animals. When they draw analogies from their own work on animals, however, to cover the behavior of human beings, and then support their conclusions with entirely unsound assertions, their work loses its value and, in fact, because of its popular appeal becomes dangerous. They are the direct descendants of the "Nature red in tooth and claw" thinkers of the nineteenth century when they allow their scientific training—in caution, in careful definition of words and concepts, in understanding of relationships between events, in logical thinking—to go up in the smoke of their enthusiasms.

The New Social Darwinism

An even more important and urgent danger in the present-day acceptance of Lorenz's ideas is the contemporary version of the movement that was called Social Darwinism. Developed under the leadership of the English philosopher and social thinker Herbert Spencer during the last quarter of the nineteenth century, Social Darwinism extended the concept of warfare in nature, a dubious concept at best, to warfare in the marketplace, a totally false analogy, and gave the burgeoning industrial world of that time a scientific sanction for free, unregulated competition. Just as in nature, the industrialists told one another, there is a struggle for existence in which the "strongest, the swiftest, and the cunningest live to fight another day," so in human society the victory goes to the fittest. "The survival of the fittest" was for the industrial barons at once the inspiration and the justification of their policies and their actions: on the one hand, explosive growth in the industrialization of society, which was naturally seen by the beneficiaries as "progress"; on the other hand, social approval of the personal qualities that made this possible—personal ambition, greed, self-aggrandizement, competitiveness, exploitation of others and indifference to their plights. If society is indeed a battle for survival then the rules of war prevail: to the victor belong the spoils, to the loser only defeat.

The inevitable accompaniment to this doctrine is that the losers are inferior to the winners by the very fact of being losers. They are not "strong": therefore they are "weak." They are not "successful": therefore they are "failures." And so widespread was this belief in our society that vast numbers of "failures" themselves were persuaded by it. Caught in the circular thinking, and not remembering, if indeed they ever knew, that the whole structure of ideas was based on a rickety foundation and held up over the years by the increasing power of those who benefited from it, the victims cooperated in their own victimization. They "knew their place," they believed in their own inferiority, and they actively supported the system that degraded them.

The broad social consequences of this doctrine are well

known: terrible poverty and enormous wealth side by side; low life expectancy and high infant and maternal mortality rates among the poor; education confined to the "upper classes"; child labor, cruelty to prisoners; and all explained away by the comfortable belief that somehow the victims of the system were themselves to blame for their misery.

When we carry this picture forward to our own times we find, with some sense of shock, that it fits neatly into the outlines presented to us by today's social warriors. Contemporary belief in the innate aggressiveness of mankind differs from Social Darwinism only in that it draws upon new material for support, and is less open in declaring its advocacy of reactionary social ideas and totalitarian political doctrines. But it is a close parallel in the justification it provides for not allowing one's self to be made uncomfortable by the problems of others.

For example, Dr. John Rowan Wilson, an English physician and writer, in reviewing Ardrey's *The Territorial Imperative* with approval and admiration, concludes: "If Ardrey is right, the assimilation of immigrants, particularly those of a noticeably different culture and physical appearance, is a more fundamental problem than we have previously believed. Racial prejudice may not simply be a matter of ignorance, which a more progressive policy will eliminate in time. Distrust of the foreigner may be an inevitable accompaniment of the group cohesion which holds our own society together. Perhaps we should stop aiming at the impossible task of trying to love and understand our neighbours. It might well be better if we kept ourselves to ourselves, barking across our fences now and then, and baring our fangs in ritualized aggression, but never going so far as to engage in open conflict."

Not only is Dr. Wilson willing to close his sceptered isle to human beings of "a noticeably different culture and physical appearance," but he seems willing to abandon "the impossible task of trying to love and understand our neighbours." Perhaps Dr. Wilson never did think highly of immigrants as neighbors, but the chances are he never said so in print before the Ardrey book gave him "scientific" sanction for his opinions.

The doctrine of innate aggression provides rationalization for the present-day business community, too. Antony Jay, an English management consultant, has written a book, *Corporation Man,* based on the writings of Ardrey and Morris, in which he endeavors to show that man's behavior in business springs not from logic or reason, a desire to support himself or his family, or an urge to master a skill, but from ancient survival imperatives: aggression, status displays, territorial defense, hunting comradeship, tribal gatherings, and appeasement rituals. Mr. Jay finds it tempting to think that the twenty-first century will prove to be the century of the Corporation Man. He foresees that international cartels will take over the affairs of the governments of the earth because human social organization, he says, is fundamentally and unchangeably hierarchical, and because dominance relationships are genetically determined.

Thus, we find racism, prejudice, and the takeover of the planet by the cartels all justified by reference to our animal heritage. Nor is that all. Think of the impact of this doctrine on criminology: naturally, a society's beliefs about good and evil are reflected more directly and more clearly in its attitudes toward its criminals than anywhere else. If the general opinion is that criminals are the embodiment of the evil in all of us, and if we see criminals as people who have done what our own base selves are urging us to do, but out of fear or cowardice cannot allow ourselves to do, then we will treat our criminals with all the loathing and repression that we feel for the evil in ourselves, and with the vengeance that we feel for someone who has done something we deeply want to do.

On the other hand, if we think of criminals as individual human beings who have for any one of a hundred possible reasons failed to abide by the specific rules that our society has made for itself, then we will set ourselves the task of trying to find out in each case what the reason was for the failure, and what can be done, if anything, for that individual to make another failure less likely.

An example of the former view was developed a century ago by Cesare Lombroso, Italian criminologist, whose three-volume work *L'Uomo Delinquente* published in 1876 had an enormous influence (translated into English in 1911 as *Criminal Man*), all based on the idea that human beings are innately aggressive. He went so far as to describe certain "physical stigmata," lobeless and small ears, receding chins, low foreheads, and crooked noses, all of which identified "the born criminal."

Dr. Edward Glover, the same psychoanalyst who described children as "egocentric, greedy, dirty, violent . . . destructive . . . opportunist . . . inconsiderate . . . domineering . . . sadistic," also referred to criminals in the same speech as displaying these same characteristics. His view of human nature included the belief that a baby is born with "primitive impulses," among which are the "instincts of aggression" which he must learn to master as he grows older. To the extent that he fails to do so, he remains a primitively aggressive individual, and he may become, among other things, a criminal. Dr. Glover's views are shared by many law-enforcement and justice-dispensing officials in Western societies, with the result that criminals have been treated by them as something less than human. The rationalization is that since the responsibility for acquiring control of his primitive impulses is his, society has no duty toward him if he fails, but only a duty toward itself to protect itself from him. Thus, down through history, we find that wrongdoers, however the term is defined in different periods and different places, are incarcerated, starved, beaten, often allowed to die, and sometimes deliberately killed.

Think, too, of the impact of the doctrine of innate aggression on education: should children be tamed and trained, and conditioned for life in a hostile world? Or should they be allowed to grow and develop and be educated for life so that their behavior will be appropriate to their surroundings? Which view society adopts will determine the kind of schools it will have. And in the light of the controversy today about the nature of human nature, it is no wonder that controversies about schools are among the most heated we have.

There is no question that a belief in the innate aggressiveness of man allows a person to condone the most extreme forms of human madness. Perhaps one of the more dramatic examples of the influence of this belief on one man's attitudes is the famous statement made in 1931 by Sir Arthur Keith, a noted anatomist and physical anthropologist, and himself a kind and gentle man (whom Ardrey likes to quote). He declared: "Nature keeps her orchard healthy by pruning: war is her pruning hook." Entirely aside from the shocking acceptance of war as a law of nature, Sir Arthur was guilty here of the error, shared later by Lorenz and Ardrey and others, of false analogy, and his statement demonstrates the dangers of such sloppy thinking. Society is not an *orchard;* nature is *not* a conscious force choosing some to live and some to die; and in any case, the metaphor is ill chosen because pruning removes old canes, weak canes, and canes that will no longer bear, so that the young and the strong may have more air and more nourishment to live. The analogy with war, where the young and the strong are always killed first, would be so inept as to be ridiculous, were it not so tragic.

It is interesting to note that the anthropologists of the time, who were on the whole in disagreement with Sir Arthur, nevertheless declined to speak out in criticism of his views. The combination of centuries of original sin, decades of Darwinism, and years of Freudianism, were, together with a certain reluctance to engage in controversy, too much to confront. Thus, Sir Arthur's view stood unchallenged.

This cannot be allowed to happen now. The subject is too important; our understanding of ourselves must go forward along lines that are distorted as little as possible by our mythologies, our personal prejudices, our misunderstandings, our unwillingness to accept responsibility for our conclusions. Our survival, perhaps, depends on whether or not we are able to achieve this. We have never achieved it, as a society, in the past; on the other hand, in the past we have never had the urgent need that confronts us now.

Here is an example of the kind of contemporary statement that will be challenged in this book. It is a statement by Professor Raymond Dart, the anatomist, from whose work and ideas Robert Ardrey, as we have already noted, took his principal inspiration. And it is an example of what happens when a moral position on original sin and an intellectual conviction about evolution come together. The two threads, twisted together, make a strong rope.

The statement was contained in the article by Dart entitled "The Predatory Transition from Ape to Man." The title was followed immediately by an epigraph of two lines from *Christian Ethics* by Richard Baxter, a famous English divine of the seventeenth century:

> Of all the beasts the man-beast is the worst
> To others and to himself the cruelest foe.

The article combines Dart's two threads—scientific-sounding data, and an evangelical fervor that would carry conviction in any prayer meeting. He endeavored to show that man has arisen "from a predacious anthropoid stock." Even though the brain in this creature was small, he stated—about 500 cubic centimeters—this "microcephalic mental equipment was demonstrably more than adequate for the crude, omnivorous cannibalistic, bone-club wielding, jaw-bone-cleaving Samsonian phase of human emergence. . . . The loathsome cruelty of mankind to man," he went on to say, "forms one of his inescapable, characteristic and differentiative features; and it is explicable only in terms of his carnivorous and cannibalistic origin. . . ."

It is this kind of statement that this book will challenge in the hope of putting to rest, at least for a time, the idea that human beings are inescapably evil. "The loathsome cruelty of mankind to man," states Professor Dart, ". . . is explicable only in terms of his carnivorous and cannibalistic origin." That human beings are capable of loathsome cruelty is not in question; every one of us can list examples from his own personal knowledge. But the second half of the sentence contains at least three errors in eleven words: "is explicable only." In this phrase Professor Dart reveals an oversimplified view of cause and effect that is shared by few if any scientific minds. No behavior pattern can be accurately explained by a single condition. In fact, to imply that behavior so complex and so generalized as "cruelty" is due *only* to man's inheritance, with no contribution from his environment, is to take a position with which very few reputable scientists would agree. Even to maintain that such behavior arises from any one factor in his environment itself is a serious oversimplification. In addition, he assumes here that behavior can be inherited; this, as we shall see, is false.

"Carnivorous . . . origin." In this phrase Professor Dart accepts as a fact that man's closest relatives among the fore-runners of man were carnivorous. This is by no means an accepted fact. Most students of the subject believe that these forms were predominantly vegetarian. In any case, to write as though the matter were settled when it is not, is to be guilty again of oversimplification, if nothing more. Humans, in any event, are omnivorous—not carnivorous.

"Cannibalistic." The idea that "loathsome cruelty" and "cannibalism" are connected is also false. Human beings have been, and indeed still are, cannibalistic, and most of us, in our culture, are horrified by the thought. However, when people have eaten other human beings it has not been because of innate cruelty, or inherited aggressiveness, but usually because of religion, superstition, hunger, adherence to tribal ritual, and a number of other reasons. When Professor Dart claims that cannibalism is a proof of innate aggression, he is guilty of either ignorance or prejudice, or both.

These points together reveal at least a carelessness that causes a reader to question Dart's methods and thinking processes. In addition, the passage suggests in its immoderate tone that the writer is so caught up in the subject that his conclusions may be unreliable. Three errors in eleven words is a higher concentration than we customarily find, even in the most devoted of true believers.

Professor Dart's statement is singled out here, in advance of more detailed criticism of the work of the writers who have presented the idea of innate aggression, to indicate the kind of statements we are dealing with, and the kind of criticisms that will be leveled against those statements. This example is given also to show something of the standards that must be maintained in the development of scientific ideas; assumptions must be scrutinized and evaluated; logic must be clear and faultless; facts must be verifiable; all the known facts must be accounted for; conclusions must follow from the evidence. Obvious, one would think. Yet the very absence of these practices is what has led to questioning the collection of untenable positions held by Konrad Lorenz, Robert Ardrey, Raymond Dart, and their followers, and to the writing of this book.

4
Instinct and Adaptation

Instinct—The "Explanatory" Principle

Instinct has been one of the most frequently employed explanatory principles of behavior in living creatures. It has the virtue of being simple and easily understood. When we narrow to human beings the question of whether instinct plays a role in human aggression, we are touching on truly important issues. It is the purpose of this chapter to inquire into the claims made by the innate aggressionists for the existence of an instinct of aggression in human beings, to describe and define instinct, to differentiate it as far as possible from adaptation and learning, reflex behavior, and thinking, and to try to determine the extent to which instinct and other factors influence human behavior and particularly human aggressive behavior, and finally to draw the conclusions that flow from all these considerations.

Konrad Lorenz and other ethologists of his persuasion hold that almost all animal behavior—and they include human behavior in this sweeping generalization—is instinctive. By that, they mean that for each act by any animal there is an arrangement already in existence within the nervous system of that animal that determines that act. To a specific stimulus, the creature will always react in a specific predetermined manner, and all members of that species will react in that same manner to that same stimulus.

The animals most closely studied by Lorenz, and from which he derived a large part of his conclusions—domesticated ducks and geese—demonstrate interesting examples of the instinctive behavior he speaks of. The "triumph ceremony" of the Greylag geese, for example, is a lengthy series of movements combined with various noises—neck stretching, head tilting, raucous fanfares, and several kinds of cackling—all leading to the establishment of specific relationships among the animals involved. These movements and sounds are "programmed," according to Lorenz, in the genes of all Greylag geese; for each small increment of the procedure there is a blueprint, in effect, filed away in the nervous system of each goose. These blueprints are transmitted from one generation to the next, are activated in all members of the species by the same stimuli, and result in identical behavior.

According to Lorenz, all animals have such genetic programs waiting within to serve what he sees as the four great drives: hunger, fear, sex, and aggression. The programs vary from species to species, of course; lions behave differently from stickleback fish in the face of hunger or fear or sex or aggression. But each species has its own program to which it adheres; all lions behave the same, and all sticklebacks, and all human beings. And they do this because of their genetic programming. Push the buttons in the right order, the lights will flash in a certain sequence, and the behavior will follow in a predetermined way.

Reasoning on the basis of such ideas about the behavior of man, Lorenz and his followers believe it is possible to understand and explain man's aggressive behavior. Lorenz tells us that anyone who understands the convincingness, beauty, and awe-inspiring greatness of the evolutionary process, cannot possibly be repulsed by either Darwin's recognition of our common origin with animals, or Freud's realization that we are still driven by the same instincts as our prehuman ancestors.

Is it, however, really possible to determine from the investigation of the evolutionary record and from the study of animal behavior why man, unlike other creatures, so frequently murders and makes war on his own kind? Is it true that the roots of aggression are to be sought in the very nature of man's biological makeup?

Quoting Sir Arthur Keith's statement, "We have to recognize that the conditions that give rise to war—the separation of animals into social groups, the 'right' of each group to its own area, and the evolution of the enmity complex to defend such areas—were on earth long before man made his appearance," Mr. Ardrey tells us, "Such an observation of a human instinct probably more compulsive than sex throws into pale context the more wistful conclusions of the romantic fallacy: that wars are a product of munitions makers, or of struggles for markets, or of the class struggle; or that human hostility arises in unhappy family relationships, or in the metaphysical reaches of some organic death force."

Certainly we have a common origin with animals. It is devoutly to be wished that we remembered more often the kinship with our fellow creatures than we do in our frequently cruel disregard of that relationship. But our kinship with other animals does not mean that if their behavior seems often to be under the influence of instincts, this must necessarily also be the case in humans.

As for Mr. Ardrey's appeal to Sir Arthur Keith's "enmity complex" and his cavalier dismissal of the military-industrial complex as a cause of war as a "romantic fallacy," it need only be said that while no such thing as an "enmity complex" exists among animals, there can be not the least doubt of the very real relation between the existence of a military-industrial complex, against which no less an insider than General Eisenhower warned, and the proneness to war. Certainly it is as absurd to attribute wars to an organic death force as it is to attribute them to an instinctive drive, but to dismiss the economic and social causes of war is to ignore the conclusions of virtually all serious students of the causes of war. The literature on the subject is vast, but no reader of the present volume should do himself or herself the disservice of failing to read Richard J. Barnet's *The Roots of War* (1973). In this book Dr. Barnet, who is cofounder and codirector of the Institute of Policy Studies, Washington, D.C., in considering how wars are brought about, writes: "Human nature makes war possible, but it is not its cause. Despite efforts of the apologists of American policy to justify permanent war by invoking pop anthropology, the view that militarism is a biologically determined aspect of the human condition cannot stand serious scrutiny. . . . The dismal view of man as a natural warrior offers a certain bizarre comfort because it absolves individuals of responsibility of identifying, much less removing, the specific political, organizational, and economic causes of militarism and war. If human beings, males particularly, have biological urges to slaughter their own species at regular intervals, there is nothing to be done. Remorse is as useless as reform."

To which we may say, "Amen." War is a continuation of politics, and conflicting political ideologies and social systems, in a world that steadily bureaucratizes the planning of "inevitable" wars, present conditions, on an international scale, that may readily explode into war. Military, industrial, and political factors are principally involved, and as

Hannah Arendt has pointed out, the use of violence for political ends represents an index of the failure of political power. In spite of the attempts of Lorenz, Ardrey, and Tiger and Fox to write a biology of politics, instinct has no demonstrable relation to war. None whatever. As Julian Huxley pointed out long ago, there is no such thing as an instinct to make war.

War, as Huxley said, is an organized physical conflict between members of the same species; as such it is an exceedingly rare biological phenomenon. Competition between two different species, even when involving conflict, is not war. Even at the most generous interpretation it may be said that there are only two kinds of animals that make war: humans and certain species of ants. War, as Huxley said, may not only be useless but also harmful to the species as a whole. Whatever benefits war may have produced in the past, modern wars, in which whole populations are starved, oppressed, and murdered while their countries are laid waste, are clearly harmful to the species. Such wars, as many observers of recent history have remarked, might even turn back the clock of civilization and force the world into another Dark Age. In such an attempt Hitler very nearly succeeded. As Huxley remarked, "War of this type is an intraspecific struggle, from which nobody, neither humanity nor any of the groups engaged in conflict, can really reap any balance of advantage, though of course we may snatch particular advantages out of the results of war." The truth is that in the perspective of biology war dwindles to the status of a rare curiosity.

There is nothing either in the nature of war or in the nature of humanity that makes war inevitable. Human aggressive impulses *can* be canalized into other outlets. Political machinery *can* be designed to make war less likely. These things *can* be done. But they are most likely to be done when people understand that war is inimical to their personal and collective interests.

Wars have an ancient history. They go back to the first city-states, and in the form of raiding earlier than that. Few states have ever existed that have not engaged in warfare. Such facts, however, do not mean that belligerency is either principally or in part due to instinctual drives. Warfare is most frequently associated with politically organized societies, and from this fact alone it would appear that whatever other factors are involved, it is political power and motivations that are the chief cause of war. As Blainey points out in his book *The Causes of War* (1974), since war and peace mark fluctuations in the relations between nations, each is more likely to be explained by factors which themselves fluctuate than by factors which are innate.

Dr. Anatol Rapoport of the Institute of Mental Health at the University of Michigan has raised some very cogent questions in this connection. He writes: "If the idea of an instinct as a determinant of behavior is to be given some benefit of the doubt, then it would be better to avoid rigorous operational definitions of the term. The basic idea, after all, is the existence of biologically determined predispositions toward certain behavior patterns. That such exist, and consequently the *tabula rasa* theory is without foundation, is, I think, not open to doubt. Why should they not exist? Are we to believe that such an immense biological gap exists between us and the other species that nothing at all has been left of our biological heritage?"

These are important questions and they deserve answers. It is, of course, nonsensical to claim that the mind of the child at birth is a blank tablet upon which experience inscribes its directions. We can also accept the fact of the existence of biologically determined predispositions toward certain behavior patterns as a nonoperational definition of instinct, although I think "influenced" would probably be nearer the mark and safer than "determined." The trouble, however, is that Dr. Rapoport, like so many other writers on the subject, proceeds to employ the term "instinct" as something very much more than a "predisposition," for in the very next paragraph he goes on to say: "And so, let us suppose that an aggressive instinct exists in man, submerged, it is true, like all the other possibly existing human instincts, by enormous superstructures of learned behavior, symbolization, etc. But it is there, nevertheless, like the sex drive."

So now a "predisposition" is transformed into a "drive," and Dr. Rapoport continues: "Might we not suppose that the aggressive instinct that has survival value for a great many species lingers in man as a maladaptive feature, which will eventually bring about his extinction? If so, the recognition of this fact is of the utmost importance."

And indeed it is, whatever the facts are ultimately proven to be. Here we may once more draw attention to a common fallacy in the reasoning of such writers. They all emphasize man's common origin with other animals and conclude, therefore, that if instincts drive animals to aggressive behavior, then instincts must also do so in humans. But this in fact represents the fallacy of the false equation.

The Assumption That Aggressive Behavior Is the Same in Animals and in Humans

The fact that aggressive behavior is exhibited by other animals is only too often taken to constitute good evidence that it must also exist in humans. But what is overlooked in that inference is that the aggressive behavior of animals is often of a very different nature from that which is defined in humans as calculated to inflict injury on a member of one's own group or species. The truth is that there are many different kinds of aggressive behavior in animals which are not to be confused with those that may be found among humans. It is, indeed, a very real question whether the aggression of other animals is significantly related to the aggressive behavior of humans. Different strains of the same animal species will, in different environments, react very differently to aggression-inducing stimuli. For the most part aggressive behavior among animals is not really directed toward inflicting injury on another animal, but rather toward the establishment of dominance relationships, the retention of food, and the like. Such aggression has been called "instrumental," and is often observable in humans, but what is found alike both in animals and in humans is that the stimuli inducing aggressive behavior are, with the exception of abnormal cases, invariably environmental. Hence, the exercise and control of aggressive behavior will to a large extent depend on the experiential background and behavioral flexibility of the animal. What appears to be stereotyped instinctive behavior in many animals often changes very rapidly within the lifetime of animals flexible enough to adjust to new environmental conditions. In spite of claims to the contrary, the causes of aggressive behavior are many; the attribution of either the origin or development of such behavior to a single cause is simply contrary to the facts. The development of aggressive behavior in both animals and in humans depends, during each phase of development, on the complex interaction between organism and environment, with, as Hinde says, "social experience playing a crucial role." Adding, "Clearly, in the understanding of these social influences lie the best hopes for coming to terms with man's propensities for aggression."

Dr. Rapoport asks why instincts should not exist in man. "Are we to believe that such an immense biological gap exists between us and the other species that nothing at all has been left of our biological heritage?"

The answers to Dr. Rapoport's questions are simple. Yes, an immense gap *does* exist between humanity and other species, a gap which has been enlarged over a period of more than five million years as a consequence of the species' unique evolutionary history. But this does not mean that "nothing at all has been left of our biological heritage." A great deal has been left. Indeed, there is hardly any form of human behavior that does not have some relation to our animal origins. But that does not mean that such a relationship in any way necessarily *determines* any form of human behavior. They may *influence,* but it is quite another matter to say that they will determine, govern, resolve, or regulate the shape, form, or content of human behavior.

One of the major differences between humans and other animals responsible for the "immense gap" between humanity and other animals is the result of the uniqueness of human evolutionary history, as a direct consequence of which humans as such lost virtually all remnants of any instincts they may have once had.

But what is an instinct? Is it something that corresponds with reality or is it an artifact created by those who are only too ready to settle for simple and simplistic explanations of complex behavior and assume that such explanations will serve as satisfactory substitutes for analysis?

The complexities of human behavior are such that they readily lend themselves to misinterpretations of every kind. It is, in part, because the phenomena of human behavior are so difficult to analyze that easy explanations are so eagerly received. "Instinct" undoubtedly constitutes the most popular of such explanations. Spiders spin webs by instinct, cats nurse their young by instinct, beavers build dams by instinct, and so on. Hence, when women nurse their young, and men "defend their country" by killing other men, they do so by instinct. Are we to suppose that when women make beds and men build dams, that such activities, too, are referable to some appropriate instinct? The absurdities of thought that have been committed in the name of "instinct" constitute an object-lesson in the systematics of confusion.

The "Sex Instinct"

Most of us who have given any thought to the matter may no longer believe in an instinct of property or philoprogenitiveness (supposing we have ever heard of it). But most people continue to believe in the unquestionable reality of the "sex instinct." Everyone "knows" from his or her own experience that there is such a thing as a sex instinct. But what everyone knows, and what one's own experience may mean, do not necessarily constitute sufficient grounds for the assumption that an innate, unlearned drive exists in each of us which causes us to seek out a member of the opposite sex for the purpose of satisfying by copulation the requirements of that instinct.

The fact is that there is no such thing as a sex instinct. Certainly a state of activity exists in the organism that is a necessary condition before a given stimulus is able to elicit a particular class of behaviors in response to certain shifts in physiological balance such as hunger, thirst, and sex. Such a state of activity is called a *drive*. A drive, then, is a tendency, initiated by shifts in physiological balance, to be sensitive to certain stimuli of a certain class and to respond in any of a variety of ways that are related to the attainment of a certain goal. A drive is a very different thing from an instinct. An instinct is a phylogenetically determined fixed action pattern designed to react to a specific stimulus in an organized and biologically adaptive way that is characteristic of a given species.

Definitions of Instinct

The most famous of all definitions of instinct, and the one that has been most widely influential in the social and behavioral sciences, is that given by William McDougall in his widely read *An Introduction to Social Psychology,* first published in 1908. In this work, which went into twenty-three editions and was reprinted many times more, instinct was defined as "an inherited or innate psycho-physical disposition which determines its possessor to perceive, and pay attention to, objects of a certain class, to experience an emotional excitement of a particular quality upon perceiving such an object, and to act in regard to it in a particular manner, or, at least, to experience an impulse to such action."

McDougall's definition of an instinct states what most people believe an instinct to be, although they might not be able to formulate their belief as programmatically as McDougall did. Virtually all definitions of instinct since McDougall, however independently devised, have largely followed the pattern set by him. For example, Professor Niko Tinbergen's ethological definition of an instinct describes it as "a hierarchically organized nervous mechanism which is susceptible to certain priming, releasing and directing impulses of internal as well as of external origin, and which responds to these impulses by coordinated movements that contribute to the maintenance of the individual and the species." There have been numerous similar definitions.

Essentially we find that most definitions of instinct embody the same assumptions. The most common of these appear to be (1) innate determiners of some kind which, (2) when affected by particular stimuli, (3) call into function certain neural, glandular, and muscular mechanisms (4) that underlie particular patterns of behavior or even "psychological states." Such definitions of instinct are invariably based on the study of behavior in "lower" animals, and not the behavior of humans. Tinbergen, suspecting that there may be a difference, is properly cautious when he comes to discuss the possibility of instincts in humans. What has been proved in other animals, he writes, has not been proved in humans. "Further, different species have different instincts. For instance, while many species have a parental instinct, others never take care of their offspring and hence probably do not have the corresponding neurophysiological mechanisms." Furthermore, "a species might lack a certain instinct because, having lost it relatively recently, it retained the nervous mechanism but not the required motivational mechanism. So long as we know nothing about such things, it would be well to refrain from generalizations."

Let it be noted that Tinbergen emphasizes that instincts may be lost while retaining the nervous mechanism formerly associated with the instinct, but no longer possessing the required motivational mechanism. These very relevant facts are seldom referred to in discussions of instinct in humans.

Tinbergen's words sound the proper note of caution. His assumption, however, that his interpretation of instinct holds for all other animals calls for the most careful, skeptical examination. The truth is that the concept of "instinct" has assumed the form of a "doctrine," and represents an outstanding example of reification—the employment of an abstraction as if it had a real existence. The revival of "instinct" as an explanatory device by Lorenz and Tinbergen has been thoroughly examined and rejected both on the basis of experimental evidence and theory, first by Professor

Daniel S. Lehrman and subsequently by almost all other students of the subject.

The trouble with Lorenz and Tinbergen, as well as with some other ethologists, is that they have considered behavior to be "innate" or "inherited," as if these words, as Lehrman originally pointed out, demonstrably referred "to a definable, definite, and delimited category of behavior." The idea that there is anything in any organism, especially in humans, whether in the genes or in anything else, that determines fixed action patterns is rejected by most students of behavior. As Professor Peter H. Klopfer, of the Department of Zoology at Duke University, has said, "The difficulty in relating behavior, however stereotyped it may seem, to genetics actually stems from an obsolete and incorrect notion of gene action. This notion which, in its essentials, holds the chromosome to be a biological homunculus [i.e., a little man seated in the chromosome] is derived from the one-gene-one-enzyme hypothesis [namely, that each gene controls the synthesis or activity of a single protein], which is in itself an oversimplification." Klopfer goes on to point out that heritable differences in behavior would become more intelligible if we viewed the gene not as a repository of data or a blueprint from which an organism could be reconstructed—that is, "an inchoate homunculus"—but rather as an information-generating device which exploits the predictable and ordered nature of its environment. And while it is erroneous to speak of behavior as inherited, it is true that it may be more or less stereotyped. But this will vary with the organism and with the behavior involved, presenting a continuum of acts, perceptions, or responses ranging from the highly plastic and variable at one end to highly constrained or stereotyped at the other. In humans the striking thing is the variability and plasticity that characterize their responses, and the very large roles experience and learning play in the establishment of even fairly simple patterns of behavior.

The "Innate" and the "Acquired" or "Learned"— A False Dichotomy

One of the difficulties in discussions of this sort is that some ethologists are wedded to outmoded ways of thinking concerning the mechanisms of behavior. The term "innate," for instance, is critical here since it is usually employed as synonymous with "instinct," while it is at the same time also used to denote the genetic predeterminance of the manner in which organic traits develop. Lorenz, for example, states that what rules individual development (ontogeny) "is obviously the hereditary blueprint contained in the genome [the chromosomal set of the organism] and not the environmental circumstances indispensable to its realization. It is not the bricks and the mortar which rule the building of a cathedral but a plan which has been conceived by an architect." The innate, says Lorenz, is what is determined by the chromosomal blueprint which reacts selectively to certain stimuli with the appropriate message leading to effector organizations equally adapted to dealing with the situation. Such innate determinants, Lorenz tells us, are the products of evolutionary processes.

The fact, however, that any characteristic of an animal is genetically based, in the sense that it has been arrived at by the processes of evolution, tells us nothing whatever concerning the influences by which that characteristic has been affected during the process of individual development. It is well established that under differing environments the genes for certain traits will express themselves differently. For example, a small elevation in temperature will change the eye color of certain crustaceans (*Gammurus*) or affect the wing length of the fruit fly (*Drosophila melanogaster*), and thus its ability to fly. In humans varying conditions in the prenatal environments of identical twins may produce substantial differences in their subsequent organic and mental development.

It is misleading to think of the chromosomal set as the blueprint which specifies the plan for the construction of the organism, unless one completes the thought "within certain environments." For the same reason it is unsound to speak of the organism as being "programmed" or "wired" for behavior. Such analogical terms convey an entirely false impression of the facts. As Lehrman has pointed out, a blueprint presents a one-to-one (isomorphic) relationship between its specifications and what is to be constructed. Each part of the structure is represented by a separate part of the blueprint, and each part of the blueprint refers only to a specific part or parts of the structure. This is very different from the relationship existing between genes and traits in animals. No structure or trait is represented in a single gene or well-defined group of genes, nor are spatial relationships between genes reflected in the spatial relationships between the traits to which the genes refer. For genes to contain a blueprint for behavior an item would have to be specified for every single piece of the act, neural, biochemical, glandular, muscular, and so on. And this is absurd. "Programming" and "wiring" similarly constitute false analogies since the former refers to something very like a blueprint or computer program which simply unfolds with growth, and the latter to a contained and insulated arrangement which is triggered into action by the appropriate stimulus. Analogies are no substitute for analysis.

The late Professor Theodore C. Schneirla, curator of animal behavior at the American Museum of Natural History, constantly warned against the "heredity-environment," "innate-learned," or "acquired" trap, and suggested that a view more closely corresponding to the facts be based on the concepts of "maturation" and "experience." Maturation refers to the contribution to development from growth and tissue development, experience refers to the contribution to development of the effects of stimulation from all available sources (extrinsic and intrinsic), including their functional trace elements surviving from earlier development.

This by no means implies that there are no genes, or that all genes are alike, or that genes have little or no influence. What it says is that development is a process of maturation and differentiation as a consequence of the interaction between genes and the environments in which they function.

Professor Gilbert Gottlieb of the North Carolina Department of Mental Health in a fascinating series of studies has shown that while the instinctive auditory perceptual responses of ducklings and other birds to the maternal call will achieve a high degree of perfection in the absence of normally occurring stimulations, such as its own vocalizations while still in the egg, full maturity of response will not be achieved unless it does hear its own chirpings. These findings lead Professor Gottlieb to conclude that even in what appear to be the most unlearned types of instinctive behavior, as in the response to the maternal call in these birds, what seems to have occurred during evolution was a selection for the entire manifold, not simply the organic part but the experiential part as well. In other words, that so-called innate behavior is experience-dependent for its full development.

This has all been summarized very well by Professor Howard Moltz of the Department of Psychology, Brooklyn College. In a wide-ranging critical examination of instinct theory, he was able to show that in the development of the individual the synthesis of response systems is brought about

by the integration of both intrinsic (intraorganic) and extrinsic stimulative conditions. Gene effects are contingent
upon environmental conditions, on experience. The classes
of relationships into which the genetic constitution is capable of entering is dependent on the prevailing environmental context. The environment is not simply benignly sup-
portive, but is actively implicated in determining the very
structure and organization of each response system.

The epigenetic view is in marked contrast with the tem-
plate conception of the instinct theorist which maintains
that instincts are innate, fixed action patterns resulting from
the virtually passive translation of genetic factors into behavioral or other traits through the medium of tissue growth
and differentiation. According to such theorists, each instinct has its locus in underlying neural coordinating centers.

But, in fact, there exist no adaptively organized responses,
either species-specific or otherwise, that exhibit the genetic
parallelism asserted by the instinct theorist. It is the inter-
meshing during individual development of genetic processes with experience that gives those genetic processes their
significance. It is this coalescence of intrinsic and extrinsic
factors "which makes each integrated response an emergent
and which thus renders it gravely misleading to conceptu-
alize maturational elements as functioning isomorphically
[i.e., in point-for-point correspondence between genic and
behavioral traits] in behavioral development."

Furthermore, since aggressive behavior in humans does
not appear to be stereotyped or to be invariable or consistent in its appearance, or capable of appearing in vacuo if it
has not been expressed for a long time, it can hardly be said
to satisfy the requirements of the Lorenzian conception of
the "innate." The epigenetic interpretation of the evidence
sees behavioral development not as an unfolding of a pre-

determined, fixed, wired, or programmed response, but as
the emergence of new phenomena and properties not contained in the genes. This is the fact the importance of which
cannot be overemphasized.

The "Sexual Instinct": A Good Example of the Role of Learning

The so-called sexual instinct constitutes an outstanding example of the role of learning in what most people take to be
a clear example of an instinctual drive. The truth is rather
more interesting and revealing than that, for while all human beings, like other animals, are equipped with all the
neurophysiological arrangements and organs which have
been evolved to function under particular conditions in certain ways we call sexual, they will, in fact, be able to respond only after a complex system of learning. The "energies," as it were, fueling the sexual drive, which are largely
hormonal, act upon a nervous system, which has to be taught
how to direct and employ those "energies" and organs. In
short, no one is born with the *ability* to perform sexually.
Nor is this an ability which will develop with age in the absence of the appropriate conditioning stimuli. The *capacity*
to perform sexually is one thing; the ability is quite another. The capacity is a potentiality which develops gradually and must be trained; that is, learning must take place
if the capacity is to become an ability. Difficult as it may be
to believe, in the second half of the twentieth century, in an
age of sexual freedom, in every civilized land for which
information is available, there are to be found grown men
and women of normal intelligence who enter upon marriage
without the slightest idea of how to go about sexual intercourse or even, indeed, know that such a thing is possible.
Almost every obstetrician, gynecologist, urologist, and mar-

riage counselor of experience will have encountered such cases.

Unless the individual learns what to do with his or her sexual feelings or impulses, there is nothing in the body, brain, or mind that will automatically lead the individual to sexual intercourse. The lack of any innate predeterminants for such behavior therefore conclusively eliminates it from the class of instincts. This is not to deny that all sorts of biological elements are involved in the development of sexual behavior, or that under normal conditions of social growth and development dispositions develop having as their object sexual behavior of some sort. But such sexual behavior requires the priming effect of learning if, for example, sexual intercourse is to be successfully accomplished. To call such dispositions "innate" is to obscure the fact that while many physiological changes are occurring in the developing individual the accompanying psychological changes frequently observed are largely influenced by cultural conditioning. Thus, for example, whether the object of sexual interest will ultimately be a member of the opposite sex or of one's own sex or of both sexes will, except in rare cases of prenatal hormonal sensitization, be culturally conditioned. Sex behavior changes observable in Western individuals, such as adolescent stress, gender identity, hypersexual activity, and the like, do not necessarily occur in individuals of other culture areas. Such changes, often attributed to "hormones" or other "innate" factors are, in any event, everywhere largely learned. Monkeys, apes, and humans, in that order, have become increasingly dependent upon learning in order to know what to do about their sexual impulses. Of course, hormones play a role in "fueling," as it were, the sexual impulses, but it is learning that determines the acquisition of the knowledge necessary for the practice of sexual relations.

"Instinct" Obscures and Oversimplifies

The terms "instinct" and "innate" oversimplify and obscure the complexities involved in the behavior they purport to define, with the net effect of confusing issues which require much fuller exploration and analysis. We agree with Professor Frank Beach that when analytic methods have been "applied to various types of behavior which today are called 'instinctive,' the concept of instinct will disappear, to be replaced by scientifically valid and useful explanations."

As Professor S. A. Barnett, of the Department of Zoology at the National University at Canberra, has pointed out, " 'Instinct' itself is a notable example of what Ogden and Richards call a nomad: it wanders from meaning to meaning, sometimes even in a single work. . . . It is indeed now sometimes urged, with good reason, that the word 'instinct' be banished from scientific writing. . . . But semantic rigor alone is a hollow achievement. . . . Ways of speaking which no longer match the needs of the time are not so much consciously discarded as neglected."

Unfortunately, as we have seen, the term "instinct," although it may be neglected by some workers, is still quite popular with many students of behavior, and for most laymen it constitutes an article of faith more solidly entrenched, possibly, than the belief in the Deity.

The layperson, following established usage and what he or she believes to be the facts, finds it easy to accept the idea of an "instinct of aggression," since it explains everything. But what explains everything in fact explains nothing. The fallacy of corrupting actualities with words or names was pointed out by the Chinese philosopher Hsun Tzu about 250 B.C. Words and names, as we well know, "stiff with years of veteran service," as William James put it, are not easily changed or displaced. The word that solves an enigma and illuminates a universal principle is likely to endure long after its fallacies have been demonstrated. We still speak of "blood" as the carrier of human heredity, though it has been known for almost a century that blood has no such function. "Race" is another such term, and there are many others like it. In connection with such matters as we are here discussing, John Stuart Mill put it very well when, in 1848, in his *Principles of Political Economy,* he observed: "Of all the vulgar modes of escaping from the consideration of the effect of social and moral influences on the human mind, the most vulgar is that of attributing the diversities of conduct and character to inherent natural differences."

There is a strong human propensity to confuse theories with facts, especially when theories are more appealing or easier to grasp than the facts. Facts constitute evidence, but, contrary to the conventional wisdom, they do not speak for themselves. Facts are reliable only if they hold up in repeated investigations of their reality; a theory is valid if it offers the best possible interpretation of the facts, that is, the soundest and most logical, and satisfies the critical judgment of independent authorities.

"Instinct" and Aggression

With respect to the problem of aggression we face two major questions. Question One concerns Lorenz's evidence for an "instinct" of aggression in "lower" animals. We ask: Is this evidence he offers reliable? (Does it include all of the important facts now available and relevant to behavior in other animals? How validly does he interpret this evidence —for example, without appealing to authority or to personal prejudices, and so on?) This is Question One.

Question Two is: How well do the evidence and the argument that Lorenz offers for other animals apply to humans?

Readers must accept the possibility that on all points Lorenz fails on the answers to Question One. For example, the theory which holds that aggression is innate is misleading since it is not really supported even for other animals. If this is the case, and we think it is, anyone (e. g., Ardrey) who answers yes to Question One had better reconsider any arguments he or she bases on Lorenz.

Lorenz himself takes for granted and abundantly rationalizes his conclusion that he has answered Question One in the affirmative. That is, he thinks he has demonstrated the soundness of his belief that "instinctive aggression" exists in "lower" animals. We doubt that he has done so, for reasons made clear in this book. Moreover, we hold that Lorenz has not demonstrated how any answer to Question One may bear on Question Two. This is not to say that a really valid answer to Question One could have some important bearing on Question Two. We agree with those writers who have stated that Lorenz's procedure of applying his doctrine of innate aggression in other animals directly to humans is naïve.

As Professor Theodore C. Schneirla wrote: "The question is not whether results concerning behavior in lower animals are applicable to man, but whether the application is as simple a matter as Lorenz's procedures imply. . . . The significance Lorenz gives his results is too great to justify his non-experimental, anecdotal treatment of the subject."

In spite of every attempt to show that instincts are in the saddle and ride humankind, all such attempts have failed for the simple reason that even in other animals behavior credited to instinct has only too often been shown to involve many other factors, such as the individual history of the organism during development, early learning, kind of later stimulation, and so on. The "evidence" for instincts in humans has been largely anecdotal or declarative, or else illusory, and for the most part based simply either on an inadequate examination of the evidence or on a simple misinterpretation of it. As Hinde has said, "The manner in which aggressive behaviour can be influenced by experiential factors is clearly a matter of rather fundamental importance, but it has not received the attention it deserves. There are, however, abundant indications of the inadequacy of Lorenz's (1966) implication that experiential influences on aggressiveness are of minor importance in most vertebrates."

Instincts in Man?

At this point let us return to Professor Anatol Rapoport's question: Why should instincts not exist in man? "Are we to believe that such an immense biological gap exists that nothing at all has been left of our biological heritage?"

Let us deal with the first question. Why should instincts not exist in humans? For the best of all reasons: because they would be adaptively utterly useless to a creature that responds to the challenges of the environment by the use of intelligence and learning. Instinct may serve a useful purpose in other creatures, creatures that still live largely in a biological universe, but in the case of humanity, which has evolved as such in a largely human-made environment, instinctive behavior not designed to meet the requirements of the human environment would have been thoroughly maladaptive, and would quickly have led to the extinction of a population constitutionally so ill endowed. Instincts, by definition, predetermine reactions to particular stimuli. In the human-made environment instincts would not only have been redundant but would have acted as so many bunions calculated to impede the pilgrim's progress. Instincts would simply have got in the way of the *responses* that were called for—not reactions but *responses*. A reaction is automatic, a response is a weighed, thought-out solution to a problem, and it is in a complex, problem-solving *human* environment that humanity evolved. If human beings ever had any remnants of instincts to begin with, they would have lost them.

That, in brief, is the answer to the question "Why should instincts not exist in humans?" It also happens to be the answer to the question of why there is such an immense gap —it has been described by some as "a quantum leap"—between humanity and other creatures. It is not that nothing at all has been left of our biological heritage, but that humans have evolved under conditions in which they have been more or less continually under the pressure of problem-solving challenges from the cultural and physical environments. As a consequence, humans have moved into a new zone of adaptation in which their behavior is dominated by learned responses, *not* by predetermined reactions. It is within the dimension of culture, the learned, the human-made part of the environment, that humans grow, develop, and function as behaving organisms. And it is the cultural environment that has exerted the greatest selective pressure in molding humans not only culturally but also physically.

Professor Clifford Geertz, of the Institute for Advanced Study at Princeton, has put it very well. He writes: "Recent research in anthropology suggests that the prevailing view that the mental dispositions of man are genetically prior to culture and that his actual capabilities represent the amplification or extension of these pre-existent dispositions by cultural means is incorrect. The apparent fact that the final stages of the biological evolution of man occurred after the initial stages of the growth of culture implies that 'basic,' 'pure,' or 'unconditioned,' human nature, in the sense of the innate constitution of man, is so functionally incomplete as to be unworkable. Tools, hunting, family organization, and, later, art, religion, and 'science' molded man somatically; and they are, therefore, necessary not merely to his survival but to his existential realization. It is true that without men there would be no cultural forms; but it is also true that without cultural forms there would be no men."

These are points of the most fundamental importance if we are to understand what the nature of humanity's evolution has been. That the later stages of the biological evolution of humanity occurred after the initial stages of the growth of culture is fully attested by the immense growth of the brain from the australopithecine average of about 500 cubic centimeters to 1500 cubic centimeters in Neanderthal man, with its apparent stabilization to around 1400 cubic centimeters in modern man. And as Professor Ralph L. Holloway, Jr., of the Department of Anthropology at Columbia University, has argued, the major changes in the brain from australopithecines to more advanced forms would have involved increasing degrees of complexity resulting from the increase in connections between neurons. Such increase in interconnections would have allowed for greater degrees of discrimination of both the cultural and physical environments, prediction, and memory *control,* as well as capacity. "That is, it would mean increasing adaptability or plasticity along essentially continuous lines." Holloway calls this aspect of behavioral adaptation "complexity-management."

What is involved is not merely adaptation to a vastly increased complex sensory input but also an increase in the ability to integrate this into a functioning individual and collective social system. Unquestionably, selective social pressures in the evolution of humanity have been focused

largely on the ability of the individual to make these adaptive adjustments. Humans, as Holloway points out, have
constituted a major part of their own environment, and the
actions of early humans within the context of the general,
more passive environment must have become an integral
part of their environment in the total sense. Selection pressures to handle the ever-increasing complexity of the total
environment are by their nature, quantity, quality, and
interconnectednesses uniquely different from anything that
goes on in the world of other animals. Natural selection has
favored increasing size of brains because it favored those
brains that behaviorally could best meet the challenges of
the total environment, but especially that part of it continuously created and rendered more complex by humans.
"Shifts," writes Holloway, "in neuro-endocrine control and
their pathways would have been attendant upon shifts of
the aggressive co-operative axis of behavior from an early
ape-like group to the hominid condition, where there was
co-operative sharing of food, probable division of labor, full
receptivity of the female, domestication of the male, and
patterned symbolic methods of social control and interaction. Thus selection pressures would have favored behavior
related to more co-operative forms of social behavior and
at the same time favored that apparatus [i.e., the brain]
most capable of handling greater environmental complexity
in terms of social and material stimulation discriminations."

The enormous growth of the brain during the first three
years of life in the human infant, trebling in weight from
birth at 350 grams to 1115 grams at the end of the third
year, suggests the immense importance of the role that
learning has played in placing a selective premium on the
increase in brain size, for it is within these first three years
that the basic learning has to be done, the basic foundations
laid for a superstructure that will take many more years to

construct. If changes in the gene pool may be regarded as a reaction, mediated by natural selection, to changes in environmental conditions, then there can be not the slightest doubt that the genetic constitution of humans embodies predispositions that have been molded over the last five million years or more to the present day by those environmental changes. And these changes have principally been of a cultural nature, in which a continuous positive feedback interaction existed between cultural and genetic change.

Culture is an agency not only for controlling but for changing the pressures of natural selection, and thus for influencing the evolution of humans both physically and culturally. The cultural processes through the agency of which such evolutionary changes are achieved are many—as, for example, through the development of tools, marriage regulations, sexual selection, social selection, cooperativeness, economic development, migration, improved child care, and the like. It is principally through cultural pressures that the behavior we recognize as uniquely human was developed. It must be emphasized that this change has been brought about not by the gradual suppression of instinctual drives, or by creating artificial barriers against them, but by an adaptively more effective means of meeting the challenges of the environment, namely, by enhancing the ability to learn, and the development of intelligence.

The High Selective Value of Human Learning

The development of learning and intelligence has been at a high selective premium in the evolution of humans, and has led to the species trait that distinguishes humans from all other living creatures—namely, their great educability. The human being's educability puts learning in the place of such instincts as in other animals may influence their be-

havior. In the evolution of humanity the rewards have gone
not to those who reacted instinctively but to those who
were able to make the most appropriate responses to the
challenges with which they were confronted. Where the
emergence of novelty, inventiveness, improvisation, origi-
nality, and thoughtful response is required, instinct is no
match for intelligence. And the development of a high intelligence was conditional upon the ability to learn and the
liberation from the body-compulsion of instinct.

For the innate aggressionists instincts are organic; they
arise within the organism; they are, as it were, parts of its
bodily (i.e., neural) structure. They are somatized, narrowly
limited, behavioral reactions. It is a main difference between humanity and other animals that the latter rely upon
the body and its capacities by which adaptation to the environment may be implemented—as, for example, by the
development of structures which may be used for defensive
purposes—whereas humanity has evolved by the opposite
principle, namely, by escape from the constricting bondage
of reliance upon organically determined predispositions, to
the freedom of what has been called "the superorganic," to
the human-made way of adapting oneself to the challenges
of the environment.

"Had our ancestors," writes J. B. S. Haldane, "had a few
million years in which to develop instincts appropriate to a
bipedal mammal I doubt if they could have become men. If
our descendants ever achieve a stable and permanent culture lasting with some little change over some millions of
years, they may develop instincts suited to it, and cease to
be men. Our relative lack of instincts has so far enabled us
to adapt ourselves to the changes which we have made and
are making in our environments." "The scope of human
instinctive knowledge is limited, and we feel the lack of it.
Free will is hard to bear. . . . Man did not arise with a set

of instincts as detailed as those of most other vertebrates, from which he had to emancipate himself. Wordsworth described this human absence of instinct as

> Blank misgivings of a creature
> Moving about in worlds not realised."

The most important setting of human evolution has been and continues to be the human cultural environment. It is because cultural response has been the most important dimension through which we have made our adaptations to the environment that "the immense biological gap exists between us and other species."

May it not be possible, Dr. Rapoport inquires, that "the aggressive instinct that has survival value for a great many species lingers in man as a maladaptive feature, which will eventually bring about his extinction? If so, the recognition of this fact is of the utmost importance."

The "Aggressive Instinct" and the Myth of the "Beast"

The recognition of the facts is, indeed, of the greatest importance. We have already seen that the attribution of instincts, and especially of an "aggressive instinct," to humans, is rather more than questionable. As for the alleged "aggressive instinct that has survival value for a great many species," what, it may be inquired, *is* this so-called "aggressive instinct" in other species? Is it the "instinct" that causes other "species" (Dr. Rapoport's word) to make war on one another, to murder and to mug, to assassinate leaders, or what? The myth of the "beast" has been long with us as a convenient scapegoat upon which to project our own sins, and so "the jungle," "the wild," and "the wild beast" have been saddled with all the worst attributes of humans and their conduct—and insult has been added to injury by attributing our sins to allegedly "bad seed" inherited from an "animal ancestry." In that sense we contrive to invest the idea of "animal ancestry" with the most pejorative of all qualities: that being an animal is in itself a mark of "bestiality." Hence, our propensity to describe peculiarly noxious human behavior as "animal," or "bestial," or even "Neanderthal." In the matter of Neanderthal man, the real truth presents us with a cautionary example of the kind of projective thinking that is so characteristic of the prejudiced mind. In keeping with the myth of the beast and the fact of humanity's animal ancestry the original describers of Neanderthal man endowed him with knock knees, a stooping gait, a bull neck, beetle brows, and a "bestial" face. And, of course, the cartoonists, following suit, invariably depicted him carrying a heavy club dragging his woman by her hair behind him. All this is completely false.

Neanderthal man, even though he was shorter than modern man, had a much larger brain. From the archeological evidence we know that Neanderthal man must have been an individual of considerable spiritual development, the first among human beings to bury the dead, and in some groups at least to do so with tenderness on a bed of flowers surrounded by objects that would make the departed comfortable on the journey to the other world. Prejudices of the nineteenth century, however, were such that virtually everything relating to our prehistoric ancestors was seen through the distorting glass of a theory that equated the prehistoric with the "primitive," "undeveloped," "brutal," and "animalistic." Not only were these traits attributed to prehistoric humanity, but what is worse, so-called primitive peoples—"savages," no less—were also invested with them. The mandarins of "superior" technological civilizations were, of course, always able to find in the "savage," and in "savage societies," what they expected to find in him and his societies. This enabled them to look down upon such "inferior" undeveloped peoples as "living fossils," "superannuated races," and "primitive men" destined to be replaced in "the struggle for existence" by "the survival of the fittest." Hence, conflict, fighting, war, and conquest were seen as "nature's pruning hook," as Sir Arthur Keith put it; for, as General von Bernhardi declared in his notorious book *Germany and the Next War,* published in 1911, war renders the only biologically just decision, since there can be no more genuine arbiter of the fitness of nations. It is to this sort of reasoning that designations such as the alleged "aggressive instinct that has survival value for a great many species" lead.

The Function of Aggression

What, in fact, do we find aggression to be in other species? And what is the "survival value" of such behavior? We have already touched upon these questions, and we underscore the answers here. Field studies during the last twenty years, on many different kinds of animals, have thrown considerable light on these questions. These studies have revealed that fighting within the group, especially among mammals, is of a very different order from that which characterizes the fighting of humans. The general conclusion, summarized by Professor V. C. Wynne-Edwards of the Department of Zoology, University of Aberdeen, is this: "Although . . . the stakes are sometimes life or death, serious fights and bloodshed are uncommon. Convention restricts the contestants very largely to displaying themselves for mutual appraisal or engaging in a harmless trial of strength, and from these actions they predict what the outcome of real combat would be without needing to fight it out. What they do is to threaten or impress one another, at the crudest extreme by exposing or even briefly using their fighting weapons—butting with their horns or baring their teeth. In the most refined examples the victor overrides the self-confidence of the loser by sheer magnificence and virtuosity." The immediate outcome of such trials of strength is seen in the establishment of hierarchical status relationships, social roles, spacing, and the like. One must, however, distinguish between the species-adaptive ends served by a particular behavior and the motivation of the particular organism performing the behavior. While aggression may ultimately be the means by which the species spaces itself out, the *intent* of the aggressive organism is not that, but to gain ascendancy by physical prowess over others. Professor Adriaan Kortlandt, of the Department of Zoology of the University of Amsterdam, puts it succinctly. "The goal of fighting," he writes, "in many species is not so much fighting in itself but rather to establish a social organisation which makes fighting superfluous." Summarizing the evidence, Professor J. L. Cloudsley-Thompson states: "Threatening gestures and ceremonial displays frequently replace actual fighting. In this way conflict tends to become ritualized and adapted, so that its function may be achieved without harm to the rivals." Finally, as Professors Ueli Nagel and Hans Kummer of the University of Zurich put it, "Aggression in animals is primarily a way of competition, not of destruction." And that is the main point to be understood about animal aggression—namely, that a principal effect of animal aggression is the establishment of organized cooperative social relationships within the group through competition, and *not* the destruction of other members of the group. It is not killing but cooperation that is the fundamental result of aggressive behavior in animals, and it is in that effect that its principal survival value lies. As Professor Edward O. Wilson of the Biological Laboratories at Harvard has emphasized, there is no universal aggressive instinct. Furthermore, that "aggression evolves not as a continuous biological process, like the beat of the heart, but as a contingency plan of the animal's endocrine and nervous system, programmed to be summoned up in times of stress."

In primate societies, aggressive behavior, on the whole, plays a cohesive role. Its principal function appears to be to keep the amount of divisiveness and aggression to a minimum; that far from desiring to inflict injury upon others, the aggressors seek to reduce the amount of aggression accompanied by a minimum amount of injury to others and as little social disruption as possible. The fighting is, for the most part, ritualized—i.e., the principals go through the motions of aggressive behavior rather than becoming involved in its actual performance. In this manner ritualized fighting limits the consequences of aggressive encounters between conspecifics, and the social mechanisms controlling aggression between individuals and groups clearly contributes to the preservation of the species. Even in extraspecific encounters bluffing and display may be positively selected.

There can be little doubt that such nonlethal aggressive behavior has positive selective value, but to jump from this conclusion to go on to say, as many have done, that humans have been the subject of the same selective pressures constitutes a nonsequitur. Humans have had a very different kind of evolutionary history from that of other primates, and while natural selection has by no means been suspended in its action upon them, that action has been mainly directed toward a different set of conditions. In humans, cooperation and altruism have been at a much higher selective premium than in other primates. Competition has by no means been attenuated, although it should be evident that cooperation are each forms of competition in which under certain conditions they become highly selectively valuable.

In a small gatherer-hunter population what possible survival value could an "instinct of aggression" have that was directed toward the destruction of members of one's own species? Such destructive behavior could threaten in a short time the continued existence of the group.

This is not to say that intraspecific killing does not occur in other groups. It does. Such intraspecific killing has been observed in gulls, langurs, lions, hippos, hyenas, macaques, elephants, and some other animals. Professor Wilson believes that humans are among the more pacific mammals as measured by serious or lethal assaults per unit of time even when our episodic wars are averaged in. However that may be, the primary purpose of aggressive behavior is not to kill, but to achieve and to establish status relationships and social organization within the group. In large populations such aggressive behavior tends to insure the proper spacing of groups, so that crowding is avoided and the food supply is kept in adequate balance.

"Spontaneity" of Aggression?

What the innate aggressionists have done is to place a wholly unwarranted emphasis on killing as a goal of aggression. But as we have seen, killing is rarely the purpose of aggression; when animals kill for food they are no more motivated by feelings of aggression than are the workers in an abbatoir who kill animals that are to be eaten by unaggressive diners. When the lioness sets out in search of prey and the housewife goes out marketing, they both have a common goal in view, the feeding of the family; aggression on such occasions no more enters into the behavior of the one than it does into that of the other. Both lioness and housewife had to learn their respective roles. Women and eunuchs both lack male sex hormones and tend to be unaggressive. Male sex hormones or androgens tend to be associated with aggressivity; hence, such androgens may be considered a "biological base" for aggression. But such a "base" does not function spontaneously, nor does it act as a primary cause of aggression. There are no drives or instincts or predispositions to kill members of one's own or any other species, although under certain conditions men can easily be taught to do so. But this is a very different thing from claiming that there exists a "biological base" which "spontaneously" causes any animal, and especially a human being, to be aggressive. "Knowledge," writes Lorenz, "of the fact that the aggression drive is a true, primarily species-preserving instinct enables us to recognize its full danger: it is the spontaneity of the instinct that makes it so dangerous." We recall that Freud thought so too. In support of the existence of the spontaneity that characterizes the "instinct of aggression," Lorenz adds: "The fact that the central nervous system does not need to wait for stimuli, like an electric bell with a push-button, before it can respond, but that it can itself produce stimuli which give a natural, physiological explanation for the 'spontaneous' behavior of animals and humans, has found recognition only in the last decades, through the work of Adrian, Paul Weiss, Kenneth Roeder, and above all Erich von Holst."

What a pity it is that Lorenz failed to inform the reader of the actual nature of this work and the kind of animals upon which it has been carried out. Adrian's work was done on goldfish, that of Weiss on axolotls (larval forms of the salamander), Roeder's on insects, and von Holst's on the oysterfish. What Lorenz omits to tell the reader is that in all these experiments what was observed was that spontaneous muscular movements occurred in the fins of the fish studied, in the grafted limb of the axolotl, and in the copulatory movements of the praying mantis, in each case before the formation of reflex arcs between receptor, intermediate, and effector nerves, so that there was no question of sensory stimuli activating the motor neurons to produce the effector muscular movements. It may be that such endogenous activity of the nervous system exists in mammals, including humans, but at the level of so complex a behavior pattern as aggressive behavior, which Lorenz equates with a fixed action pattern—that is to say, an innate, coordinated sequence—that will express itself spontaneously, it is very unlikely that anything like the spontaneity that Lorenz claims exists. To extrapolate from the motor movements of insects, fish, and larval salamanders to the aggressive behavior of human beings is quite unjustifiable.

The threshold for aggressive behavior can be progressively lowered by learning so that it may come to appear as "spontaneous"; but that, again, is a very different thing from claiming spontaneity to be innate, requiring no "push-button" stimulus to set it off. Individuals socialized in violent environments are likely to become so habituated to violent feelings and behavior that their conduct may sometimes appear spontaneous. But even in the most violent cases the violence is always triggered by some external cause. Lorenz dilates on the necessity of periodic expressions of aggression, and tells the story of his deceased aunt, who regularly progressed from quarreling with her maids to discharging them after a final violent episode. He also observed, as a prisoner of war, the so-called polar disease or expedition choler, a condition which often appeared in men who were dependent on each other, but who were prevented from quarreling with strangers or people outside their own circles of friends. Such damming up of aggression, according to Lorenz, becomes dangerous, for there then follows an extreme lowering of the threshold of aggression. One becomes irritated by the small mannerisms of one's best friends. The man with insight removes himself from the proximity of the irritants. "But the human being without insight," Lorenz tells us, "has been known to kill his best friend."

Anecdotal observations of this kind are not without interest, but field or experimental observations are likely to be more dependable. I cannot recall any such systematic observations made on man, but those that have been made on rats and Siamese fighting fish do not support Lorenz's anecdotal "evidence." Van Hemel and Meyer placed rats in an operant chamber in which responses were reinforced by the presentation of a mouse, which the rats nearly killed. The rats were then satiated with mouse killing, and then deprived of mice, for one, two, or four days. Following such deprivation, it was found that the rate of killing was unrelated to the amount of deprivation. There was no increase in killing as a result of deprivation. In Siamese fighting fish Roger N. Johnson found no relation between the amount of deprivation from viewing conspecifics and their aggressive behavior following release from isolation: in fact, they performed the threat response less often rather than more after the longest period of deprivation.

But we need not turn to fish and rats for support of the fact that periodic expressions of aggression are unnecessary in order to avoid spontaneous overflow. There are plenty of prisoner-of-war records available from both the first and second world wars in which the "polar disease" to which Lorenz refers was not observed. There were the prisoner-of-war camps in which organized games, sports, entertainments, and escape projects provided socially deeply involving experiences. Under such conditions, and without the least necessity for the venting of aggression, the men had little time for brooding or allowing the secondary consequences of their imprisonment to result in intragroup conflict. On the contrary, what seems to have been pre-eminently brought out under such conditions was an extraordinary spirit of cooperation. The same was true of the Uruguayan footballers whose plane was wrecked high in the Andes, and who for seventy days lived isolated from the rest of the world in amity and cooperation.

As for Lorenz's aunt, there is no need to resort to the hydraulic theory of spontaneous aggression to explain her outbursts. There is a much simpler explanation than that. As Erich Fromm has said, the lady was clearly an exploitative narcissistic character whose impossible demands led to extreme anger and uncontrolled behavior. This type of character has also been similarly discussed by Dr. Gregory Rochlin in his book *Man's Aggression: The Defense of Self,* without resort to innate spontaneous aggression.

The Hydraulic Model of Aggression

Lorenz's hydraulic energy model of aggression is one among many of his hypotheses that have been severely criticized in the past, but to this criticism he makes no response. The trouble with all energy models is that they tend to be identified with physical energies which are directed toward discharge in action, thus allegedly "reducing" the "pressure" and bringing the behavior to an end, instead of through the change that is produced in the stimulus situation. As Klopfer has observed, the notion that aggression accumulates and requires discharge, as if it were a fluid liable to seep through the cracks in the cranium, is untenable. "We 'contain' aggression," writes Klopfer, "about as much as a radio 'contains' the music we hear issuing from it." In fact, a very complex external input has to be introduced into the device we call a radio before it is able to transmit the sound waves we receive as music. Aggression no more "flows" or "overflows" from any organism than music does from a radio. Hydraulic models of aggression are erroneous and obfuscating. Reviewing the evidence, Professor J. P. Scott, of the Department of Psychology of Bowling Green University, succinctly states the facts. "Lorenz's hydraulic model," he writes, "with its concept of a releasing stimulus, which lets loose an accumulated volume of energy, has no counterpart in the nervous system of any known animal." In spite of such criticism Lorenz continues to argue that humanity's problems arise in large part because this energy of aggressiveness, finding no proper outlet, overflows into forms of destructive behavior. Such destructive redirection of aggression may be aimed against oneself. Lorenz tells us that in 1955 he produced a paper "On the Killing of Members of the Same Species," in which he wrote "that present-day civilized man suffers from insufficient discharge of his aggressive drive. It is more than probable that the evil effects of the human aggressive drives . . . simply derive from the fact that in prehistoric times intra-specific selection bred into man a measure of aggression for which in the social order of today he finds no adequate outlet."

The Utes

As an example of the problem of "the hypertrophy of aggression owing to intra-specific selection," Lorenz cites the observations of Denver psychoanalyst Sydney Margolin, who, according to Lorenz,

> made very exact psychoanalytical and psycho-sociological studies on Prairie Indians, particularly the Utes, and showed that these people suffer greatly from an excess of aggression drive which, under the ordered condition of present-day North American Indian reservations, they are unable to discharge. It is Margolin's

opinion that during the comparatively few centuries
when Prairie Indians led a wild life consisting almost
entirely of war and raids, there must have been an extreme selection pressure at work, breeding extreme aggressiveness. That this produced changes in the hereditary pattern in such a short time is quite possible.
Domestic animals can be changed just as quickly by
purposeful selection. Margolin's assumption is supported by the fact that Ute Indians now growing up
under completely different educational influences suffer in exactly the same way as the older members of
their tribe who grew up under the educational system
of their own culture; moreover, the pathological symptoms under discussion are seen only in those Prairie
Indians whose tribes were subjected to the selection
process described.

Ute Indians, we are told, suffer more frequently from
neurosis than any other group and Margolin found, again
according to Lorenz, that the trouble was undischarged aggression. Violence toward people outside the tribe, and even
manslaughter, "belong to the order of the day," although
attacks on members of the tribe are extremely rare, for anyone killing a member of the tribe is compelled to commit
suicide. The Ute, according to Lorenz/Margolin, are particularly prone to accidents, and this accident-proneness is
thought by Lorenz to result from repressed aggression. The
Ute rate of motor accidents is alleged to exceed "that of
any other car-driving human group."

Omer C. Stewart, professor of anthropology at the University of Colorado, who has been studying the Ute since
1930 and is our leading authority on this people, can agree
with nothing in Lorenz/Margolin's comments on the Ute.
Margolin's views on the Ute appear not to have been published, but Professor Stewart has published a good deal on

this tribe, and moreover has commented directly on Lorenz/ Margolin's statements about this people.

Stewart disagrees with the Lorenz/Margolin "facts" as well as with their conclusions. In the first place, the Ute are not Prairie Indians; they are Mountain and Great Basin Indians. In the second place, they did not lead "a wild life consisting almost entirely of war and raids." In such activities they were involved only occasionally, and differed in no significant way from other Indian tribes. The Ute were neither a violent people nor addicted to war. They collaborated with the U.S. Government in nearly every way, and became aggressive only under severe provocation. The Ute did not have a rule compelling the suicide of the murderer of a fellow Ute. As for the Ute accident rate, it is high, says Stewart, because the excessive use of alcohol is high. Stewart challenges the statement that the Ute neurosis rate is abnormally high, and concludes: "Margolin's statements of fact which are subject to testing concerning the Ute Indians are simply not correct. Others are questionable."

Dr. John Beatty, of the Department of Anthropology of Brooklyn College, also finds the Lorenz/Margolin claims not in accordance with the evidence. While it is true that intra- and extra-group murders are rare among the Ute, suicides occur more frequently. The most common "crime" is drunkenness. As for the alleged "extreme selection pressure" which worked at "breeding extreme aggressiveness," Beatty points out that this would require a closed population, or else intermarriage with other aggressive groups. But the fact is that the Ute married with members of the pacific Pueblo groups, and the Bannock and Snake Indians living to the West who, again, were unaggressive peoples.

As for wars and raids, these were highly ritualized activities. The most common reasons for raiding were wife-stealing and horse-stealing. Killing and scalping occurred, but Grinnell states that "neither the killing nor the scalping was regarded as an especially creditable act. The chief applause was won by the man who could first touch the fallen enemy. In Indian estimation the bravest act that could be performed was to count coup on—to touch or strike—a living unhurt man and leave him alive, and this was frequently done."

Again, questioning the high motor-accident rate among the Ute, Beatty points out that the quality of the automobiles the Ute are able to afford may be a factor more relevant than aggression in the analysis of the causes of their accidents. He also believes that the questionable higher neurosis rate is in any event difficult to assess in view of the very real cross-cultural differences, and furthermore, where neurosis exists among the Ute it would be equally valid to ascribe the condition to general deprivation and despair, the consequence of the destructive social conditions under which they are forced to live.

Lorenz could hardly have chosen a worse example than Margolin's "very exact" studies to sustain his claims, either for "the spontaneity of the instinct of aggression" or as evidence of the self-destructive effects of aggression unable to find adequate discharge, or, finally, for the intraspecific selection of breeding and extreme aggressiveness. The marriage patterns of the Ute simply play havoc with Lorenz's attempt to provide a genetic basis for their alleged inbred aggressivity.

Having thoroughly surveyed the evidence, both experimental and observational, Professor J. P. Scott in his book *Aggression* (1958) concludes: "The important fact is that the chain of causation in every case eventually traces back to the outside. There is no physiological evidence of any spontaneous stimulation for fighting arising within the body. This means that there is no need for fighting, either aggressive or defensive, apart from what happens in the external environment. We may conclude that a person who is fortunate enough to exist in an environment which is without stimulation to fight will not suffer physiological or nervous damage because he never fights."

The Nonaggressiveness of Retarded Children

Were the spontaneity of aggression a fact and were it anything like as powerful as Lorenz suggests, one would expect severely mentally retarded children to be particularly aggressive since their power of inhibition is generally low. The exact opposite is, in fact, found. The mentally severely retarded and children with Down's Syndrome (mongolism) are seldom aggressive. Down's children are especially noted for their amiable disposition, and are usually described as "friendly, cheerful, harmless and affectionate. . . . They are not as a group distinguished by aggressiveness." Autistic children are especially notable for their unaggressiveness and avoidance of all aggressive situations.

One would have expected, according to the theory of innate aggression, that being less inhibited than normal individuals, the mentally retarded would tend to exhibit a much higher frequency of aggressive behavior than unaffected individuals. But the fact is that they behave aggressively much less frequently. This alone constitutes a telling argument against the Lorenzian idea of the spontaneity of human aggression. Not that under unfavorable conditions the mentally deficient cannot be taught to be aggressive; they can be. But it is only when they are taught as the result "either of a limited, unsympathetic environment on the one hand, or over-indulgence, and lack of discipline and training on the other [that] they may be difficult, bad-tempered and destructive."

In his painstaking investigation and report on autistic children Gerhard Bosch concludes "that the inability of autistic children to defend themselves against others cannot be adequately explained as cowardice, timidity, or inhibition in the characterological sense, but rather we can say that counter-attack or defense is impossible because the child has no experience of attacking or defensive relationship with others."

Clearly, these cases indicate that there must be some learning and outside stimulus to produce the aggressive behavior. In the absence of the learning and stimulation the behavior simply does not develop. Such observations on the mentally retarded—and especially on autistic children, who are not usually mentally retarded—indicate that while the neurological elements are available for organization to function as aggressive behavior, unless they are so organized aggressive behavior will not appear spontaneously.

Children and Aggression

In the normally well cared-for healthy child spontaneous aggression is not observed. Charlotte Bühler has pointed out that cooperative behavior among children is more basic than competitive response. She found that the latter type of response in her group of observed children did not make its appearance until about the third year. All investigators have found that aggressive behavior tends to increase as the child grows older. Lauretta Bender, professor of pediatrics at New York University Medical School, finds that far from being inborn, hostility or aggression in the child "is a symptom complex resulting from deprivations which are caused by developmental discrepancies in the total personality structure such that the constructive patterned drives for action in the child find inadequate means of satisfaction and result in amplification or disorganization of the drives into hostile or destructive aggression." "The child," she writes, "acts as though there were an inherent awareness of his needs and there is thus the expectation of having them met. A failure in this regard is a deprivation and leads to frustration and a reactive aggressive response."

Indeed, the creativeness of the organism is directed toward maturation in cooperativeness. Bender calls it "the inherent capacity or drive for normality." And as she says, "The emphasis on the inborn instinctive features of hostility, aggression, death wishes, and the negative emotional experiences represents a one-sided approach which has led our students of child psychology astray."

The late Professor Abraham Maslow, the humanistic psychologist, in an article entitled "Our Maligned Animal Nature," published in 1949, wrote: "I find children, up to the time they are spoiled and flattened out by the culture, nicer, better, more attractive human beings than their elders, even though they are of course more 'primitive' than their elders. The 'taming and transforming' that they undergo seem to hurt rather than help. It was not for nothing that a famous psychologist defined adults as 'deteriorated children.' . . . Could it be possible," Maslow inquired, "that what we need is a little more *primitiveness* and a little *less* taming?"

Similarly, Professor Katherine Banham, who during the course of twenty years studied over 900 children from four weeks to four years of age, concludes that children are born with outgoing affectionate drives, and that "they only become preoccupied with themselves, withdrawn or hostile as a secondary reaction, when rebuffed, smothered with unwanted ministrations, ignored or neglected."

None of these investigators would claim that there are no neural bases for aggression, or that constitutional differences do not exist in the disposition to express aggression. But what they would, I think, all agree on is that those neural bases and constitutional dispositions must receive a certain amount of stimulation before they can be mobilized to function in aggressive behavior, . . . that children will simply not react "spontaneously" with aggression but that aggressive behavior has to be provoked, and that its development into full-fledged aggression will depend on the subsequent training children receive in the expression of aggression.

When children pull the wings off a fly, there are those who see in such behavior the evidence of "innate" depravity. There is a failure to understand that the child may simply be interested in discovering how the fly works, in much the same way and for much the same reasons as he does when, at an opportune moment, he takes the family's treasured grandfather clock to pieces and attempts to put it together again. What he is displaying is not "innate aggressiveness" but curiosity, the most precious of intellectual traits. In the same manner he may behave with what appears to be cruelty toward small animals. But, in fact, there is generally no more intention to hurt the animal than there is to hurt the grandfather clock. It is affection for small animals that is the outstanding characteristic of children. When cruelty is deliberate in children, it is not innate aggression that is expressing itself but externally induced adaptive reactions to the pressures of parents, teachers, siblings, and the general living conditions which bear down upon the child. As Curran and Schilder put it many years ago:

> The development of the child is not seen merely as a maturation process but as a continuous process of social experimentation by which after trial and error, final construction is reached. . . . It should be stressed that the child is not merely aggressive but that he has a genuine and lively interest in the well-being and existence of those around him. . . .

There is a process of gradual organization of aggressive tendencies into a socially accepted concept in which the attitude of the surroundings is of paramount importance. The psychological situation of the child leads to the final crystallization of his aggressive tendencies.

In environments in which attitudes and conduct are such as to meet the child's need for support and involvement, aggressive behavior is seldom seen in children.

The genuine cruelty of which so many children have been known to be guilty is too easily attributed to innate aggression, when in virtually every case it can be traced back to the unfortunate social experience of the child. At a meeting of the Medical Association for the Prevention of War, in London in 1966, the discussants on "Aggression in Childhood" agreed that behind aggressive behavior there is always torment. The aggressive child believes that the world is against him and is therefore full of fear. Assuming attack to be the best form of defense, he employs the only forms he knows—vituperation and physical violence. These, at least, bring him a certain sense of achievement. What such children need beyond all else is reassurance. And, the discussants concluded, if there is any single specific in the therapy of maladjusted children, it is love. This may sound naïve, they added, but nothing can abate aggressive behavior as successfully.

As Drs. Nevitt Sanford and Craig Comstock have put it:

The child's natural potential for aggression does not become a source of destructiveness toward himself or others until aggressive impulses having specific objects and modes have been built up through experience. The crucially important experiences are losses or denials of love, weakness and humiliation, unjust pun-

ishment, threats of bodily harm—experiences which the
child interprets as having catastrophic implications.
Love and gentleness and firmness are the counters to
such experiences, but such are the exigencies of childhood that the generation of some aggressive impulses is
virtually unavoidable. The child still needs the parents'
help in learning to control these impulses, to express
them in relatively nondestructive ways.

However we may conceive the contribution of nature
and of experience to the generation of the child's aggression, there is no store of aggression which has to be
drained off in one way or another. . . . Aggression,
far from being drained off, is likely to become its own
stimulus, for aggressive behavior leads to feelings of
guilt, which may be suppressed by more aggression.

Lauretta Bender, summarizing her forty years of observation of children, reiterates: "Destructiveness and hostile
aggression in a child is a complex symptom caused by developmental pathology which disorganizes the normal constructive patterned drives, so that inadequate gratification leads
to frustration." And she emphasizes, if theories of innate
aggression were correct, instances of children causing a
death should not be uncommon. In her many years of experience she has been able to collect only thirty-three cases
in which children had been responsible for a death. In only
eight cases was it possible to investigate the background of
these children psychiatrically. In these eight cases the conclusions were striking. In each case the death was accidental
and unexpected by the child. All these children had experienced early social deprivation, and were also suffering
from such conditions as schizophrenia, encephalitis, epilepsy, and primary learning disabilities.

In more recent years, with the rapid increase in social disorganization, there has been a considerable increase in homi-

cides committed by juveniles. This fact in itself points to environmental factors as being closely related to aggressive behavior. Juvenile crime rates of every kind in civilized societies are reflections of conditions in the home as well as in society.

Psychotic Adults

A propos of our discussion of mentally retarded children as well as the autistic reference may also be made to psychotic adults. In his Reith Lectures, Professor G. M. Carstairs remarked that "we shall be free of fear of each other only when we recognize, and abate, our own destructive impulses." This remark elicited a response from a psychiatrist who chose to remain anonymous. He reported that he had never encountered an aggressive person among the six hundred psychotic patients he had treated. He protested against the indictment of all of humanity as being characterized by either original sin or aggressive propensity. "And I object," he wrote, "in spite of the apparently overwhelming evidence in favour of this indictment. As I see it, this evidence consists of the terrible acts of a few people, on the one side, and the flood of words and phantasies culled by psychiatry and history on the other." He goes on to point out that it has become fashionable to take a pessimistic view of man's nature, a view which is not merely incorrect but which also muddles research and creative thinking about our nature, since, if we believe that we have the answer to a problem, we shall not go on searching, as we must. With this pessimism goes the feeling that all politicians are corrupt, so why bother, with the resultant feeling of futility and despair. War is inevitable, so don't think about it. Crime is unavoidable, so let's restore the death penalty. Races and nations will always be opposed to each other, so let us each cultivate our own gardens, for there is not much else we *can* do, for we are all intrinsically bad, and there is nothing that can be done to alter that.

This pessimism, this apathy, as our psychiatrist says, amounts in fact to the symptoms of a depressive illness. "The ghost of self-lacerating melancholia wrings its hands," and the world goes to pot. In such a mood the new soothsayers and shamans, the innate aggressionists, carry a message which allays anxiety, removes guilt and encourages "business as usual."

The Nonadaptive Value of Murderous Behavior

"Our remote ancestors were probably . . . very aggressive," write Washburn and Hamburg. The probabilities, evaluated not alone on the basis of human behavior everywhere, especially the behavior of foraging and gatherer-hunter peoples, seem to us to indicate that our remote ancestors were probably very unaggressive. What possible causes could there have been to have produced such murderous conduct, and what possible advantage could there have been to a small population resorting to the kind of aggressiveness against their fellow humans that the innate aggressionists attribute to them? That the making of tools suddenly triggered off the bloody behavior attributed by the innate aggressionists to early man seems to us highly improbable. Yet, as we have seen, the innate aggressionists have seriously made that claim. And this in spite of the fact that there exist many peoples today who seldom or never use their tools as weapons with which to kill their fellow men. The fact that such peoples exist does not, of course, necessarily disprove that tools may have been employed as weapons for homicidal purposes by our remote ancestors. It simply seems to us, on the basis of the facts, extremely unlikely.

"Some" and "All"

As evidence that man is naturally aggressive and enjoys the destruction of other creatures, Washburn and Lancaster cite the fact that some anglers will use the lightest fishing tackle in order to prolong the fish's futile struggles, so that they might "maximize the personal sense of mastery and skill." "War," they write, "has been far too important in human history for it to be other than pleasurable for the males involved." The ease with which boys can be interested in hunting, fishing, fighting, and games of war constitutes a measure, according to these authors, of the extent to which the biological bases for killing have been incorporated into human psychology. This view is based on Hamburg's notion that the importance of a behavior for survival of the species is measured by the ease with which it is learned and its pleasurability. This may represent a perfectly sound principle, but its validity has yet to be established. However that may be, it seems quite unjustifiable to endow the whole human species with the kind of pleasure that some anglers may take in prolonging the painful struggles of the fish they catch. Other human beings have been appalled by the idea of fishing in this or in any other way. In the instance of anglers who prefer light tackle it is probable that most of them have never even asked themselves whether fish have any feelings at all. Certainly a sense of struggle, of mastery and skill may give them a feeling of euphoria, but it is unlikely that they feel in any way aggressive toward the fish.

As for the ease with which boys can be interested in hunting, fishing, fighting, and games of war, again, it is not all boys who can be so interested. Those who can surely do not exhibit such interest because of any biological bases that have been incorporated in their psychology, or because of any aggressive drives they may experience, but rather because it is something that boys in their culture are encouraged to do whenever they have the opportunity. They take pleasure in these exercises not because either in the past or in the present those exercises in any way contribute toward the survival of the species, but because the playfulness of these activities is satisfying in itself, and in a variety of other social ways which have nothing whatever to do with killing or aggression. There are individuals who enjoy inflicting pain on animals and on other human beings, but these persons are always abnormal and seriously disturbed. The few who may not be—if there are any such—are simply misguided. Both kinds, in any event, can hardly be accepted as evidence for the existence of biologically based aggression.

Robert Claiborne in his excellent book *God or Beast* has characterized the innate aggressionists' use of what he calls "the Evasive We" in describing the sins of a few as if they were those of the species as a rhetorical device of schlock sociology. He believes it is the political purpose of the "Evasive We" to shift responsibility for social evils from some to all. This may well be its purpose in some cases, but it is certainly not so in all. We may rather suspect its misuse in most cases to be due to a profound misreading of the facts of life, equivalent to the equation of the part with the whole. The great majority of people do not and never have exhibited the kind of behavior with which the innate aggressionists invest "us." We may safely join Mr. Claiborne and his friends in claiming that most of us have never had the least desire to be violent in any shape or form or to control large areas of land or people—indeed, not even *small* areas and a few people. "We" are not violent. On the basis of history and everyday experience "we" repudiate the suggestion. *Some* people *are* violent—but let us not confuse "some" with "all."

Inhibition

Lorenz makes the point that among animals instinct involves mechanisms that inhibit violence against members of their own species, but that such mechanisms have not evolved in human beings. This may well be, but it does not mean that human beings do not inhibit behavior. They do so every day, if not every hour, of their lives, in every area of their activity. They do it the way they do everything else, by choosing, on the basis of everything that has happened to them, either consciously or unconsciously, either thoughtfully or impulsively, either wisely or foolishly. They refrain from hitting one another; they decline to betray their friends; they give up their heart's desire for someone else's dream. The list is endless of human behavior that is characterized by the inhibition of some hostile act. And all of it comes from the human side of a human being, and it takes the place of the instinctive inhibition of the insect, or the goose, or the dog.

The fact is that Lorenz, Ardrey, and the other innate aggressionists have failed entirely to make their argument that aggression is an instinctive behavior pattern in human beings. Even in animals, as innumerable studies have shown, behavior is not as instinctive as the innate aggressionists believe it to be. In human beings especially, in whom innate influences on many forms of behavior are capable of total or almost total control or modification by environmental influences, aggression represents the expression of the interaction between genetic potentials and environmental, social environmental, experiences. It is because this is the fact that we can have every hope that with the proper understanding based on such facts we shall be able to deal sensibly with the problem of human aggression.

5
Cannibalism and Aggression

Is Cannibalism an Evidence of Innate Aggression?

> Of the Cannibals that do each other eat,
> The Anthropophagi, and men whose heads
> Do grow beneath their shoulders,

Lorenz and Ardrey speak with what sometimes gives the impression of Pentecostal ardor, for if it could be shown that prehistoric humans were cannibals, *that* would constitute yet another proof of their view of innate human nastiness. "Cannibalism," Mr. Ardrey tells us, "has been a prevalent pastime throughout all the human record." One can only wonder what evidence Mr. Ardrey has for that statement. Cannibalism has occurred in many societies, past and present, but that it was at any time either "prevalent" or a "pastime," there is good reason to doubt. A few "exceptions" might be allowed, but not more.

Cannibalism in various ways and to various degrees is practiced among many nonliterate peoples. The practice ranges from ritual token cannibalism, in which one eats a small portion of a dead member of a family from a feeling of affection or veneration, to the rare kind of cannibalism of some Highland New Guinea tribes who actually enjoy raiding other peoples and eating those they have killed. Ronald Berndt has vividly described the horrifying cannibalistic practices of such tribes in New Guinea in his book *Excess and Restraint* (1962). But such cannibalism is extremely rare.

The Evidence

That the australopithecines were any more cannibalistic than apes or any other more recent forms of men is very unlikely. Chimpanzees will occasionally eat one of their own dead infants or an infant belonging to another group, but this is rare and has not been recorded for any other ape. Cannibalism has been suggested in the case of Solo Man from the Upper Pleistocene of Java. In some of the skulls of Solo Man the great foramen (foramen magnum) at the base of the skull has been enlarged, to permit, it has been conjectured, extraction of the brain. Such enlargements had also been found in the skulls of Peking Man (*Homo erectus*) excavated at Choukoutien near Peking, belonging to the Middle Pleistocene, and dating back some 350,000 years. Many of the long bones had also been split open, with the object, it is thought, of extracting the marrow. "Peking Man," Lorenz informs us, "the Prometheus who learned to preserve fire, used it to roast his brothers: beside the first traces of the regular use of fire lie the mutilated and roasted bones of *Sinanthropus pekinensis* himself."

This statement is typical of Lorenz's cavalier way with archaeological and anthropological facts. The truth is that of the many human bones and bone fragments recovered at Choukoutien, only one fragment, according to Weidenreich, showed the doubtful evidences of burning. Dr. Kenneth Oakley of the British Museum (Natural History), one of our leading authorities on these matters, concluded that "in the Choukoutien deposits . . . only animals' bones were in a charred or calcined condition." Not only has Lorenz been careless in checking the facts; he has also drawn conclusions from them which are thoroughly contraverted by the actual finds. This is not to say that fragments of charred bone of prehistoric men do not occur. They do. They have been found, for example, at Krapina in Yugoslavia. Here in a rock-shelter in a deposit which dates back some 40,000 or more years, the much fragmented skeletal remains, many of them charred and calcined, of some twenty individuals of Neanderthal type were found. Most authorities believe that these were the remains of one or more cannibal feasts. Whether the individuals involved were "brothers" eating each other or whether they were eaten by members of another band, it is not possible to say. That cannibalism was practiced occasionally in prehistoric times is certain; that it was habitually practiced is improbable, and not very likely that it was usually done from aggressive motives. From the fact that man hunted and ate other animals it does not follow that he also hunted and ate other humans.

It is quite possible that Peking Man and Solo Man sometimes resorted to cannibalism: it would be surprising if, on occasion, they did not. It is possible that prehistoric humans experienced periods of famine. Under such conditions the most civilized of humans have been known to resort to cannibalism in order to survive. The Donner Pass and the Nobile Expedition tragedies are but two of many historic examples. More recently, in December 1972, the amateur football team survivors of an air crash high in the snow-covered Andes in Chile stated that they had eaten the flesh of their dead comrades in order to stay alive. "When the moment came when we did not have any more food," said one of the survivors, "or anything of that kind, we thought to ourselves that if Jesus at His last supper shared His flesh and blood with His apostles, then it was a sign to us we should do the same—take the flesh and blood as the intimate communion between us all. It was this that helped us to survive."

Intimate communion or not, this was under the circumstances the most sensible thing to do. The prohibition against cannibalism is, of course, a civilized prejudice. The fact that cannibalism is regarded with horror among civilized people is entirely due to conditioning, but even that can be overcome and rationalized away under threat of imminent death from starvation.

The cultural bias in these matters is amusingly illustrated by an account given in a missionary's travelogue of many years ago. In it the author, speaking of an African tribe, writes: "Once, when told by a European that the practice of eating human flesh was a most degraded habit, the cannibal answered, 'Why degraded? You people eat sheep and cows and fowls, which are all animals of a far lower order, and we eat man, who is great and above all; it is you who are degraded.' "

The innate aggressionists claim that the evidence of prehistoric cannibalism constitutes additional evidence of our ancestors' innate depravity; in fact, it constitutes nothing of the sort. It is naïve of these writers to believe that prehistoric humans roasted and ate other humans because they felt hostile toward them, or that the bare fact of cannibalism constitutes the least evidence of innate depravity.

The Cultural Significance of Cannibalism

The evidence suggests that prehistoric cannibalism was mostly practiced for ritual purposes, and that probably mainly under the pressure of starvation was it sometimes indulged in as a life-saving expedient. The rarity of cannibalized fossil human bones would suggest as much.

There are many reasons why the dead have been eaten among different peoples. As Dr. Hermann Helmuth has stated in his study "Cannibalism in Paleoanthropology and Ethnology," even in so narrowly circumscribed an area as aboriginal Australia we encounter different reasons for the practice of cannibalism. "Together with the view," writes Dr. Helmuth, "that one incorporates into oneself valuable qualities, the feeling of belonging together, the idea of helping to preserve the way of life, the means of transmission of the soul, and of participation of the dead man in the life of the tribe, also play a role. Thus, friendship with the dead man, respect, and love also bear a relation to the consumption of human flesh by other humans."

Among many South American peoples it is the custom to burn parts of the body and mix the ashes with their drinks. This serves to preserve for the tribe the life located in the body, and to insure that the life separated from the body secures a new abode.

The motives for the practice of cannibalism throughout the world are, as one would expect, extremely varied, and Helmuth sums them up as follows: (1) love and affection, (2) judicial cannibalism, (3) hate and scorn, (4) for the purpose of acquiring power, (5) the idea of continuity, (6) magico-ceremonial, and (7) funerary.

Having surveyed the varieties of cannibalism throughout the world, Helmuth concludes that the assumption cannot be sustained that "the broken bones of *Sinanthropus* (Peking Man), the Neanderthalers, and diluvial man" constitute evidence of hostility of men toward each other. "The belief in a transmission of qualities, fear of revenge, punishment for crimes, repetition of a myth, as well as a certain love and a feeling of belonging together, or complete indifference on the part of the subject toward pain and the essence of the object eaten, are not connected with aggressive feelings. The assumption of aggressive feelings or aggressive behavior of man toward his fellow men is not justifiable without certain conditions, since this assumption too represents nothing else but an application of ideas deduced from a present situation to a past one. With the same justification one might argue that an Indian or an Australian practicing patrophagy [the ritual eating of members of one's own tribe] could imply a long history of friendly, loving feelings and affection" (p. 250).

In the light of Helmuth's survey those who cite cannibalism as one of the principal evidences of the innate nature of human aggression will find little support for their views in the facts. It is one thing to write airily about cannibalism in general, as if it were always or most often motivated by hostility, but it is quite another to consider the varieties of cannibalism on a worldwide scale, and find that it is often motivated by love, respect, and loyalty. It may also constitute an evidence of quite awful aggressiveness, but aggressiveness not necessarily motivated by hostility. It may often be motivated by ritual indifference, as is quite clearly the case among the many headhunting tribes of New Guinea. In the groups described by Berndt in *Excess and Restraint* the cannibal raids on other tribes were generally regarded by the cannibal raiders as great fun. But even here they could hardly be described as a pastime.

Dr. T. Jacob of the Department of Physical Anthropology of the Gadjah Mada University College of Medicine, Jogjakarta, Indonesia, in a study entitled "The Problem of Head-Hunting and Brain-Eating Among Pleistocene Men in Indonesia," has seriously questioned whether most of the breakages around the foramen magnum found in pithecanthropine and Neanderthaloid skulls were made by humans. He points out that pithecanthropine skulls have never been found in a living site in Indonesia, but that all specimens had been transported by rivers hundreds of thousands of years ago together with stones and boulders. Under such conditions the comparatively thin facial bones and base of the skull around the foramen magnum would suffer most. Volcanic eruptions, accidents, a forceful animal bite on top of the head resulting in *contrecoup* (that is, damage done to a part opposite the site of impact), expansion of soil within the skull, stone falls, breakage during excavation or transport, and the like, could all account for damage done around the foramen magnum. Without denying the possibility of sporadic incidental cannibalism, Jacob concludes that there is no convincing evidence that Pleistocene men were cannibals and ate the brains of their fellow men. Jacob points out that the pithecanthropine long bones were either almost complete or broken transversely and not split longitudinally, a condition which has generally been attributed to the attempt to extract marrow from the bone. Since the femoral bones were not broken while in the fresh state, Jacob considers such attempts at extraction unlikely; the more probable explanation he believes to be the numerous obstacles encountered by the bones while being transported by rivers to their ultimate site of deposition.

An additional point to emphasize is that since in almost all pithecanthropine skulls the region of the foramen magnum is broken away, this in itself would indicate that the breakage was accidental, for the same reasons that apply when in so many cases the top of the skull alone is found, namely breakage of other parts due to their comparative thinness. It is unlikely that the greater number of the members of a prehistoric band had their facial bones deliberately destroyed and the basal openings of their skulls enlarged. If the latter was done at any time, the former was certainly un-necessary. In later skulls of Neanderthaloid type, such as the Steinheim am Murr (about twelve miles west of Stutt-gart in West Germany) skull, the face remains, and in the somewhat later Ehringsdorf (near Weimer, Germany) skull the lateral walls and occiput remain, with the base missing. In both skulls there is evidence of injury, the right orbital region in Steinheim, and on the top of the head frontally in Ehringsdorf. These injuries have been interpreted to be of human origin, but in fact it is impossible to say.

Jacob believes that head-hunting and ritual cannibalism originated at a more complex level of cultural development than the pithecanthropine, when populations were at a higher density level. In this latter connection it is interesting that cannibalism is a rare phenomenon among gatherer-hunters. Among some forty living and recently culturally extinct gatherer-hunting peoples I have surveyed, cannibal-ism apparently occurs only among the Australian aborigines. It never occurred among their closest physical and cultural relatives, the Tasmanians. The cannibalism of the Austra-lian aborigines was mostly of a ritual kind. No one was ever killed in order to be eaten, but once an enemy had been slain it was the custom among some tribes to eat the body.

It is strange that, except for a remark by Coon that few hunting peoples are cannibals, the extreme rarity of canni-balism among gatherer-hunters seems to have gone quite unnoticed. And yet that is a fact of great significance, bear-ing out, among other things, Jacob's suggestion that can-nibalism tends to appear at more complex levels of society than those of Pleistocene gatherer-hunters. It also suggests that early man no more frequently indulged in cannibalism than did more recent gatherer-hunters.

In prehistoric times periods of severe drought and famine occasionally doubtless led to cannibalism, as has happened in most societies. Among the Kalauna of Goodenough Island off the eastern coast of New Guinea, instead of resorting to conflict in their disagreements or demanding compensation for offenses, it was the custom to present their enemies and offenders with pigs and yams in order to shame them. When famine threatened to destroy them the traditional response was for parents to exchange their children to eat.

In passing it may be noted that while human flesh may serve as both an emergency source of protein and calories, even a small population could not have indulged in regular people-eating as a staple item of nutrition, since there simply would not have been enough people to satisfy the caloric requirements of the consumers.

The discussion of cannibalism by those who have cited it as an evidence of the innateness of aggression simply exhibits their relativistic naïveté and bias. Not all peoples have been taught to feel the way civilized people do about eating other people. It is really quite unsound to project upon prehistoric humans the standards of taste and morality prevailing in civilized societies. For prehistoric humans it was acceptable, under certain conditions, to eat human flesh, and there was nothing either in the way of taste or morality that forbade it. It is, indeed, only civilized societies that can afford such refinements of taste and morality. It is very probable, therefore, that when, on occasion, prehistoric humans did eat their own kind they customarily did so with no more feeling of aggression than civilized humans experience when eating a steak.

As for "the mutilated and roasted bones" of Peking Man of which Lorenz speaks, dramatic and prejudicial as those words are, the facts are capable of quite another interpretation than that given them by Lorenz. Dr. F. M. Bergounioux of the Institut Catholique of Toulouse points out

that there is no trace of teeth marks in any of the long bones
of Peking Man, and the large number of skulls and jaws, of
at least forty individuals, suggests they were brought to the
Choukoutien site intentionally. Furthermore, the back of
the base of the skull, the occipital part, was deliberately
raised by successive fractures, as if there had been an attempt to reach the brain. "This suggests," writes Dr. Bergounioux, "funeral rites of the type known as 'two stage,'
which were still observed among the Buginese on the south
coast of the Celebes, before their conversion to Islam in the
eighteenth century. The body of the deceased was carried
far from the dwelling and left out in the open, sheltered
from beasts of prey. When the body had dried out the head
could be detached easily, without the need even to cut the
cervical vertebrae. (No vertebrae were found at Choukoutien.) The skull was then solemnly carried to the village,
carefully washed, and became a kind of protective divinity
of the family of the deceased. Sometimes only the jaw was
preserved, and it was worn around the neck, suspended
from a cord, like a medal. Acts of ritual anthropophagy were
associated with this cult; the occipital hole (foramen magnum) was enlarged with blows from a club on the base of
the skull, then the brain was devoured by those who wished
to assume the merits of the dead man. Certain anthropopha-
gous tribes in Central Africa practiced similar rituals for a
very long time."

Far from the crass aggressive cannibalism that the innate
aggressionists like to think of as the explanation for these
jaws and broken skulls, they reveal the existence of a widespread funerary cult which lasted for hundreds of thousands
of years, as evidenced by precisely similar finds at a Neanderthal site like Monte Circeo on the Mediterranean coast,
some forty miles south of Rome. Here a single skull with
its base broken open was found surrounded by a circle of

stones. This is a late Neanderthal site dating back to the first phase of the last glaciation some 40,000 years ago. Another single Neanderthaloid skull, found at Steinheim, also has the base of the skull around the foramen magnum broken away. So does the Neanderthaloid skull found at Ehringsdorf together with artifacts of late Acheulian type. One cannot be certain that the brain was always eaten—after long exposure of the body it would not always be in an edible state—but in any event the removal of the brain through an opening in the base of the skull in a freshly killed individual is an enormously difficult and laborious task. In the autopsy room and in the dissecting room the brain is taken out of the skull by first removing the flaps of the skin and adjacent tissues from the top and sides of the skull, and then sawing all around the upper part of the skull until it is possible to chisel through the inner table of bone and lift the skullcap off the outermost portion of the membrane, the dura mater, enveloping the brain. Even so, it takes considerable skill and practice to be able to remove the brain contained with its membranes or even without them. No anatomist, and I speak as a teaching anatomist of many years' experience in the dissecting room, would ever think of attempting to extract a brain from the base of the head. This laborious way of extracting the brain suggests that the main object was the preservation of the skull as intact as possible. By contrast, chimpanzees of the Gombe National Park, who regard the brains of their juvenile baboon victims as especially succulent delicacies, care nothing for the preservation of the skull, and so extract the brain by biting away the skull top and eventually eating the whole of the skull.

It is probable, as I have said, that most brains were not edible after the body had been allowed to lie for some weeks or months in the open or even in a cave, and that, therefore, while the enlargement of the base of the skull may have been made in order, among other things, to extract the brain, its shrinkage, depending upon the climatic conditions, could have been quite considerable. During glacial periods, however, an exposed body would have been more likely to have been preserved, and under such conditions it would have been less difficult to extract the brain through the artificially opened base of the skull. Even then it would have been no easy task. Eating the brain may have been an important part of a ritual, but the indications are that the breaking open of the skull to reach it was not done so much for cannibalistic purposes as for the ritual celebration of a complex religious and widespread cult of skulls. A principal reason why we find so many skulls and comparatively few parts of the remainder of the skeleton is that the skull was preserved and venerated, as the onetime dwelling of the magic principle that animated it. What does one think before the face of death? Is this all that remains of a living being who is no longer capable of hearing, of seeing, of speaking? He is cold, rigid, and still. Do men at death vanish into husks and the formless ruin of oblivion? No nonliterate people ever believed this, and we may be certain that no prehistoric people ever thought so. Speechless, sightless, deaf, and forever silent, the dead one is nevertheless a formidable presence. "He appears to be jealously guarding a formidable secret," writes Bergounioux, "which none can take from him without assuming his substance. And thus they believed that the head, the organ of command, so expressive yesterday and today fixed in its fearsome rigidness, must be the object of special veneration. And, in order to cover themselves with its guardian protection, the idea occurred to them to carry a few bones of the deceased about the person, like a talisman."

And, so, the cult of skulls. It was and remains very widespread. The late Dr. Alberto Blanc of the Institute of Human Palaeontology, Rome, drew attention to the fact that identical breakage of the skull is produced by many of the peoples of Melanesia and Borneo, with the object of extracting the brain and eating it for ritual and social purposes. In New Guinea a man may be killed in order that a name shall be given to a newborn child. The skull of the victim is opened at the base and the father extracts the brain, bakes it with sago, and eats it. The skull is kept in the home as a sacred object until the bearer of its name dies. Dr. Blanc emphasized that "this gruesome custom is practiced by tribes that are not particularly bloodthirsty or aggressive and have rather high morals; the ritual cannibalism is performed as a strict obligation toward the community, on the one hand, and the newborn on the other."

It is quite possible that skulls may also have been used as vessels, that blood was drunk from these ready-made bowls, as part of a magic ritual. From such magic rites, it has been more than once suggested, descends the Holy Communion of the Christian Church, as a modified but very real survival. "This *is* My body; this *is* My blood."

We conclude, then, that cannibalism cannot justly be cited as evidence of man's innate aggressiveness. A critical examination of the evidence reveals that while some prehistoric humans, members of some contemporary nonliterate peoples, and on occasion some civilized individuals have eaten others, and sometimes killed them in order to do so, the overwhelming body of evidence indicates that this seldom was done from motives of hostility or aggression. Occasional ritual cannibalism is one thing, while cannibalism under conditions of starvation is quite another; both are relatively rare. There is considerably more evidence to show that cannibalism was more often practiced from motives of respect, tradition, and both love and affection, than it was from any feelings of aggressiveness.

When, however, the evidence has been prejudged without a thorough examination of it, and one is a true believer in the doctrine of innate aggressiveness, it is easy to see in cannibalism the confirmation of that doctrine. Inquiry into the reasons for the occasional practice of cannibalism throws a very different light on its motivations, and fails to provide any support whatever for the doctrine of innate aggressiveness.

6
Weapons or Leopards?

Broken Bones and Fractured Hypotheses

In his book *Adventures with the Missing Link* (1959), Raymond Dart elaborates in detail on the evidence which convinced him that *Australopithecus* was not only a predatory carnivore but also a killer of his fellow man. In a chapter entitled "The Anatomy of Murder" Dart describes an adolescent australopithecine jaw which had been split on both sides and all the front teeth "knocked out." "This dramatic specimen," he writes, "instantly prompted me to study the murderous and apparently cannibalistic manner of life of these violent creatures" (pp. 106-7). The jaw, Dart believes, "was bashed in by a formidable blow from the front and delivered with great accuracy just to the left of the point of the jaw."

Other australopithecine skulls found at Sterkfontein, near Johannesburg, "showed that they too had been shattered shortly before death by skull-smashing shocks" (p. 110). Dart found that the ridges of many antelope humeri fitted perfectly into the depressed fractures. This confirmed Dart in the belief that these bones were the principal implements employed by the australopithecines in killing baboons, the very same which, according to Dart, they also used to kill their fellow men. "They were murderers and flesh hunters; their favorite tool was a bludgeon of bone, usually the thighbone or armbone of an antelope" (p. 113).

Sharp penetrating parts of bones, such as the ends of horns and the sharp ends of broken bones, were, as Dart sees them, used as daggers. To impress this upon the reader there is a drawing (p. 113) of two "australopithecines fighting with bone club and dagger."

The tools and weapons which the australopithecines are believed by Dart to have manufactured from bone, teeth, and horn, he has named as belonging to "the osteodonto-keratic culture"—that is, the bone, teeth, and horn culture. Most authorities do not accept Dart's view that the australopithecines really used these portions of the skeleton of animals as tools and implements or weapons. In his book *African Genesis* (1961) Mr. Ardrey writes: "It was Raymond Dart's durability, tenacity, and unshakable belief in his own rightness that in my opinion made possible our present knowledge of human origins" (p. 22). Indeed, Johannesburg, australopithecine land, and Raymond Dart were for Mr. Ardrey the Road to Damascus. It was under the tutelage of Dart that Ardrey underwent that conversion which has made him the most widely read apostle of the new litany of original sin. His own writings constitute an exegesis on the gospel according to Dart rather than according to Lorenz. It is, therefore, uniquely right that Ardrey should address his Epistles to the Laity from Rome rather than from Bavaria. Mr. Ardrey freely and generously acknowledges his intellectual debt to Dart, and Dart has been quoted here at some length in order to indicate something of the nature of that debt.

The question we have to discuss here is not, however,

either one of apostolic succession or doctrinal heterodoxy, and still less whether the australopithecines were characterized by an osteodontokeratic culture. The question, rather, is whether the animal bones, teeth, and horn discovered in association with the australopithecines were employed by them against their fellows in the manner and for the purposes attributed to them by Dart.

While there is no longer any doubt that some, at least, of the australopithecines made stone tools, there is not the slightest genuine evidence that they ever used them as weapons.

Few authorities agree that the baboons whose fractured skulls Dart describes were killed in the manner which he claims. Baboons are formidable creatures. They are possessed of decidedly dangerous canine teeth, and are quick, intelligent, and agile. It is difficult to imagine how they could be killed in the manner described by Dart. A full-grown adult chimpanzee is no match for an adult baboon. Under natural conditions chimpanzees occasionally kill and eat juvenile baboons, but they strictly avoid conflict with adults. Chimpanzees kill by biting, snapping the neck, or beating the infant's head against the ground or a tree trunk. Most of the fractured baboon skulls described by Dart are those of adults. But even if it were to be granted that baboons were killed by australopithecines with the humerus of an antelope, are we to conclude from this that the australopithecines deliberately manufactured weapons in order to kill their fellow australopithecines as well?

The innate aggressionists, Dart, Ardrey, Lorenz, and others, assert that they did. "There is evidence," writes Lorenz, "that the first inventors of pebble tools, the African Australopithecines, promptly used their new weapon to kill not only game, but fellow members of their species as well."

In his article "The Predatory Transition from Ape to

Man," an article which Mr. Ardrey tells us "no regular
scientific journal would touch," and which finally found a
place in a rather peregrine journal that shortly afterward
ceased publication, *International Anthropological and Linguistic Review,* the author emphasized, as we have seen, the
carnivorous habits of the australopithecines in particular
and of humankind in general. I have already quoted a passage from this article in the preceding chapter. This concludes with the statement that man is to be numbered
among the deadliest of the Carnivora, implying that this
deadliness is a heritage from allegedly deadly australopithecine ancestors.

Mr. Ardrey echoes Dart. "The human being," he writes,
"in the most fundamental aspects of his soul and body is
nature's last if temporary word on the subject of the armed
predator. And human history must be read in those terms."
"What Dart put forward in his piece was the simple thesis
that man had emerged from the anthropoid background for
one reason only: because he was a killer."

These words speak for themselves. They require no
underscoring. ". . . emerged from his anthropoid background for one reason only: because he was a killer." It is
a view to which it is possible to hold only if one is unaware
of or ignores the large amount of evidence that is now available, drawn from many different sources, which tends to
throw a very different light on the causes of the emergence
of humanity from anthropoid origins.

On Tools, Implements, and Weapons

The innate aggressionists speak of "tools," of "weapons,"
and of "armed predators" without ever clearly defining
what they mean by those terms. When an animal hunts
other animals it is a predator and its objects are prey. The

aggressionists convey the impression when they speak of early men as "armed predators" that the latter spent a good deal of their time preying on other animals, and devoted not a little of that time to preying on each other. Both for animals and early men this is highly improbable. To this day, among gatherer-hunter peoples hunting forms about one-fifth to one-fourth of the total time devoted to the acquisition of food. As for reciprocal destruction among the australopithecines, there is no evidence that this occurred any more frequently among them than it does among contemporary gatherer-hunter societies (see pp. 164-192). The question has been raised: Can a species be characterized as predatory if only a small proportion of its time is devoted to hunting? We think not. The development of hunting in early humans was preceded by the development of food-gathering. The combination of gathering with hunting was a development that followed later.

In the matter of the alleged use of "weapons" by the australopithecines against their fellows, Mr. Ardrey chooses to identify "tools" with "weapons," and makes no distinction between them. He writes: "We must keep in mind that when any scientist writes the word 'tool,' he as a rule refers to weapons. This is a euphemism" (p. 306). This statement is simply not true. Scientists endeavor to distinguish between tools and weapons. They do not usually indulge in linguistic analgesics such as euphemisms.

Mr. Ardrey tells us that euphemisms "are normal to all natural sciences." Are they? It would have been helpful had he produced a few examples of such normal "euphemisms." In any event, euphemism or not, some tools may be used as weapons and even manufactured for such purposes; the tools of early man, however, do not have the appearance of weapons, but look very much as if they were designed to serve mainly as working implements. Knives were designed to cut, scrapers to scrape, choppers to chop, and handaxes to dig and cut. That such tools could be used as weapons is true, even though they could serve as such only when one was in immediate contact with the creature who was to receive the blow. There is no evidence whatever that australopithecine tools were designed or used as weapons.

One need only familiarize oneself with australopithecine tools to realize the unlikelihood of their being devised as weapons with which to kill animals. Pebble tools are simply too small for such a purpose. It is possible that they may have used other objects for such a purpose, but there is no evidence for this. Does the possibility, then, remain that australopithecine tools were devised as weapons with which to kill other australopithecines? The answer is that this is highly improbable, for these implements would have been thoroughly useless in anything other than hand-to-hand encounters. Contemporary gatherer-hunter peoples do not engage in such hand-to-hand combat, and there is no good reason to believe that australopithecines or other types of early humans did so. The likelihood is that encounters of any kind between early groups of humans were infrequent, simply because they tended to be isolated from each other, so that on this ground alone there could have been no reason for the manufacture or use of tools as weapons.

But Dart has urged the bludgeon in the form of the antelope humerus or the thighbone, as well as the dagger made from "the end of horns and the sharp ends of broken bones." "Round holes in skulls and casts," are Dart's evidence that these "murderers and flesh eaters" (p. 113) used the sharp ends of broken bones as daggers.

Even if it were found that antelope bones of the fore and hind limbs, the humerus and femur, may have been used to kill baboons, it is quite another thing to posit the use of "daggers" for any purpose whatever. A dagger is a very sophisticated kind of instrument, and there is no evidence of its existence, let alone use, throughout the Paleolithic. It is, therefore, questionable that australopithecines ever made or used such instruments.

There has been a great deal of imprecision in the use of the term "weapon." Its employment at once suggests aggression, for there is no other reason for the existence of such an instrument than its forseeable use either offensively or defensively. So let us attempt clarification of the meaning of this word. A word should be defined by what it does, the action it serves to describe or produce. It is the use to which a tool is put that gives it its meaning, and the word employed to describe that use should distinguish the different purposes to which a tool may be put that has been designed to serve a particular function.

All weapons are, of course, tools, but all tools are not weapons. When, then, does a tool become a weapon? A tool is defined as "any instrument of manual operation." A weapon is "an instrument of any kind used in warfare or in combat to attack and overcome an enemy." These are the distinctions made in the *Oxford English Dictionary*.

Is a tool employed for the purpose of killing an animal a weapon, or is it an implement—that is, a tool or instrument? Is the three-balled enthonged bola, used by Neanderthal man, and possibly before him, to enmesh the legs of birds and other animals, a weapon or an implement? Is a spear a weapon or an implement? I suggest it is an implement when used to spear an animal; a weapon, when used to spear another human. Any object when employed to attack a human, no matter what its customary use may be, becomes a weapon. But no tool employed by humans to kill an animal is properly regarded as a weapon.

It is not a taxonomic, a classificatory, difference based on physical characteristics that determines the distinction, but *the attitude of mind o*f the individual involved toward the object of his attention. Animals are hunted principally for food. Humans, for whatever reason, seldom are attacked for the purposes of consumption. It is not weapons with which animals are hunted, but implements, though the same implements may become weapons when they are turned against humans.

That australopithecines devised weapons to be used against their fellows would seem to be extremely unlikely: first, because those tools would not easily lend themselves to such usage; second, because such tools appear to have been made for practical domestic use; and third, there is no supportable evidence in fossil australopithecine bones of injuries that could have been inflicted by such tools.

"Man," Mr. Ardrey tells us, "is a predator whose natural instinct is to kill with a weapon" (p. 316). One can only wonder. Does man also have a natural instinct to write with a pen? The answer would appear to be not. Writing is not much more than 5,000 years old, and that, presumably, would not be enough time for an instinct to establish itself. But since our nearest relations have no instinct to kill with a weapon, several million years must have elapsed during which, by natural selection, those individuals who were proficient in the use of weapons and showed themselves to be the most adaptively fit in so doing, were selected for survival and eventually became the australopithecines, born with a natural instinct to kill with a weapon.

This all seems highly improbable, the natural instinct, the killing, and the weapon. Perhaps Mr. Ardrey is a Lamarckian and believes in the inheritance of acquired habits, such as the habit of killing with a weapon. If he is, he stands alone in that belief, and it seems to me he has brought forth no evidence to justify it. As we have seen, the very existence of instincts in man is highly questionable, and whatever predispositions humans are born with are most unlikely to be directed toward killing. On the contrary, the evidence points in the very opposite direction.

"Sticks and Stones"

There are many objections to the unwarranted, and almost certainly erroneous, assumptions concerning the aggressive behavior of the australopithecines. For one thing, there is really no evidence that australopithecines ever killed other australopithecines. It is possible they may have done so on occasion, but the kind of certainty with which Professor Dart and Mr. Ardrey express themselves on the subject is based solely on their inferences from the appearance of a number of australopithecine skulls which could have been damaged in ways quite other than those they assert. Of the forty australopithecine skulls thus far recovered at least half have been alleged by Dart (1949), Ardrey (1961), and L. S. B. Leakey (1961) to have met their death by deliberate violence from other australopithecines. Since 1949 Dart seems to have changed his mind regarding the frequency of violent death among the australopithecines, for in 1965 when Professor Joseph Birdsell asked him how many austra-lopithecines he thought had been murdered, he replied, "All of them." Perhaps Dart was just trying to make a point. In any event, most of the fractured skulls, according to him, showed depressed breaks, corresponding to the two condyles at the end of an antelope humerus, with radiating fractures from the depressed area, and the conclusion "obvious" that these injuries had been inflicted with such bones. This seems a plausible enough inference, but it happens to be a precarious one.

Accidental falls against a rock can produce depressed fractures of the skull; so can rocks falling on the skull; even a collision with another head can produce such a fracture, as can accidental blows and deliberate ones inflicted shortly or considerably after the time of death; so too can falls and injuries inflicted by animals. And so, also, can various objects pressing against the skull long after death, as, for example, heavy soils, stones, and rocks in the soil in which the skull lies. It is often extremely difficult to distinguish between deliberate and accidental injury to the skull, especially in cases in which the fracture is depressed and could have been caused in several different ways. The possibility that the australopithecines indulged in reciprocal violence is not only non-proven but so remote that it would be at the very least reasonable to consider possible other explanations. Here we don't have to go far.

Much light has been thrown on this matter by Dr. C. K. Brain of the Transvaal Museum, Pretoria, South Africa. In a study entitled "An Attempt to Reconstruct the Behaviour of Australopithecines: The Evidence for Interpersonal Violence," Dr. Brain has reported his observations on the skulls of australopithecines said by Dart and others to bear the evidences of injuries inflicted by other australopithecines. Brain suggests that in most cases the damage attributed to deliberately inflicted blows may well have been produced by post-fossilization effects. For example, the presence of a stone in contact with a skull may result in damage restricted to the area of contact only, while the rest of the skull may remain intact. From his examination of the fossils Dr. Brain concludes: "There does not seem the slightest doubt that the localized damage suffered by these and a large number of other fossils from the australopithecine caves resulted simply from pressure applied to a heterogeneous matrix in which the bones were enclosed. . . . In my opinion the damage on all these specimens could have resulted from influences other than inter-personal aggression."

Australopithecine populations were small, about twenty or thirty individuals in a band, so that on the face of it, it would seem highly improbable that they made a habit of smiting each other on the head. They were certainly intelligent enough not to mistake each other for baboons. Professor Joseph Birdsell, of the Department of Anthropology of the University of California at Los Angeles, thinks that the thickness of the cranial vault may have come about in man as a consequence of his addiction to reciprocal head-smiting, that early men with thicker skulls enjoyed a much better chance of surviving than those with thinner skulls. This theory will hardly stand critical examination since the thickness of the skull bones varies considerably in different human populations, and in any event, as Tobias has shown, both the juvenile and adult representatives of *Australopithecus* and *Homo habilis* had extremely thin skulls two million years ago. Thick skull bones make their first appearance in *Homo erectus*, well over a million years later. In spite of their thick skulls Professor Franz Weidenreich believed the evidence showed that most of the *Homo erectus* population found at Chou-Kou-Tien near Peking died from violent blows to the skull. Furthermore, if baboons, who have quite thin skull bones, were as banged about by australopithecines as the Dartians claim, how is it that they have managed to survive to the present time with their skull bones not in the least thickened?

Carnivores and Broken Bones

The claim that many prehistoric skulls show the evidences of fatal blows inflicted either with a blunt instrument or a glancing sharp one, has been examined by Mrs. Marilyn Keyes Roper, in a detailed study published in 1969 entitled "A Survey of the Evidence for Intrahuman Killing in the

Pleistocene." Mrs. Roper's conclusion is that "some intra-
hominid (perhaps intraspecific) killing probably occurred
in the Lower and Middle Pleistocene and that sporadic intraspecific killing probably took place among *H. sapiens* in
the upper Paleolithic" (p. 448). In his comments on Mrs.
Roper's survey Professor Adolph Schultz writes: "I share
the author's scepticism regarding the supposed prevalence
of intrahuman killing in the Pleistocene, for I am convinced
that the action of carnivores offers a more likely explanation
for most of the cranial injuries found in fossil men. That
the early hominids might have occasionally killed their own
kind with primitive weapons is, of course, quite conceivable,
but has not been proved. It appears more reasonable to assume that at least the great majority of early men with supposedly fatal cranial injuries were the victims of contemporary large carnivores." As Schultz points out, large predators
can break a human skull with a single blow or pierce it with
their teeth and claws more easily than can any weapon or
bone or stone. A predator's paw crashing down on the skull
can stave in the more delicate base around the occipital condyles without damaging the top of the skull itself.

Schultz also points out that man-eaters usually leave the
head uneaten, a fact which may explain the frequency with
which the skull alone is found without any remnant of the
remainder of the skeleton. Furthermore, many carnivores
choose caves for their dens, to which they could easily bring
a body to be devoured. In some European caves the skeletal
remains of bears, hyenas, lions, and other carnivores have
accumulated in immense numbers together with the broken
bones of many other animals. Mollison has convincingly
shown that Rhodesian Man was probably killed by a large
carnivore.

It would perhaps be claiming too much to assert that all
evidences of injury in the skulls of early humans were in-

flicted by animal predators. Some of these injuries may have
been the result of accidents, and it is remotely possible that
some may have been inflicted by other humans. Schultz's interpretation of the evidence indicating that the killing of
early humans by their fellow men was rare, and that carnivores were more likely to have been responsible for the killing, has been thoroughly ignored by the innate aggressionists in spite of the very significant substantiating evidence. Professor Schultz is the world's leading authority on
the anatomy of the apes, and his considered judgment in so
important a matter as the interpretation of the meaning of
cranial injuries in early humans is hardly to be lightly
passed over, much less ignored.

Mr. Ardrey allows that not all australopithecines could
conclusively be shown to have met their death by purposeful violence. "But," he says, "a curious case of what could
only have been intentional armed assault" came to his attention when Dr. Kenneth Oakley of the British Museum
(Natural History) gave him a plaster cast of a small portion
of an australopithecine skull from Swartkrans. "The skull
showed two small round perforations, about an inch apart.
The holes could not have been of animal origin, since no
carnivore has canines set so closely together. . . . The living australopithecine had been struck by something, not
only once but twice, from different directions."

Ardrey is mistaken on all points. The small round perforations happen to match perfectly the distance between
the canine teeth of leopard mandibles. Dr. C. K. Brain has
studied the australopithecine and carnivore remains from
Swartkrans, and in particular the original of the cast to
which Mr. Ardrey refers, and in his report published in
1970, Dr. Brain concludes: "I believe that it is more likely
that the two holes were made simultaneously by the canine
teeth of a carnivore about 33 mm apart. . . . It can natu-

Fig. 1. Reconstruction showing how the observed damage to the skull of a Swartkrans *Paranthropus* child could have been caused by a leopard. The leopard's lower canines are thought to have penetrated the parietal bone of the dead child while it was being dragged to a feeding place. (Courtesy of Dr. C. K. Brain and *Nature*).

rally not be proved," Dr. Brain adds, "that a leopard (or any other specific carnivore) was responsible for the damage to the fossil skull, but, considering the various lines of evidence from Swartkrans, it is very probable that leopard canines did, in fact, produce the holes." The evidence, Dr. Brain concludes, suggests that the australopithecines at Swartkrans were probably preyed on by leopards, just as leopards prey on human beings today. He believes that such predation was probably much more prevalent at a stage of evolution when australopithecines were neither physically formidable nor protected by weapons of an advanced technology.

To conclude, then, an examination of the evidence suggests that many of the cranial injuries found on the skulls of some early humans were probably the result of causes quite other than those to which the innate aggressionists have attributed them, and therefore they cannot be cited to support the arguments of those who believe in their particular interpretation of the phylogenetic and instinctual bases of aggression.

7
Cooperation

Evolution

When we look back over our history and trace as best we can our evolution from humanlike ape, to apelike human, and finally through various stages to the creature we see around every day, we are struck with an important realization: that cooperation and competition both were responsible for that evolution.

First, a caveat: although we know numerous things about our ancestors from bones that have been dug up around the world, the remains at camp sites, and the evidences of hunting and eating habits, we don't yet know as much as we will eventually know. The fossil record remains incomplete, accidental finds still play an important role in the expansion of knowledge, and there are still long periods from which we have no evidence at all, or only small bits of bone on which to erect substantial structures of surmise. Nevertheless, we have other important sources; our rapidly increasing knowledge of the behavior of the great apes, our nearest relatives among the nonhuman animals, and a considerable body of knowledge about present-day foodgathering-hunt-

ing peoples. These peoples live, more or less clearly approximately the way our ancestors lived during a great part
of human evolutionary history, and they afford us some insight into the basic questions of human nature and human
culture. Thus, recognizing the limitations of what we know,
but using a combination of scientific method, logical thinking, and observations of relevant present-day creatures, we
arrive at reasonable deductions concerning our animal forebears, about early men, their ways of living, and the general
principles that governed their behavior.

An important thing to recognize about the evolution of
men from animals is that the process was gradual and continuous and relatively slow. There never was a moment
when a creature—an ape—suddenly stood up on its hind legs
for the first time, spoke a word for the first time, picked up
a piece of fruit in its newly developed hands, had a thought
in its newly developed brain, and was human. The evolution of humans was undoubtedly a gradual process, but it
was by no means as slow as has customarily been thought;
nor did it proceed in the straight line or the arborizing fash-
ion in which it is often depicted. It appears, rather, more
closely to have resembled a reticulum in which there was a
good deal of crisscrossing and new developments, so that
sometimes more advanced forms were living cheek by jowl
with their less advanced related types. For example, fairly
large-brained types, looking quite modern for so early a
form of human, were found at East Lake Rudolph, Kenya,
in 1972. The skull ("Skull 1470") has a cranial capacity of
about 750 cubic centimeters, and dates back almost three
million years. Another form of early human, *Homo habilis,*
from Olduvai Gorge in Tanzania, dating back 1.85 million
years, has a cranial capacity of 650 cubic centimeters. These
forms were contemporaries of a variety of australopithe-

cines, more than forty specimens of which, ranging in age from one to three million years, have been found at East Lake Rudolph.

From the fossil record as we know it today, meager as it may be, the evidence suggests that the evolution of humans was rather faster than has been generally supposed.

When fossil specimens were rare the evolutionary distance and the time periods between different forms of man such as *Homo erectus,* Neanderthal Man, and *Homo sapiens* appeared considerable. With the many discoveries that have been made during the last twenty-five years, both the evolutionary distance and the time-periods between the various forms of early human have been appreciably reduced, even though the total time over which human evolutionary history has extended has been greatly increased, from one million to about five million years.

In addition to the gradualness of the human evolutionary process, another important factor to recognize is that whole populations of people were changing over that enormous period. It was not a single ape that eventually evolved into a single human who then became Adam for all future human beings. The process was very much more complex than that, and much more interesting. It took place within groups widely separated from each other, at first apparently only on the continent of Africa but later in Europe and Asia as well. It involved adaptation to many different changing conditions, accidental genetic mutations that proved useful in specific places at specific times and were therefore retained, learned patterns of behavior that were culturally transmitted from generation to generation. And it involved a degree of chance, too; there must have been times when changing conditions—sudden climatic changes, for instance —and the creatures' ability to adapt were running neck-

and-neck, and a fortuitous discovery and the presence of a particularly bright leader made the difference between survival and extinction for a group.

Cooperation

Through the wide variety of conditions prevailing over all those millions of years and all those wide spaces of the earth's surface, a single thread is discernible. It is the thread of cooperation and mutual aid. If that thread had not been there, or if in its place had been a thread of competition and mutual hostility, our species would never have achieved humanity. Had our forebears been natural killers of each other, they would have had a hard time surviving. And had they not developed the physical attributes and the intelligence to cooperate with each other, they might well have been killed off by other predators. A necessary factor for human evolution was cooperation among individuals; without it we would not have evolved.

Consider our remote ancestors and the way they lived. They were forest-dwelling monkeys, whose most interesting features from an evolutionary point of view were their hands, their eyes, and their brains. Living in the trees as they did, all these features were valuable, and were developed over tens of millions of years as the qualities most likely to succeed in the trees in a tropical forest. Hands were uesful for grasping branches and holding on, and reaching food at the end of the branches. The better the ability to grasp, the less chance of falling and killing oneself; and the longer one lived, the more offspring there would be to inherit those useful grasping hands.

Specialized sight is also useful in the trees. Primates, unlike many other animals, see in color; also, unlike others, they have both eyes in the front of the head—and thus have binocular vision—instead of one eye on each side. Binocular vision makes it possible to see in three dimensions, and thereby to judge depth and distance. Both the perception of color and the ability to judge distance are clearly useful if your life includes a substantial amount of leaping from branch to branch among the trees. Animals who possessed both these qualities were likely to live longer and to have more descendants than those whose eyes were less well developed. Thus grasping hands and acute vision gradually came to be part of the natural endowment of those primates.

And they led inexorably to the third important adaptation: an increasingly active brain. Arboreal life was good for the development of the brain; it was a life filled with surprises, and every surprise called for some quick response, with a reward for correct responses and possibly a fatal penalty for incorrect ones. Birds flying through the empty air, fish swimming through unchanging waters, animals walking along the steady ground were faced with no such challenges as the monkeys met dozens of times a day. Moving swiftly from branch to branch, catching, swinging, hanging, falling unexpectedly, encountering suddenly a rotten branch, having to judge from a distance the strength and flexibility of several possible routes—all that adds up to a precarious way of life, and the creature with the quickest responses and the greatest ability to make correct decisions and to survive incorrect ones is the creature most likely to live long enough to pass on its genes and its braininess to its offspring.

These abilities were useful to apes, too, when their lives gradually changed from arboreal life in the forest to following a quite different kind of existence, largely on the ground in the more open, drier country of the savannas. This change came about, not because the forest apes decided to move to a new location, but because the forests where they lived gradually changed into savannas, and the apes, because they were bright, adaptable creatures, adapted to the change.

Over a period of about 20 million years, the climates all over the world became drier: the rain forests grew less wet and parts of them opened up into areas that were half-wooded, half-grassy; the sections that had been partially forested became the dry savannas where some of the apes and early men eventually found their home; broad plains and steppes of pure grassland appeared where once there had been woodland; and the driest sections of all became desert. All these changes forced corresponding changes in the animals, who depended on climate for their food. Those animals who were adapted to live in the open grasslands, which came to take up more and more of the earth's surface, naturally increased in number and variety—antelope, deer, horses, cows, elephants, goats—and their predators, the lions, the leopards, the wolves, and foxes. Important among all these inhabitants of the dry savannas were the primates; and most important—at least to us—among the primates were the australopithecines, our close relatives if not ancestors.

Australopithecines were, for want of a better term, ape-men, but men nonetheless—about four feet tall, with a brain somewhat larger than that of a present-day chimp and quite possibly with some power of speech. They were primarily vegetarians—fruits, roots, seeds—although they also ate birds' eggs when they came upon them, and even small, slow-moving animals or the young of larger animals. We know about this part of their diet because at Olduvai Gorge, where Dr. L. S. B. Leakey and his wife Mary had been digging since 1930, and where they found the remains of australopithecines and other early forms of humanity, they found also the bones of baby pigs, baby antelope with the long bones split open in order to extract the marrow, rats, mice, frogs, lizards, snakes, tortoises, and birds.

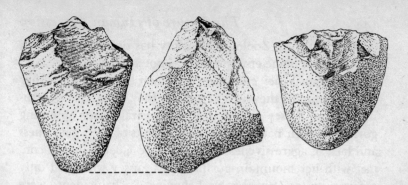

Fig. 2. Pebble tools from Bed I, Olduvai Gorge, Tanganyika. (Courtesy of the British Museum [Natural History]).

On the other hand, the australopithecines were something more than apes. They stood up and moved about on their hind legs, for example, which gave their ever-developing hands freedom to explore, to hold objects up for inspection, to poke, to squeeze, to reach, to grab, and thus to feed the curiosity that even then was becoming an important mechanism for learning and understanding and adapting.

Also, these creatures had begun to use tools routinely. Not only that, they even made some of them out of stone, and used them as implements for digging and related purposes.

Amiability

As they developed away from their ancestors, however, it is conjectured that the australopithecines retained something of the amiable disposition that characterizes the great apes today. Gorillas, especially, portrayed in comic books and popular literature as hideous menacing creatures, are, in their natural habitat and even under congenial conditions of captivity, peaceful, loving creatures. Dr. George Schaller of the New York Zoological Society has described them in their natural home environment as not at all aggressive, and has said that if they encounter a human being, or any other strange animal, they will retreat if they have an opportunity. Dian Fossey who has spent several years observing gorillas in their native habitat also speaks of their gentleness and lack of aggressiveness. During some 3,000 hours of contact with her mountain gorillas Miss Fossey witnessed only a few minutes of aggressive behavior. Such incidents were generally initiated by protective adults when their young approached her too closely. In all instances the "charges" proved to be bluff. Carl Akeley, the explorer, who had much experience with mountain gorillas, described the gorilla as a "normally perfectly amiable and decent creature. I believe that if he attacks man it is because he is being attacked. He will keep away from a fight until he is frightened or driven into it." He also said, "The gorilla lives in amity with the elephants, buffalo, and all the wild creatures of his neighbourhood, and in the Mikeno region, the natives drive their cattle into the gorilla's mountains in the dry season of the year without molestation." "The first living gorilla I ever observed," added Akeley, "was in the Zoölogical Park in London many years ago. It was very young and its chief aim in life seemed a desire to be loved. This has seemed to be the chief characteristic of the few live gorillas that I have seen in captivity. They appear to have an extremely affectionate disposition and to be passionately fond of the person most closely associated with them." These observations have been thoroughly confirmed by all investigators who have had prolonged experience with gorillas.

Jane van Lawick-Goodall, the young Englishwoman who has conducted such interesting and widely reported studies of chimpanzees in Africa, has made similar observations on her subjects. "It is one of the most striking aspects of chimpanzee society," she writes, "that creatures who can so quickly become roused to frenzies of excitement and aggression can for the most part maintain such relaxed and friendly relations with each other." She points out that these frenzied "fights" between chimps seldom result in anything worse than the loss of a bit of hair, or a scratch or a cut from a fall in the melee.

Another important characteristic of primate behavior, and of the behavior of our australopithecine relations, is sociability. This should come as no surprise: sociability and amiability go together often. With the exception of a few of the small-bodied nocturnal primates, the bush-babies, lorises, and tarsiers, all members of the order live in groups, spend almost all their time in groups, and carry out all their projects—eating, copulating, raising their young, protecting themselves from foes—in groups.

The Group

So important is group living to the higher primates that when individuals are separated from their groups, they suffer. R. A. Butler, in a study of "Curiosity in Monkeys," has demonstrated that to a monkey the simple sight of another monkey is more welcome than food. And Harlow, in his many important studies with rhesus monkeys, has shown the deep psychological harm that is done to the young of that species when they are separated from their parents. This sometimes happens in the wild. Jane van Lawick-Goodall tells of a little male chimpanzee who had lost his mother and who became progressively more isolated, neurotic, stunted in growth, and who eventually died of a polio infection. In this area, human beings are very like their forebears: the most severe punishment short of death our society metes out to wrongdoers is solitary confinement. And loneliness is widely considered the most severe malady one can suffer. We are true primates in our emotional reliance on each other.

This characteristic has had great significance for the evolutionary development of our species, and as we discuss the various aspects of primate and human dependence on other primates and other human beings, we will be demonstrating at the same time how our evolution could not have taken place in anything like the form it did without this emphasis on cooperation and mutual aid. The group-living of early australopithecines is one of the important factors that led these humanlike apes, or rather apelike humans, slowly toward the achievement of abilities that made them invincibly human.

Hunting, for example: this activity could never have developed without a high degree of cooperation among the members of a group who were working together for the mutual good. Forest-dwelling ancestors of humankind probably did little hunting of animals, except for insects, eggs, and an occasional slow-moving animal; the luxuriance of the vegetation available to them kept them predominantly vegetarians. But as the trees thinned out, and the grass took over, and small animals were more plentiful than greenery, these ape-men extended their hunting activities to include a larger repertoire of small animals. And as the animals grew in size, variety, and number, the australopithecines became more proficient. And because they preferred to be together rather than apart, they hunted together.

Hunting in groups—even in small groups of perhaps half-a-dozen or more—turned out to be an effective way to get food. If we are to judge from the behavior of Gombe chimps, these creatures were certainly capable of working out for themselves the effectiveness or efficiency of group hunting, but even if they were not, the evolutionary conditions would have sufficed to do their thinking, as it were, for them: groups that hunted together and shared their food were healthier groups; the individuals in those groups tended to live longer than individuals who went out alone after an animal, and the groups that did the best job all around tended to prevail.

Present-day collateral relatives of the australopithecines still hunt this way now: Dr. Geza Teleki has reported recently that the hunting behavior of wild chimps in the Gombe National Park is highly cooperative; while dominant males may eat for some time without sharing, in general the sharing of meat is quite unaggressive to the extent that dominant males have been seen begging food from subordinate males.

The same principle—that groups are better than individuals—applied when it was necessary to protect themselves from other hunters. A group is clearly better equipped to stand off predators than a single individual ever is. The australopithecines may not have been able to talk, in the sense of using words, but they certainly made sounds to one another, as apes do today, and many of these sounds have specific meaning: "Danger!" And a predator would have to be bold indeed to take on a band of powerful ape-men who had been alerted and were ready to fight.

Fighting among australopithecines is unlikely to have been any more frequent than it is among apes. Their ability to flee from dangerous situations was well developed, and flight rather than fight would in many cases have been to their advantage. In this connection, the function of the group is again evident: flight of a group is safer by far than flight alone for each individual in the group, and primates, who can take refuge in trees where few predators can follow them, are particularly well suited to flight.

Learning

Perhaps the most important function of the group in the evolution of early humans was in the area of learned behavior. It is possible to learn alone, of course, by trial and error, but it is much easier and quicker to learn from watching others. It is also safer and contributes to greater length of life, since sometimes learning by trial and error is too slow. By the time you've learned the lesson, it may be too late.

There is no question that learning from other members of the group is an important component of the lives of all primates, and the learning is not restricted to the young. Primate adults teach each other, too. We may here draw attention to the studies of the groups of Japaneses macaques who have lived and been observed for many years in a semi-wild state on an island near Japan. One exceptionally bright female monkey in that group figured out for herself how to wash sweet potatoes; these were dropped at feeding stations as they were when just dug from the ground. She took them to the edge of a stream and let the running water clean them. Within a few years, all the females and males who fed with the mothers and young were washing their own sweet potatoes. The same female figured out, too, how to separate out the grain from the sand it was lying on—also by washing it. The others who had learned to wash the potatoes also learned how to do that.

Irven DeVore has reported the reaction of a troop of baboons to automobiles. Two of the troop had once been shot dead from a car. Eight months later the troop was still afraid of cars, and would shie off whenever they saw one. When threatened by men they run away. When threatened by lions they flee to the trees. Such behavior obviously represents several kinds of learning—from observation, from adult to adult, from adult to young.

We see in the car-avoidance episode another value of the group: the advantage that accrues when many individuals learn from a single experience. An individual baboon living alone, and shot from a car, would have died in a vacuum, so to speak. Its death would have done no other baboon the slightest good. Whatever lesson it learned would have died with it. That baboon had companions, however, and they saw that creature—noisy, stinky, and shooting flame—and saw their companion die, and made the connection for themselves and for all baboons who came after them for eight months. Their suspicions, communicated to younger baboons, altered the behavior of that troop and would serve them in good stead for years to come.

When that episode is translated broadly into the more normal happenings and hazards of primate life, it becomes clear that long before the emergence of the first true human beings, even before the development of the australopithecines, the patterns of cooperative living had been established and individuals were helping each other survive.

One of the early forms of humanity, *Homo erectus,* is believed to have made its appearance about a million and a half years ago, give or take a few tens of thousands of years. The difficulty with dating is considerable, partly because by the time *erectus* appeared the species had become more widely scattered: there have been fossil remains found throughout Africa, Europe, and even in China. When we take into account that evolution depends upon circumstance and environment, upon the challenges met and surmounted, and upon chance mutations in the genetic material in each group, we can recognize that different groups would have evolved at different rates.

One positive consequence of the wide scattering of *Homo erectus* was that the demands made upon them by the more rigorous climates of other places resulted in several major developments: clothing, cave-dwelling, and eventually, fire. In even the moderate climates of Europe and Asia the winters are cold and vegetation dies down completely for several months of every year, and this led, too, to more sophisticated hunting. In short, we now begin to see the pattern of life that we know as that of early humans.

In tropical Africa, clothing was never necessary, and the australopithecines wore no more clothing than the apes. In the cold of European winters, the hides of animals were needed, and were adopted. Groups took to living in the mouth of caves as protection against wind and snow and cold. And some time during the period of *Homo erectus*, perhaps half-a-million or more years ago, they began to use fire for warmth and for cooking food. It, too, like hunting, was probably accidental at first: a tree struck by lightning, twigs rubbing against each other till they ignited, or even hot ashes from a volcano, and the tending of these fires must have become a cooperative venture sooner or later.

The development of hunting among early humans and its later extension to the hunting of large animals probably served to intensify the importance of cooperation in the lives of these people. Cooperation enhanced their chances of developing and evolving and eventually becoming something more than apes.

It is not necessary to maintain, as Lorenz and Ardrey do, that human beings enjoy killing animals in order to explain *why* they kill animals. In their early development they killed animals, as their descendants still do, in order to eat. Our own methods of animal slaughter are farther removed from our daily lives; not many of us, for example, personally participate in the killing of the beef and chicken that

daily come to our tables. But animals are killed, as they were
in the days of our animal forebears, so that we may eat, even
though it is no longer necessary to eat meat in order to survive.

Incidentally, killing animals for sport is another matter.
For some this is sport, in the same sense that football is
sport, and both are enjoyed by many human beings. Taken
on a global scale, however, not a large percentage of people
is much interested in killing other living things for fun. In
any case, the subject is not relevant to a consideration of
hunting as it applied to early man, who killed animals in
order to eat.

Thus, from necessity, various groups of these people
around the world began to learn to be serious hunters.
Wherever they could, they evidently preferred to hunt herd
animals of moderate size—deer and horses—for the very good
reason that it is easier and safer, first, to find the animals
and, second, to kill them when there are a great many in
one place. Larger animals that travel singly are harder to
find, and much harder to track down and, because of their
size, to kill in safety. In either kind of hunt, however, the
hard work was lessened and the result was surer and more
plentiful when several hunters cooperated in the enterprise
than if a single man went out alone. We can imagine, then,
a band of early men—say about a half-dozen or so—stalking
and killing and dividing up enough meat to keep all of them
in protein for several days at a time.

Meantime, back at the hearth, the women were beginning
to live the kind of lives that women have tended to live
ever since—as caretakers of the young and, perhaps for the
first time ever, also of the elderly, the injured, and the ailing,
and literally as keepers of the home fires. With the strongest
and swiftest members of the group—the men—out stalking
the meat, the women stayed behind. Their main occupation,

in fact, was gathering, and from that fact we derive the ap-
pellation that such groups have been known by: hunter-
gatherers. Since, in such societies to the present day, most
of the food is supplied by gathering (except among Arctic
peoples), mostly by women, and far less time is spent in
hunting, I prefer to call such societies "gatherer-hunters."
In these societies the men were not always successful in the
hunt, and except when the ground was frozen and covered
with snow, the stay-at-home women, taking their children
along with them in the pattern we still recognize, roamed
the nearby countryside for fruits, berries, roots, and edible
vegetation of whatever kind. They brought these back
home, where they met the men coming in from the hunt
either with or without the meat; the group then divided up
the available food and ate it together.

The whole question of the division of labor between the
sexes evidently goes back to our earliest days as human
beings. And without taking a position here concerning
whether or not present-day women should remain in the
cave keeping those fires burning, it is sensible to point out
that during prehistoric times such an arrangement was necessary for survival. Natural selection, in fact, greatly favored
those individuals and those groups who cared for their
young for extended periods, and whose tribal lives were organized on the highly cooperative principle of mutual support between men and women.

Big Brains, Immaturity, and Dependency

The reasons for this are several, and closely intertwined.
Basically, the major reason is physical: as human beings
needed to adapt themselves to changing environments, and
as they did so, those creatures who were the brightest—that

is, those who had the best and biggest brains—survived the longest and left the greatest number of descendants. As the brains of human beings thus gradually grew larger, their heads, of course, also grew larger. We have only to picture in our minds the sloping foreheads of the apes, and compare them with the present-day eggheads to see how much larger our heads have become in relation to the rest of our bodies.

A larger head and a larger brain are fine endowments, but they presented a major difficulty: that of being born. A child with a large-size brain could not possibly be born through its mother's birth passage and pelvis. The answer, from the point of view of evolution, was a compromise: the female pelvis broadened somewhat to accommodate the larger head of the fetus; the infants were born with considerably less than their full brain size and development. In chimpanzees, to give a rough comparison, babies are born with 65 percent of their adult brain capacity; in the australopithecines the percentage was about 50; in modern humans the figure is about 25 percent. That is, a modern human baby has about one-quarter the brain size it will eventually develop. A related fact of significance is that in contrast to the young of other animals, a human baby is immature, undeveloped, and in fact, as we all know, entirely helpless.

This evolutionary development has had two important consequences. One is the changed shape and functioning of the female—the broadened hips and rather rolling gait that is typical of the human female are the direct results of the need to accommodate the enlarged brain. This change has brought to females a disadvantage in walking and running. Women do not walk and run as easily and swiftly as men, whose legs and hips are designed solely for locomotion. Thus when hunting swift animals is in question, it is reasonable that the men in the group be the ones to do that job, leaving other jobs for the women.

Growing Young—Neoteny

The other major consequence of this whole development turned out to be that extended maternal care paid high dividends, and thus contributed to the prolongation of the child's dependency. The human infant must be fed and protected for years if it is to survive. To contribute to that end the human mother has not only been elaborately prepared during pregnancy but she must also learn a great part of her maternal role.

Since it is important for us to understand how the growth and intensification in interdependency came about in the human species, we must consider the evidence for this in somewhat greater detail.

When we compare the developmental periods of apes and humans, infancy, childhood, adolescence, maturity, and later adulthood, we find that their duration in humans is greatly prolonged in comparison with the same periods in the apes, as may be seen from Table I. This extension of the

TABLE I

Length of Gestation and Postnatal Growth Periods and Life Span in Ape and Human

Genus	Gestation (days)	Menarche (years)	Eruption of first and last permanent teeth (years)	Completion of general growth (years)	Life span (years)
Gibbon	210	8.5	?—8.5	9	30
Orang-utan	273	?	3.0—9.8	11	30
Chimpanzee	231	8.8	2.9—10.2	11	35
Gorilla	252	9.0	3.0—10.5	11	35
Human	266½	13.5	6.2—20.5	20	73

periods of development in human beings has come about by
a biological process known as *neoteny* (from the Greek *neos,*
new, and *teinein,* to stretch). In short, the periods of development in humans are stretched out by the retention of
fetal or juvenile ancestral traits into the later developmental
stages of descendants. The young chimpanzee, for example,
looks very much more like an adult human being than does
the adult chimpanzee (see Figure 3). The human being re-
tains and maintains the promise of the young anthropoid
or infant human in its later stages of development, whereas
the ape does not. This is true not only for such physical
traits as the retention of the large brain of the fetus and
child, the rounded skull, flat face, small teeth, late eruption
of teeth, relative hairlessness, thin nails, small jaws, and
many similar morphological traits, but it is also true of behavioral traits, such as prolonged immaturity and dependency, prolonged playfulness, curiosity, love of fun, imagina-
tiveness, experimentalness, and inventiveness.

The one developmental period which is about the same
in duration in humans and apes is the gestation period, the
period spent in the womb. Taken in relation to the duration
of human postnatal developmental periods, the duration of
gestation within the womb should last, as Kovács has shown,
22 months instead of nine months. Owing, however, to the
explosive growth of the brain during the ninth fetal month,
and the narrowness of the mother's pelvic outlet, the human
fetus must be born when it usually is because otherwise its
head would grow too large for it to be able to pass through
the birth canal, and that would spell the end of the fetus
and of its mother. That contingency is avoided by the birth
of the human fetus when its brain reaches a volume between
350 and 400 cubic centimeters (or roughly the equivalent
amount in grams). However, at birth the human infant's
gestation is only half completed. The human infant is very

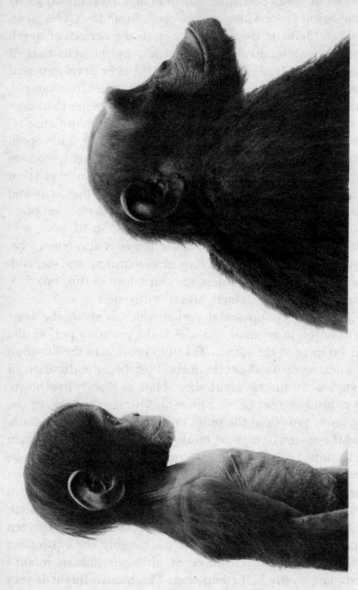

Fig. 3. Showing how humanlike the juvenile chimpanzee is, compared with adult.

immaturely developed, as is evidenced, among other things
more obvious, by the inadequate development of its enzyme
system and its consequent inability to metabolize adequately
anything other than colostrum and maternal milk, the absence of fatty (myelin) sheaths around nerve fibers, an inability to raise itself up until about six months of age, and
an inability to walk until about 14 months of age. All this,
and much else, testifies to the human infant's extreme immaturity as compared with infants of the great apes.

The human infant, like the newborn marsupial, appears
to have completed only half its gestation within the womb.
The newborn marsupial has the advantage of spending the
second half of its gestation period within its mother's pouch
(marsupium). The human newborn is lacking in such a marsupial advantage, and is therefore in a very much more
critical position than the newborn marsupial in relation to
the environment. *Uterogestation,* gestation within the
womb, has been completely symbiotic, but whereas the
newborn marsupial (which has to find its way into its mother's pouch), once in the pouch, has only to suckle, rest, and
sleep there, the human neonate must have all the arrangements made for it if it is to continue to survive during the
exterogestative period that follows birth. *Exterogestation,*
the continuation of gestation outside the womb, lasts for at
least ten months—that is, up to the time when the infant begins to crawl about by itself. The human infant, however,
requires many more years of attention from its parents than
does the infant of any other primate before it can begin
to negotiate the world for itself.

The point I am attempting to establish here is that humans, because of the greater duration of their early dependency, higher potentialities for intelligence, and sensitivities,
are considerably more in need of tender loving care, and
for an appreciably longer time, than any other animal, and

that because this has been so over the five million or more years of human evolution, a high premium has been placed on the ability to minister to the dependent needs of the infant.

The Tendency to Cooperation

The natural tendency of primates to be sociable and somewhat cooperative was developed among early humans into ways of living that promoted cooperation, and further developed among the groups of these humans into techniques and practices in which cooperation was not only the preferred mode of living but actually became essential for survival. There was cooperation among the men on the hunt as they worked with each other to find and kill the animals they tracked; there was cooperation among the women as they spread across an area, searching and gathering the fruits and nuts for the rest of their diet; cooperation between the groups of men on the one hand and groups of women on the other, as they divided the increasingly complex work that became necessary to continue living; cooperation among all the adults so that the children would grow up in health and safety and learn what they needed to know; and cooperation among all members of a group so that for the first time a person with a broken leg or an illness could survive because there was a safe place to recover and companions to give aid.

Speech

One of the most effective tools for cooperation was, and remains, speech. What form of early human was the first to attempt speech as we know it today—words and sentences expressing thoughts about the past and the future as well as communication about the present—we do not know. Our primate ancestors, of course, were capable of communicating with each other, as primates are today, with vocalizations, grunts, and wordless shouts meaning "Get out of my way," or "Here comes something!" And until very recently it was believed that these creatures were unable to develop speech because of their limited brain power. More recently it has been suggested that a more likely explanation is their lack of the proper physical arrangements in the throat, mainly the tongue and the pharynx, to make the sounds necessary for speech. A chimp named Washoe, for example, has recently been taught a sign language used by deaf and dumb people and in a period of two years has learned over thirty words. Sarah, another chimp, was taught to use one hundred and thirty cardboard symbols, standing for objects, actions, colors, and even grammatical relationships such as "If such-and-such, then this-and-that." It is therefore not the brain that prevents speech among chimps.

We conjecture, therefore, that somewhere along the road from apehood to humanity the necessary physical characteristics were gradually developed, and human beings began the talking that has characterized them ever since, the principal behavioral trait that distinguishes them from all other animals.

They did not, however, suddenly burst into speech, any more than they suddenly dropped down out of the trees and began living on the ground. Speech, like other developments, was a long time coming. Lieberman, Crelin, and Klatt have conducted some interesting studies in this connection by comparing the pharynx of modern man with the pharynx of modern infants, who can make only limited noises, and with what can be deduced from the study of a fossil Neanderthal skull. Their conclusions are that Neanderthal men, who supplanted *Homo erectus* some 200,000 years ago, spoke very much more slowly than modern man, perhaps only one-tenth as fast, and were more limited in the sounds they could make. The suggestion is that they used much the same sounds that babies make. *Homo erectus* would have been more limited still, they surmise. It is concluded that *erectus* was able to use speech, but just barely, and that Neanderthal man was able to communicate more precisely, but still not fluently. These, however, are rather precariously based hypotheses. Dr. Marjorie Le May of Harvard University Medical School has argued that endocasts of the brain of the skull of the Neanderthal man (the old man of La-Chapelle-aux-Saints) studied by these investigators indicate that he possessed all the necessary neurological requirements for the development of speech. Furthermore, as Dr. Le May cogently points out, modern adults with flattening of the base of the skull and projection of the jaws, characteristics which are supposed to reduce the ability to speak, have no problems with enunciation. Hence, the conclusions of those who have argued a late or poor development of speech in prehistoric humans are invalidated. It is, in fact, quite possible that speech originated quite early in the evolution of man as a consequence of the necessity principally of communicating the fundamental skills of toolmaking and tool usage. However that may be, the importance of speech can hardly be overemphasized in a discussion of the development of human beings, because speech is inextricably bound up with thinking. In fact, speech makes possible the act of complex abstract thinking. And it is complex abstract thinking that constitutes the major gulf between nonhuman animals and human beings.

Among nonhuman animals thinking plays nothing like the role it does in humans. As the forms of life grow more complex, the weight of the power to adapt to circumstances, which eventually becomes conscious thought, grows also, and eventually outweighs this power of instincts, until finally, in human beings, instincts account for little behavior, if any, and thinking and learning for almost all of it. And speech is one of the major factors which make that possible. Later conditioning, with very little thinking, may come to serve as a substitute for thinking, as it does in modern societies of humans.

According to some students in this field—and there are many who may disagree—thinking is a kind of silent speech; that is, it is not possible to think about an object until that object has a name. What is that flickering thing that is hot, and consumes other things, and then, unless it is fed, disappears? "Fire." When we try to think about something without using the word for it, we begin to see something of the difficulty of thinking without speech; and we *know* there is a word for it. Our ancestors did not; and it took them a long time to find all those words.

After words for objects, there were words for actions. And after that, words for qualities, and constructions to express relationships. And with each new word or group of words accompanying the sound came the understanding, the intellectual effort, the thinking, that gave the word meaning and that connected it with other words and other concepts.

"Next time we go out after deer, you go around behind and drive them toward me." "Don't pick that berry; the baby got sick when she ate it." These sentences represent several advanced achievements: an awareness of "next time"; the ability to think that *this* was caused by *that;* a different ability to think that this *will be* caused by that. Speech has helped to make all that possible.

Conversely, thinking increases language skills. As the brain developed and grew in complexity, human beings became able to imagine things for which there were no physical entities present, and for which no names had been given. Thus, people began to construct religions and magic and superstitions. A life after death, for example, appears to have been contemplated as early as the Neanderthal people: when they buried their dead, they included some tools and food for the dead to take along wherever they were going.

Of all the evidence we have of the supremacy of cooperativeness in the development of human beings, speech is surely the most convincing. Speech is by nature a cooperative venture; it is designed to put one into touch with others; without someone to talk to, talking is meaningless. Without someone to answer, talking is profitless. Talking presupposes at least two persons who are on good enough terms not to interrupt the conversation with violence or hostility. Conversely, the development of speech argues strongly for an awareness on the part of early humans for this tool to make cooperation more effective. Had they been basically hostile creatures, they would not have wanted speech, or needed it, or developed it.

The development of speech represented a giant step forward. The invention of speech brought other inventions in its wake. Tools became more elaborate, and tools with which to make other tools. Speech served as a whetstone upon which to sharpen one's wits. Increasingly, as human beings became more human—that is, as they developed their speech, intelligence, and social organization—they became increasingly interdependent; they needed each other more. For the most part a single instinct-driven insect can survive without other insects. A human alone has a much more difficult time. He or she would never even survive infancy without a caretaker. Humans as they grow need people to teach them. When they are adult they need people to talk to, and work with, and plan with. They need other people to help them with the large projects they are constantly creating. They need comfort from other people when they worry about what happens after death. They need someone to play with them. When they are ill or injured, or the victims of hurricane or famine or accident, they need someone to succor them.

Conversely, and even more interestingly from the point of view of those people who believe in innate aggressiveness, human beings from the earliest times needed not only to be cared for but they also needed to care for others. The evolutionary process, which had brought us to a state of development where we must live cooperatively or disappear from the earth, has also brought us to a state where we *want* to help each other. As a result, we do help each other, and we have done so since our earliest human days, and even before.

Primates, after all, take care of their babies, and not only because the babies demand it but because they want to. Female monkeys will hand a newborn baby monkey around among themselves in a way that is touchingly like a human group of the same kind. And male baboons and gorillas, when danger threatens, will protect the young and the females of the group to the point of taking the danger on themselves, and even being killed in the process.

Early men, on a hunting trip, likewise, shared their kill, not only among all the hunters present whether or not they had participated in the actual killing, but among the women and children and the elderly and ailing who were back home.

Looking at this kind of behavior from the point of view of evolution, we may say that natural selection favored those individuals and those groups who had some natural inclination toward taking care of babies and of helpless adults. In any group those who took care of each other would survive longer, much longer, than a group that was characterized by mutual hostility, lack of trust, and violence. This latter group would, in fact, either break up and scatter and cease to live as a group, thus exposing each individual to the increased stresses of solitude, or the group would become extinct simply as a result of people killing each other. Or both. The former group, accustomed to taking care of each other, would teach its younger members to do the same, and nurture would thus reinforce nature, and the strains of mutual aid and cooperation would be strengthened and transmitted from generation to generation.

Contemporary Gatherer-Hunters

We have one more source of information about human beings as they probably were during the millions of years between the australopithecines and modern humans: the nonliterate gatherer-hunting peoples scattered about the earth today. If we are indeed innately violent, if we are really creatures driven by genes to murder our own kind, if we are indeed incapable of controlling the hostile forces within ourselves, we should see these characteristics demonstrated here in these people. Their societies are uniformly small. They usually have no belief in gods. They are uneducated by our standards. People like the Tasaday who are primarily food gatherers live as close to nature as it is possible for human beings to live. They are, if anyone is, natural man.

And they are peaceful. And friendly. And cooperative. They share their food and their belongings with each other and with strangers. They play with their children. They take care of the elderly. Their relationships with each other are close and loving. They care. They cooperate.

Let us briefly survey these peoples. Before doing so let us briefly relate what is to follow to a statement by Lorenz in *On Aggression* in which he writes: "When man, by virtue of his weapons and other tools, of his clothing and fire, had more or less mastered the inimical forces of his extra-specific environment, a state of affairs must have prevailed in which the counter-pressures of the hostile neighboring hordes had become the chief selecting factor determining the next steps of human evolution. Small wonder indeed if it produced a dangerous excess of what has been termed the 'warrior virtues' of man" (p. 343).

"Hostile neighboring hordes"? But it is highly improbable that any hostile neighboring hordes existed in any significant sense, for the simple reason that the number of individuals in a foodgathering-hunting population is usually limited, scarcely ever exceeding more than a small number of families living together. Examples of such populations are the Eskimo, who until recently were exclusively gatherer-hunters, various Malayan groups, the Punan of Borneo, the Pygmies of the Ituri Forest, the Hadza of Tanzania, the Birhor of Southern India, the Bushmen of the Kalahari Desert, and the few remaining Australian aboriginal populations. "Hordes" are the invention of nineteenth-century antiquarians and desk anthropologists.

There exists no evidence whatever of hostility between neighboring prehistoric populations. Such hostilities may occasionally have occurred. If they did, it is extremely unlikely that they were frequent. Populations in prehistoric times would have been few and far between, and when they met it is no more likely that they greeted each other with hostility than do gatherer-hunter peoples today.

Paul Shepard, visiting professor of environmental perception at Dartmouth College, has cogently resumed the facts. He writes:

Courtesy links bands of hunters. When they meet, usually at the boundaries separating their respective areas, they are peaceful and cordial. Because of the quasi-territorial face-off, and because the serious matter of

mate selection and marriage is frequently part of these
meetings, they are highly charged affairs. Tensions are
buffered by fixed procedure, by more or less formal ceremony, and contests of skill and courage. These vary
greatly, allowing for all the kinds of personal involvement and conflict within the overriding rules conducive
to harmony. The meeting is cause for celebration; danc-
ing, information exchange, companionship, courtship,
and trade are carried on. . . . Unlike farmers, their
population is not chronically underspaced. Since men
are not by nature territorial, hunters do not repel in-
vading bands.

The Tasaday

Perhaps among the best known, because most recently discovered and publicized, "primitive" people are the Tasaday of
Mindanao in the Philippines. This people, numbering 26
individuals of whom 13 are children, impressed everyone
who came into contact with them by their friendliness and
utter lack of aggression. Discovered in July 1971, Kenneth
MacLeish wrote with enthusiasm shortly after meeting
them: "[They are] as perhaps the simplest of living humans, and those closest to nature . . . gentle and affectionate. . . . Our friends have given me a new measure of
man. If our ancient ancestors were like the Tasaday, we
come from far better stock than I had thought."

And indeed all that we know of gatherer-hunter peoples
is that they more closely resemble the Tasaday in their relations with their fellow humans than does the dismal picture
of our ancient forebears fantasied by the innate aggressionists.

The Tasaday were first discovered in 1966 by a hunter
named Dafal, who came from a southern Philippine tribe.
Between 1966 and June 1971, in which latter year Dafal lead

an official party, including anthropologists, to the Tasaday, he had visited them ten times, and his contacts have never been less than friendly. In his book *The Gentle Tasaday,* John Nance, who spent some seventy-three days over a period of three years among the Tasaday, found them to be "inspiring emblems of social peace and harmony, of, simply, love." "Their love," he writes, "was everywhere—for each other, for their forest, for us—for life." "They are altogether a loving, gentle people. They have no weapons, and no apparent aggressive impulses."

Nevertheless, Nance found that "the children showed the egotism one might expect—arguing over a stick, crying for food, slapping at one another" (p. 188). Dr. Irenäus Eibl-Eibesfeldt, who briefly visited the Tasaday remarked to Nance that he had observed "classic" aggressive behavior between toddlers—striking at one another or pretending to, tugging at opposite ends of a stick (p. 438). The key question, therefore, for Nance was how the Tasaday managed aggression in their children so that they grew up to be essentially loving adults.

The answer seems to be fairly clear: they discourage aggressive behavior, reward cooperative behavior, and set models in themselves for their children to imitate.

Mai Tuan, leader of the largest tribe in the area, the Tboli, and a surprisingly urbane man, remarked that he had traveled far and wide—to Japan, Indonesia, Hong Kong, Singapore, Manila, and all over the Philippines—"and everywhere there are good people, and some bad ones, too. But the real goodness—the best people I've ever seen anywhere are the Tasaday. Ah, the way they live. Alone. Their home is good. They have clothes easily. They don't argue among themselves. They are truly virgin people. And when they look forward, they look forward together, and they love things together. None tells them that this is not good or that is not good. They seem to forget themselves as individuals, they do not even know themselves as individuals" (p. 217).

Peggy Durdin, who spent some time among the Tasaday, says, "Among the most quickly discernible traits are their capacity for affection (and relaxed expression of it), and their sense of humor. Adults and children do not seem afraid of being openly loving. . . . It is a pleasure to watch Tasaday behavior toward people they like. . . ." "The Tasaday live this partly communal life in very close quarters year after year, as their ancestors told them to do, with remarkable harmony. I found no one who had heard them exchange harsh words or even speak sharply to the young. In the face of something displeasing they seem to use the tactic of evasion: they simply walk away."

What the innate aggressionists will make of the Tasaday, with their ability to live without weapons and without aggression, it will be interesting to learn.

The Tasmanians

The aboriginal Tasmanians, whom the British singlehandedly managed to exterminate by 1873, were a remarkably peaceful people. Robert Thirkell, who lived among them for many years, "found them an inoffensive race of people." He never considered it necessary to carry firearms to protect himself against them. Thirkell considered any injury sustained by the white settlers entirely occasioned by their own ill-usage of the females. Even George Arthur, the lieutenant-governor, appointed to drive them from their ancestral hunting grounds, described the Tasmanians as "a noble-hearted race." Nevertheless, the attempts of the Tasmanians to defend themselves against their oppressors were met with the most brutal punishment and, within seventy-five years of the first fatal impact, total extermination.

The attempts of the Tasmanians at self-defense against the whites merely succeeded in getting them denounced as "warlike" and their "benefactors" thought of as the injured party. As the Reverend Thomas Atkins wrote, after visiting Tasmania in 1836:

> Indeed from a large induction of the facts, it seems to me to be a universal law in the Divine government, when savage tribes who live by hunting and fishing, and on the wild herbs, roots, and fruits of the earth, come into collision with civilized races of men, whose avocations are the depasturing of flocks and herds, agricultural employments and commercial pursuits, the savage tribes disappear before the progress of civilized races. . . . Indeed, they have not complied with the conditions on which "the Lord of the whole earth" granted to the first progenitors of our race the habitable world. "For God blessed them, and God said unto them, be fruitful and multiply, and replenish the earth and subdue it."

The Reverend Thomas Atkins was speaking for millions of white men then and later, voicing the sentiments that many more millions share with him across the length and breadth of the Anglo-Saxon world. Today the doctrine is called by its proper names, the Christian "ethic," "imperialism," and racism.

The Bushmen of Southwest Africa

The Bushmen of Southwest Africa have been somewhat romanticized. They are not quite as gentle as many of us have been led to believe, but nor are they as violent. The Bushmen, who live on the edges of the Kalahari Desert in Botswana and Southwest Africa, occupy a land which is anything but the flat, harsh, dry, hostile, forbidding country of

thirst, heat, and thorns, of hunger and death, it has been
painted. Water *is* a problem, but it is a problem that is
continually being solved. Food is, in fact, abundant, and
life is leisurely. Life is neither nasty, brutish, nor short. The
Bushman shares food with others and, repressing any feelings of jealousy and possessiveness, lives peaceably enough
with his fellows and with his neighbors. Professors Richard
B. Lee and Patricia Draper both found that the !Kung
Bushmen deliberately choose not to live in large groups in
order to avoid the conflicts that frequently arise in such ag-
gregations. The human press among the !Kung, with an
average density of thirty people in the camps at about one
person per 188 square feet (as compared with 350 square
feet generally considered as desirable), is notably not associated with any recognizable symptoms of biological stress.
This may be due to the option the Bushmen enjoy of moving from one band to another. Band fission of this type
appears to be a common technique among band-level peoples which they employ to avoid conflict. Individual Bushmen are capable of anger and even of losing their temper
to the extent of indulging in violence, but such occasions
are comparatively rare. As a Bushman witnessing such a loss
of temper remarked, "If you want to help people don't get
angry with them. Keep calm." Professor Draper writes me
that one of the mechanisms that work against violent con-
frontations between hostile individuals is the bickering
which is endemic to !Kung life. The !Kung neither brood
nor keep silent about interpersonal problems. They scold,
complain, make speeches, and so on. She thinks that this has
the effect of reducing tensions before they reach dangerous
levels. "It is also true," Dr. Draper continues, "that physical
attack and domineering behavior are strongly devalued by
the culture and that these behaviors are rare and not readily
available for children and adolescents to model themselves

after. Overall, I would say that the everyday potential for violent behavior is much lower among the !Kung than it is for ourselves or for the neighboring Bantu peoples in the Kalahari."

Dr. Draper, who made a special study of the matter, found that !Kung parents do not punish children physically. "Among the !Kung," she writes, "there is an extremely low tolerance for aggressive behavior by anyone, male or female." "Competitiveness in games is almost entirely lacking, and the players appear to come into a game for the sheer joy of it and for practicing their own skill at it."

Quarrels occur, but like summer showers they soon blow over and serve to clear the air. No malice is borne, and the deep involvement in each other is clearly exhibited whenever any mischance or accident befalls a member of the band. There is no aggressiveness toward other groups, no raiding, no war. From past experience the Bushmen are aware that white men are likely to be dangerous and so their tactic is to avoid them, to make themselves invisible by concealment or flight. While each group has its own specific territory, which the group alone may use, they respect the territories of others scrupulously, and there is no fighting between neighbors.

When quarrels do break out between members of different bands, they are almost invariably on account of adultery. Men may fight their wives, women may fight women, and men other men. Wrestling to the ground may occur, and they may hurl sexual insults at each other. If matters get heated enough someone may shoot a poisoned arrow, with lethal effect. But when this occurs hostilities cease and everyone joins in a trance dance, a kind of ritual healing of wounds. Such band quarreling is, however, rare.

The point to be emphasized here is that while intragroup aggressiveness occurs among Bushmen, they avoid all intergroup friction. To use Lorenz's phrase, "whatever counter-pressures of the hostile neighboring hordes" they might possibly be exposed to, the Bushmen successfully avoid them simply by making themselves scarce, and for a band of some twenty or so individuals that is not so difficult.

Dr. Irenäus Eibl-Eibesfeldt has attempted to show that the claims made by various anthropologists that the Bushmen are both nonterritorial and aggression-free are mythical. He quotes older investigators and a more recent one to the effect that Bushmen groups were and are territorial. He is quite correct about the territoriality. But in the matter of aggression his case is not so good, in spite of the photographs he shows of young children in aggressive acts. The difficulty arises out of Dr. Eibl-Eibesfeldt's rather wide definition of aggression. For him aggression is any act which leads to the establishment of a dominance-subordination relationship. Intent to, or not to, injure or the actual injury of another does not enter into his understanding of the meaning of aggression. Whatever the intent of the behavior, if it results in the submission or withdrawal of the other it is, according to Eibl-Eibesfeldt's understanding of the term, aggressive behavior. This is a perfectly permissible definition of one form of aggression, but it is not that to which the innate aggressionists have devoted their attention—namely, the infliction of injury upon the other. However that may be, Eibl-Eibesfeldt, who has studied the !Ko Bushmen and the G/wi as well as the !Kung, reports that he observed many forms of aggressive conduct among children. There can be no doubt from his descriptions and photographs of such incidents that these were indeed aggressive acts. But nowhere does Eibl-Eibesfeldt consider the possibility that some elements of learning entered into the behaviors he describes. So that until he or others go back into the field and study the behavior of children with the necessary allowance for the possible effects of learning, his observations cannot be accepted as disproof of what he calls "the myth of the aggression-free hunter and gatherer society." No one with any knowledge of the facts has ever claimed that children are incapable of aggression or that such aggressiveness as they may exhibit is free of the influence of innate factors. What is here claimed is that such aggressive behavior is not primarily determined by innate factors, and that gatherer-hunters tend to appear peaceful when compared with peoples who are economically more developed.

Eibl-Eibesfeldt is impressed by the non-belligerency of the Bushmen. He concedes that they belong to "those people whose culture shapes them according to a peaceful ideal." What he finds striking is not so much their lack of aggression as their efficient way of coping with it, their friendly interactions, and their leisurely way of life. "One could say," he concludes, "that these people have more time at their disposal to be 'human' in a friendly way, while we are losing the capacity to a greater and greater extent."

We are indebted to Dr. Eibl-Eibesfeldt for making these points so well for us.

Professor Robin Fox of the Department of Anthropology of Rutgers University tells us that the "Pueblo Indians, Eskimos, Bushmen have all been cited as examples of non-violent people, and all turn out to have high rates of personal violence." He cites no evidence for this statement, except to say that "the Bushmen have a higher homicide rate than Chicago!" (*sic*).

Let us consider the facts. Professor Richard B. Lee, whose span of fieldwork among the !Kung Bushmen covered the years 1963–69, recorded 33 case histories in which people came to blows. For the period 1920–69 Lee obtained information on 15 major fights in which 22 people were killed, the last fatal fight occurring in 1955. These figures are derived from a total base population of 1300 !Kung Bushmen living in flexible social groupings of from 10 to 50 individuals.

Lee found that a bystander or third party is more likely to get killed in a Bushman fight than a principal in an argument. There is a general unpredictability about who gets killed, and Lee suggests that Bushman fighting may perhaps best be considered as a running amuck or temporary insanity, rather than as an instrumental means-end behavior.

In fifty years Bushman homicides totaled 22, which would work out at a rate of 34 per 100,000 people. If one compares this with the U.S. homicide rate, and takes into consideration the fact that in the United States many people recover from attempts on their lives owing to superior medical care, that large numbers of attempted homicides go unreported or are attributed to other causes, that many deliberate homicides are caused by means that are never recognized, to which one may add deaths caused by American intervention in the affairs of foreign nations, then the comparable American homicide rate rises to about 100 per 100,000 of the population.

All observers of the Bushman are agreed that the fear of violence is a prominent feature of their life. Hence, nothing came as a greater relief to them than the setting up of a headman's court in 1948, a court to which they could bring their serious conflicts for adjudication. Homicides occurred in 1952 and 1955, but none have occurred since then.

The point here is not that the Bushmen are nonviolent, but that while they are capable of violence they fear its consequences and have taken full advantage of the opportunities provided to control any violent impulses they might

experience, preferring to have their serious conflicts resolved peacefully. Far from surpassing Chicago in its homicide rates, the Bushmen were and are rarely homicidal. As
Lee says, the balance sheet distinctly favors the savage who,
even in the absence of other superordinate means of social
control, manages to keep the violence rate low, so that for
all their poisoned arrows the !Kung bushmen remain "the
harmless people" after all.

Professor Fox goes on to tell us that a book was written
about Bushmen called *The Harmless People*, "which only
goes to show," he writes, "that while anthropologists might
be nice folks who like to think well of their fellow men,
they can be poor guides to reality."

The truth is that *The Harmless People*—a delightful
book—was not written by an anthropologist but by a travel-
writer, Mrs. Elizabeth Marshall Thomas. Mrs. Thomas did
not bestow upon the Bushmen the name which serves for
the title of her book. It is the name, freely translated by Mrs.
Thomas, by which the Bushmen call themselves, *Zhu/wasi*
or *zhu twa si*,* as Professor Fox might have discovered had
he read the first chapter of Mrs. Thomas's book. In this
instance, at least, Professor Fox is not a dependable guide
to reality.

The Eskimos

The Eskimos are perhaps the most written-about gatherer-
hunter people of all. Everyone who has lived among Eskimos and has written about them has always done so with
unfailing admiration and enthusiasm. Living, as they do,
in the most inhospitable lands in the world, in icy waste-

---

* Professor Patricia Draper, who knows the Bushmen well, suggests that
"Just folks" might be a closer translation. Personal communication.

lands in which during the dark winter nights the temperature falls to 50 and 60 degrees below zero, the Eskimo (as
he was) is perhaps best described in the words of Admiral
Peary. Writing of the Eskimos of West Greenland, he says:
"They are savages, but they are not savage; they are without
government, but they are not lawless; they are utterly uneducated according to our standard, yet they exhibit a remarkable degree of intelligence. In temperament like children,
with all a child's delight in little things, they are nevertheless endearing as the most civilized men and women, and
the best of them are faithful unto death. Without religion
and having no idea of God, they will share their last meal
with anyone who is hungry, while the aged and the helpless
among them are taken care of as a matter of course. They
are healthy and pure-blooded; they have no vices, no intoxi-
cants, and no bad habits—not even gambling. Altogether
they are a people unique upon the face of the earth. A
friend of mine calls them the philosophic anarchists of the
north. . . . To Christianize them would be quite impossible; but the cardinal graces of faith, hope, and charity they
seem to have already, for without them they would never
survive the six-months' night and the many rigors of their
home."

No one, in so few words, has better characterized the Eskimo. The distinguished authority on the Eskimo, Dr. Kaj
Birket-Smith, in his book on these peoples describes them
as individualists who consider nothing "more repulsive
than aggressiveness and violence," and he makes the point
that "far-reaching helpfulness among camp-fellows is an
inevitable duty."

For every Eskimo tribal group or band the story is the
same. In the latest book by an anthropologist on an Eskimo
family, with whom she lived, Jean Briggs tells us how the

Utku of the Back River, northwest of Hudson Bay, early in their relationship would have nothing to do with her because she lost her temper with some visiting fishermen who carelessly broke one of the Eskimo canoes. This unseemly and frightening display of wrath, even though it was aimed at uninvited intruders who had irresponsibly damaged one of her host's most prized possessions, caused her to be ostracized for some three months. Stinginess, unhelpfulness, and bad temper, in the Utku view, are three of the most damning traits that could be ascribed to anyone.

Nevertheless, some people do occasionally become angry, and quarrels occur between individuals, between bands, and with other groups, but these seldom result in violence of any kind—although murder is not unknown. The traditional manner of settling disputes is by contestants' "assaulting" each other with reproachful songs. This is done to a musical accompaniment, and is a source of much delight to those present. It is a form of "aggression" from which the civilized world could greatly benefit were it possible to persuade it to adopt this engaging convention.

Among the East Greenland Eskimos, for example, the song contest is the customary means of settling a dispute or grudge. Even the murder of a relative may be resolved in this way, especially if the relative seeking satisfaction feels himself so proficient a singer that he is sure of victory. Since skill in singing is greatly admired, and the artistry of the performer so absorbs the interest of the audience, the cause of the contest tends to be forgotten, and the focus of attention is entirely upon the wit and skill with which the contestants attempt to outsing each other. He who delights the audience most and receives the heartiest applause is declared the winner. Singing ability, indeed, equals or outranks gross physical prowess, and brings great prestige.

From the many accounts of the culture that we have it is quite clear that aggressive behavior occurs in all Eskimo groups. However, in most of them early conditioning against it tends to limit its expression.

African Pygmies

The Pygmies of the Ituri Forest of Central Africa inhabit a world that for them is good, living as they do in the warm embrace of the forest in peace and amity with all about them. The MaMbuti, as they call themselves, average less than four and a half feet in height, but what they lack in height they make up for in strength and toughness.

Colin Turnbull, who lived among the Pygmies for three years, says of them, "Cooperation is the key to Pygmy society; you can expect it and you can demand it, and you have to give it. If your wife nags at you at night so that you cannot sleep, you merely have to raise your voice and call on your friends and relatives to help you. Your wife will do the same, so whether you like it or not the whole camp becomes involved." Anger may arise, quarrels may start, children may be slapped for doing something wrong, but anger does not last long, grudges are not borne, quarrels are evanescent, and occasional chastisement of one's wife is as far as any form of violence goes. The Pygmies are unaggressive both emotionally and physically, as is evidenced by their lack of any form of warfare, feuding, witchcraft, and sorcery. Turnbull believes that the kinds of quarreling, spouse-beating, and similar activities that go on within the anything but quiet Pygmy camp constitute outlets which, together with the explicit concern for the avoidance of aggression, are designed to provide "insurance policies" against intentional, calculated aggression. It will be recalled that a similar explanation for the general lack of aggressiveness among the !Kung Bushmen was offered by Professor Patricia Draper.

The Australian Aborigines

At the time of their discovery in the late eighteenth century there were many hundreds of tribes or bands of Australian aborigines, and what we know of them from early records and later field studies makes it clear that they were, and such of them as remain are to this day, a highly cooperative and unaggressive group of peoples. As W. E. Harney, who lived the greater part of his life among the aborigines of Arnhem Land, Northern Territory, remarked, "Did you ever see a native fight? All day it will go on, with plenty of running about and talk and natives scruffing one another, but very little bloodshed. Although they throw spears and boomerangs about, it is very rarely that a person is seriously injured. Of course, we think it silly. Understand, however, their kinship rules and you will notice that the talkers are the protectors, whereas the actual combatants are kept away from each other. Knowing this, the latter will roar and shout and try to break away; but they are never let go until their tempers have cooled off. Implicit in their behaviour is the wise principle of 'Arbitration.' "

Of the Pitjantjatjaras of Ernabella in Central Australia, to call upon yet another representative Australian example, Wilfred Hilliard writes that they fight ceremonially, following the rule of turn and turn about. In fights between women and those between men "the fight clears the air and there are no grudges. Once their quarrel has been settled, the ex-combatants assist each other to receive first-aid!"

Warfare (defined as armed conflict carried on by members of one social unit against another) and feuds (defined as conflict between particular families or groups of kin) sometimes occurred among Australian aborigines. Usually the conflicts were over a woman or over a death believed to have been caused by sorcery practiced by a member of another band or tribe. Typically, as Spencer and Gillen described the scene, the attackers entered their opponents' camp fully armed but fought with words, not weapons; after a time things would quiet down, and the affair subsided. Occasionally, however, they would come to blows, or the avenging party would wait in hiding to spear the victim or spear him after he had been ceremonially handed over by his own group.

As our leading students of the Australian aborigines, Professors A. P. Elkin of the Department of Anthropology at the University of Sydney, and Ronald and Catherine Berndt at the University of Western Australia at Perth, have emphasized, territory is important to the aborigines neither politically nor economically. The tribe as a whole seldom, if ever, makes war. This is a concern of local groups or clans. There are no wars for territorial aggrandizement. War was, in fact, as G. C. Wheeler showed many years ago, infrequent in aboriginal Australia.

In fact, students of the Australian aborigines all agree that they are a particularly gentle, generous, kind, and noble-hearted people. On occasion the aborigines were capable of carrying out a sanctioned killing in much the same manner in which a state-appointed executioner executes a condemned prisoner. Such killing, however, partook more of the nature of a retributive enforcement of a penalty than it did of an aggressive act. As Buss has pointed out, injurious attacks upon others may not be considered aggressive if they occur within the context of a socially accepted custom or role.

The Control of Aggression

The two dozen or more gatherer-hunter peoples, in addition to those already described, however much they may vary culturally, nevertheless exhibit much the same general tendencies in the matter of aggressiveness. Possible exceptions are the Ona of Tierra del Fuego and the Andaman Islanders. There was much quarreling and feuding in Tierra del Fuego within the band among the Yaghans and between bands among the Ona, usually over the theft of a woman or because of trespass. Unlike the other peoples I have described, the Ona bands, of which there were some thirty-nine, each had a leader whose authority was especially evident when conflict of any kind threatened or occurred. Furthermore, since the Ona forbade marriage of both paternal and maternal cousins, they had no ambassadors, as it were, in other bands, because interband cousin marriage was forbidden. These two facts, the emergence of a band leader and the prohibition of cousin marriage, constitute part of a political situation which, as Coon puts it, "marks a transition between a bilateral, loosely organized system which lacked firm authority to a unilateral one in which leadership was more nearly crystallized. It also marks a change from disorganized brawls and fights starting with individuals to concerted raids and ordeals between groups."

The Andaman Islanders, who live on the islands of the tip of the coast of Southern India, are pygmies, who also had band leaders or chiefs exercising power over these, one for the coastal and one for the island bands. Killings within the band were rare, but were more frequent between bands. By 1911 superior band chiefs had disappeared and the population was so reduced that there was no longer a sufficient number of bands left to indulge in the luxuries of feuding and fighting. Radcliffe-Brown states that fighting on a large scale seems to have been unknown among the Andamanese, and that their only fights among themselves were brief and far from bloody, where only a handful of men were engaged on each side and rarely more than one or two were killed. "Of such a thing as war in which the whole of the tribe joined to fight with another tribe" Radcliffe-Brown could find no evidence.

Even though in most ways the gatherer-hunter peoples I have described may be socially more advanced than were prehistoric gatherer-hunter ancestors, their ways of life are much nearer to theirs than to ours, and tell us a great deal more about the ways of life of our prehistoric forebears than we could possibly glean from any other living source. What the gatherer-hunter peoples tell us is that although on occasion prehistoric men were capable of aggressive behavior, they for the most part almost certainly led peaceful lives, that they must have been highly cooperative and deeply involved in the welfare of their fellow men.

The possibilities are high that if any people stands closest to our prehistoric ancestors it is the foodgathering Tasaday of Mindanao, undoubtedly among the gentlest and most unaggressive people on this earth. What can have happened in their case to that reservoir of aggressiveness with which writers like Lorenz and Ardrey would have us suppose that all human beings are endowed? Can it be that the Tasaday have learned to control the expression of aggression? Or is it possible they may have lost the genes associated with the potentialities for aggression? Or is it that since they have no weapons they have never developed "killer genes"?

The probability of gene loss is low. Control of aggression is very much more likely, and an even more likely explanation seems to be that from infancy the Tasaday has learned to be cooperative and unaggressive, so that seldom, if at all, has a Tasaday been called upon to harness any tendency toward aggression. One learns to be unaggressive simply by not being aggressive.

Learning is the process whereby enduring changes occur in the behavior of the organism as a consequence of experience. One can learn to be unaggressive just as one can learn to be aggressive. There is no ineluctable necessity about aggression. It is not something that must inevitably develop and mature. Humans are no more wired for aggression than they are for organized homicide.

Control of aggression is clearly exercised by many peoples. Indeed, aggression is controlled by individuals in most societies. But that is a very different phenomenon from the behavior presented by the Tasaday, who may be unaggressive because they have never learned to behave aggressively. This is not to suggest that they lack the biologic potentialities for aggressive behavior, but it is to suggest that in the Tasaday world those potentialities have not undergone those organizing stimulations necessary for the development of aggressive behavior. What seems to be most likely is a combination of this explanation with the theory of control —namely, that the Tasaday have learned to be cooperative and unaggressive and have also learned to control such feelings of aggression or aggressivity they may experience on certain occasions. These occasions are likely to be few—first, because they have been trained in cooperation; second, because they have been trained out of any tendencies toward aggression; and third, because they are seldom exposed to conditions that would be productive of aggression.

Why are gatherer-hunter peoples on the whole characterized by so little aggression? Can it be because they have so little to be aggressive about? Can it be that while humans live in small groups in precarious relation to the environment cooperation becomes a necessity, that any undue aggressiveness might fatally upset the delicate balance that the small group must preserve if it is to maintain and perpetuate itself?

I think it not only can be but is highly probable that in the course of human evolution as a gatherer-hunter the highest premium was placed by natural selection on cooperative behavior, and a negative premium on aggressive traits.

It is difficult to conceive of any useful function that aggression would have played either between members of the prehistoric band or between bands in the sparsely populated regions of the earth in which humans lived. Indeed, as J. B. S. Haldane pointed out in his book *The Causes of Evolution* (1932), "In so far as it makes for the survival of one's descendants and near relations, altruistic behavior is a kind of Darwinian fitness, and may be expected to spread as a result of natural selection."

It could, of course, be argued that once such fitness had been established within the group, fitness could be further enhanced by trial by combat, in which the worthiness of the one or the other group to survive and bequeath its genes to succeeding generations could be tested. This has indeed been argued by Dr. Robert Bigelow in a book entitled *The Dawn Warriors* (1969). Bigelow suggests that humans evolved both as intragroup cooperators and as intergroup aggressors, whose most deadly enemies were human foreigners. "The survival of our species," he urges, *"now,* depends on our ability to suppress the urge to kill our enemies." Professor Richard D. Alexander of the Department of Zoology of the University of Michigan has expressed similar views, and so has Professor Edward O. Wilson of Harvard.

The facts do not support such arguments and claims. Does the reader of this book have an urge to kill his enemies? Whatever the answer, the record of history bears vivid testimony to the fact that virtually everywhere when nonliterate peoples for the first time encountered white men they welcomed them with every sign of friendship. If some of these peoples were in conflict with neighboring bands or other groups, it was certainly not because they were foreigners but because of some grievance, fancied or real; not because they were driven by some "urge to kill" their enemies but because from past experience they had learned that some form of aggressive behavior constituted the appropriate means of dealing with the situation. Some peoples have learned that the appropriate response is with nonaggressive behavior. It depends upon the culture and its particular history. Aggression, the existing evidence suggests, occurs only in cultures in which the individual is conditioned in aggressive behavior.

Other Peoples

Among peoples practicing some form of agriculture, such as the Papago Indians, the Hopi, the Zuñi, and the Pueblo peoples generally, any form of aggressive behavior is thoroughly condemned. So, too, it is disapproved among the Semai of Malaya and neighboring tribes. The Punan of Borneo, the Land Dayaks of Sarawak, the Polynesian Tikopia of the Western Pacific, even under conditions of famine and considerable social change, preferred to express their anger in words rather than in physical violence. The Lepchas of Sikkim in the Himalayas, a nomadic pastoral people, are most gentle and unaggressive, living at peace with their neighbors and among themselves, in spite of a life that is hard and continuously trying. The Polynesian Ifaluk of the Western Pacific are another such gentle people, although life for them is much easier than it is for the Lepchas. Marston Bates describes the Ifaluk as "the most completely nonaggressive society imaginable." On their small coral atoll the Ifaluk have enjoyed the greatest freedom from contact with civilized people of any of the Pacific Islanders. Kindliness, security, and serenity are the outstanding traits of the Ifaluk personality. "Every child was a member not only of a family and a household, but of the whole island society. A child crying would be comforted by the nearest adult." "Curiously," adds Bates, "the children, though 'secure,' were far from obnoxious—in fact, it would be difficult to imagine a more delightful bunch of kids. The 'sibling rivalry' that seems to plague every American household was conspicuous by its absence—the mannerly, non-aggressive character of Ifaluk society extended even to the five-year-olds."

The outstanding characteristic of Tahitians of French Polynesia, according to Robert Levy, the anthropologist who has most recently studied them, is gentleness, defined negatively as behavior in which manifest hostility or violence is unusual. Between the years 1940 and 1962 there was only one serious crime, a murder. And for the period before that the only other similar crime, according to the older people, occurred in 1928. Self-aggression in the form of suicide is also rare among Tahitians, though common among Chinese of the Society Islands. Physical fights are infrequent and, when they do occur, not particularly violent. Lack of fighting is particularly striking among children. Play is highly energetic, involving much joking and, in same-sex play, body contact, and mock aggression, such as pushing or a tug at a girl's pigtail. When a critical or irritating remark is occasionally made, its recipient will either ignore it or, rarely, withdraw crying. He disengages.

On two occasions Levy witnessed conflict situations among children, in which the customary style of expressing a threat in a carefully ineffectual manner was followed. The offended boy chases his tormentor but never catches him, while other children look on with serious expressions. The pursuer soon gives up and throws a small piece of coconut husk at his antagonist, but carefully misses.

Levy observed that among the Piri and Roto (fictitious names for the two villages he studied) people in public were as nonviolent when drunk as when sober. At home, however, when drunk, they were often more fractious.

"The generalized and culturally valued timidity" of the Tahitians is related to the negative view they take of anger. If you are angry it is better to tell it and get it out of your system. This serves the double function of securing relief and of avoiding further trouble. Such arrangements for minimizing the interpersonal effects of anger seem to work very well.

Many other nonviolent peoples, like those of Tibet and Subarctic, the Lapps, the peoples of much of Malaya, and others such as the Arapesh of the Sepik River in New Guinea, all testify to the fact that aggressiveness is not a necessary characteristic of humanity.

All these peoples, like the rest of us who share the human heritage, are quite capable of violence and hostility. But these peoples have learned, as we have not yet learned, to handle their potentialities for aggression, so that it never or seldom expresses itself in overt violence, especially physical violence. All these peoples disapprove of it. Aggression does not occur in societies in which it is the habit not to be aggressive. Whether by trained control or otherwise, clearly such nonaggressive behavior is learned in cultures in which it is the habit to be nonaggressive. In such societies the biological potentialities for aggression are socially reinforced by the kinds of experiences which are permitted in them. In any event, in societies in which it does not occur, learning plays a dominant role, to such an extent in nonaggressive societies that the biological potentialities are simply given no chance to develop.

The fact that such great variability is encountered in the expression of aggression in different societies, ranging all the way from complete nonaggressivity to quite high rates of aggression, itself constitutes evidence of the substantive role that cultural conditions play in that expression. There is no overriding "human nature," no biological imperative, that instinctively determines the paths of aggression an individual or a people will follow. Since there is no stereotypy about human aggressive behavior, and since it is neither consistent in its appearance nor invariable in its expression it cannot be innate. Modifications in cultural pressures can make the most substantial changes in the behavior of a customarily aggressive people or one that is customarily cooperative. An instructive and terrible example of the latter is represented by the Ik of eastern Uganda. These people suddenly found themselves traumatically displaced from their traditionally hunting nomadic way of life on the plains to a totally different environment in the mountains, where they were told to go ahead and farm the rocky soil. Their failure to become farmers overnight, largely due to the sterile land to which a bureaucratic government had consigned them, quickly led to a breakdown in their old habits of cooperation. In his book *The Mountain People,* Colin Turnbull tells the shocking story of the resulting dehumanization of these people. When Turnbull visited them, he found them in the midst of a two-year drought, and starving. Some of them starved to death before his eyes, with the nearest water a scummy hole some five miles away. Life among the Ik was horrible: children were abandoned at three years of age to take care of themselves; the elderly and the feeble and the ill and the dying were laughed at and were knocked away when food was distributed; misfortunes were jokes; strangers were enemies.

Mr. Ardrey has cited Dr. Turnbull's book with glee, asserting that it attacks the central assumption of those who believe that the vices and aggressions of contemporary humans represent distortions of human nature brought on by social forces. My own reading of Dr. Turnbull's book led me to quite another conclusion. During a meeting with Dr. Turnbull he referred to Mr. Ardrey's misreading of his views. On my asking him whether he would be good enough to write me what he had said, he at once did so, and with his kind permission I reproduce his communication to me here.

Dr. Turnbull writes:

> I cannot for the life of me think how the Ik material can be twisted to support any argument that mankind is inherently nasty or violent. There is no doubt that by our standards, the Ik *are* singularly nasty. But that, I would have thought, was clearly a response to the nastiness of their situation, and a *necessary* response at that. As to violence, the remarkable thing is the absence of it in their lives . . . what there is is confined to verbal violence, perhaps accompanied by gesticulation . . . but much of that is directed at the winds, so to speak, rather than at individuals or objects, or events.
>
> What the Ik tell me is not that man is *inherently* nasty, merely that we have as much potential for nastiness as we do for goodness, for unsociality as for sociality. . . . I come to see all these qualities as survival techniques in given contexts, related to the technological range of possibilities and alternatives. In their given context, at their level of technology, sociality for the Ik became dysfunctional. The apparent violence of a mother toward her child was, I believe, a necessary

part of that child's education toward survivability. And the crux of the matter is that the Ik have had to re-order not only their economic lives, but their emotional lives, and the mother has to undo, both for herself and for her child, whatever emotional bonds are created during those two crucial years of breast-feeding, during the third and final year. So that at the end the child emerges emotionally independent and economically prepared for a solitary life.

In the book of course I gave my own emotional reactions, and I did regard the Ik with horror, as savage and violent (at such times). . . . Evidently I did not do a good enough job in bringing out the underlying message that the savagery and violence were in myself and my own attitudes rather than in the Ik.

The dedication contains the key . . . for the Ik, whom I learned not to hate. Because not knowing love they equally do not know hate. And that is perhaps the most frightening potential that the Ik show to lie in what we so glibly call "humanity" . . . an almost total dispassion.

Until now most social contexts, except in emergency situations, demand cooperation for survival . . . so for man's long history he has cooperated and been social. As technological advances have been made, cooperation became less essential, individuals had greater scope through their usage of machines, and now finally we cooperate with machines far more than we do with humans . . . and even with many of our human contacts we cooperate in a mechanical rather than human manner. Cooperation has become indirect rather than direct; we become categories rather than humans. Under these conditions . . . aggravated by population density in urban areas . . . I can see technological "progress" leading us closer and closer to that ultimate human potential for inhumanity. . . . As for the Ik, it may for us well become the only way we can survive, emotionally and economically.

In fact, the story of the Ik demonstrates once more the thesis of this book: that the way people behave is a reflection of what happens to them, not a reflection of their innate drives. Before their enforced consignment to their new land, the Ik, according to Turnbull, were generous, compassionate, and honest. After they were deprived of their traditional way of life, the only life they knew how to live, they turned not hostile but indifferent to each other and to outsiders. Turnbull himself concedes that their behavior was probably the only possible way they could meet their predicament, that each individual had to scramble for himself in order to survive at all.

The story of the Ik demonstrates another point, too: that indifference to one's fellow humans is *not* the quality that guarantees survival. For the Ik are doomed. Another generation or so and the Ik will be no more on this earth. Their misfortune was that a blind and uncomprehending bureaucracy compelled them to adopt a way of life that circumstances made it impossible for them to achieve. The whole group was forced into a situation they could not handle, and their response has been to split wide open, to neglect their children, to abandon their earlier habits of compassion and cooperation. And as a result they will soon be extinct.

Perhaps this has happened before in the course of human history. When groups were not able to handle their misfortunes together, perhaps they died separately and the group vanished. If that has indeed happened—and there is no reason to suppose it has not—then those of us on earth at this moment are the descendants of people who had first of all a certain amount of luck in the conditions of their lives: not too much famine, not too much natural catastrophe, not too sudden a change in climate, and at least so far not irremediably too stupid and blind a government. And we are also the descendants of those people who, given that certain amount of luck, helped each other through whatever did come to them.

Let us make clear once more that this is no claim that human beings are innately generous and helpful, any more than they are innately hostile and violent. There are within all of us potentialities to be helpful, just as there are within us potentialities to be violent. But the point of this discussion is that the cooperative drives have played a vastly more important role, during the five million or so years of evolution from ape to human being, than have our potentialities for violence.

8

The Brain and Aggression

The Limbic System

Since aggression is so widespread in the Western world students of the nervous system have applied themselves to discovering whether there might not be something inherent in the structure of the human brain that could perhaps explain such behavior. In recent years there has been a tremendous increase in the number of studies designed to throw some light on the possible neurological bases of aggression. There are today many investigators in experimental neurology and the neurosciences generally who claim to have located areas in the brain which represent the neurological bases or substrates of aggressive behavior. The part of the brain most generally associated with aggression is called the limbic system. This portion of the brain, also called "the visceral brain," is said to be structurally primitive compared with the dense layer of cells known as the gray matter, the neocortex, which, like the rind of an orange, encloses everything within it. The limbic system, which surrounds the brain stem, is shown in Figures 4 to 6. Some comparative neuroanatomists have recognized a triune development of the

193

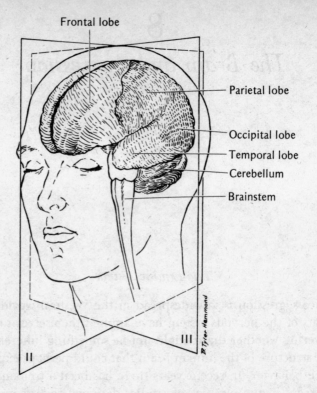

Frontal lobe

Parietal lobe

Occipital lobe
Temporal lobe
Cerebellum
Brainstem

Fig. 4. Three-quarter frontal view showing location of the brain within the head and the four major lobes of the cerebrum. A cut made along Plane II, called a midline section, reveals the anatomical relationships shown in Fig. 5. Similarly, a cut along Plane III, called a coronal section, reveals the structures shown in Fig. 6.

brain, the reptilian brain, the old mammalian brain or paleocortex of which the limbic system is an outgrowth, and the new mammalian brain or neocortex or "thinking cap." The limbic system forms, as it were, a ring on the inner aspect of the brain, the lower anterior part of which is known as the amygdala. The amygdala is situated deep in each temporal lobe, and has been strongly identified with

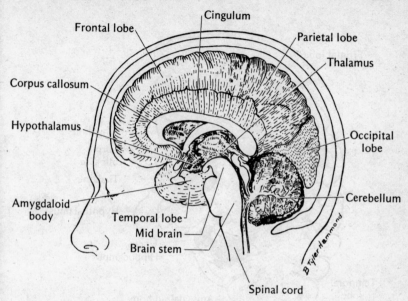

Fig. 5. Midline section (Plane II of Fig. 4) through brain illustrating gross physical relationship between structures involved in the control of aggressive behavior. The location of the amygdaloid body is shown in dotted outline.

aggressive behavior. At one time or another various parts of the limbic system have been associated with aggression, even though there are some who question the very existence of such a system. There exists, however, a basic unanimity that such a system is recognizable as a morphological entity.

The results of many neurological studies will inevitably lead some to conclude that the brain is "programmed" or "wired" for aggression, and that therefore those who claim that aggression is instinctive or innate in humans are essentially right. The claim is that if actual "centers" in the brain for aggression do not exist, something very like them does.

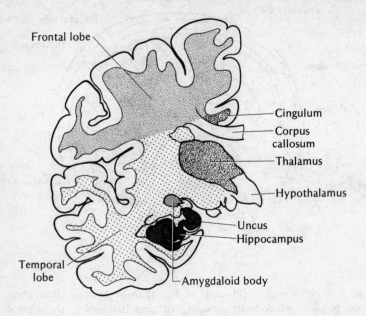

Fig. 6. Coronal section (Plane III of Fig. 4), showing the right half of the brain. The visible limbic structures include the amygdaloid body, hippocampus, hypothalamus, thalamus, and cingulum. (Courtesy of Drs. C. Boelkins and J. F. Heiser, and Little, Brown & Co.)

"Centers"?

Such investigations, largely conducted on experimental animals, deserve the most careful consideration and scrutiny for several reasons—first, because they will help us understand better what is involved in aggressive behavior, and second, because misapplied to the interpretation of human behavior there is a danger that such investigations may lead to the kind of "higher phrenology" or faculty psychology that several generations ago identified various bumps on the head with the seats of certain faculties. Phrenologists claimed that behavioral traits—"faculties," they called them —like combativeness, destructiveness, benevolence, parental love, and so on, were located in circumscribed areas of the brain. Like modern neuroscience, phrenology was based on the belief that the anatomical and physiological characteristics of the brain have a direct influence on behavior. Thirty-seven faculties were located in as many different "organs" of the brain, each of which was believed to affect the size and contour of the cranium. Hence, the degree and development of any region of the head was taken to indicate a correspondingly well developed faculty or propensity for that region. That being so, a fairly accurate character analysis, it was claimed, could be made by studying the shape of a subject's head. Such claims were quite unfounded. Yet scientists who look for "centers" in the brain that they believe turn various behaviors on and off are doing much the same thing, although in a somewhat more sophisticated way.

The fact that one can produce a particular behavioral effect by destruction or stimulation of a particular area of the brain has often been interpreted to mean that the structural basis of the behavior is located there. But that may well constitute a misinterpretation of the facts, for when brain tissue is removed one is dealing with a reorganized organ with different properties, chemical as well as structural. Behavior may have been altered because the operation interfered with blood supply or with fiber connections to different regions of the brain. Professor Richard L. Gregory, discussing the limited nature of the conclusions that can be drawn from brain lesion studies, offered an interesting analogy. Suppose one had never seen a radio and wanted to know how it worked. To find out you remove a resistor and hear static as a result. Would you be justified in concluding that the resistor is a "center" whose function in the normal circuit is to inhibit static? A similar line of argument applies to stimulation studies. It is possible to elicit some specific behavior by electrical or chemical means, but why this can be done is unclear. Stimulation may alter electrical or chemical activity at some considerable distance from the electrode. Electrical and chemical stimulation are, in any case, abnormal events, and this also needs to be taken into consideration. Electrical stimulation produces an abnormal situation because it causes all the cells in a given area to fire at the same time. Chemical stimulation is abnormal because at least ten times as much of a presumed transmitter substance is required to produce the effect that would be needed if that substance were produced by and released in the nervous system. It is also clear that chemical stimulants must be working at sites a long way from the point at which they are introduced.

The inferences that have already been drawn by many investigators concerning the neurological bases of instinct and aggression have, in my opinion, gone far beyond anything the evidence warrants and, unfortunately, those inferences have already been misused. Combined with the claim that aggression in the human species is instinctive, the neurophysiological findings would *appear* to make the case for innate aggression complete.

The view seems to be gaining ground that there exist areas in the brain which when stimulated, regardless of situation, context, or previous experience, give rise to violent or aggressive behavior. The conclusion is, therefore, drawn that these areas of the brain constitute the neural bases or substrates of violence and aggression. The words "bases" or "substrates" seem readily transmutable into "cause" or "causes," that is to say, a necessary and fundamental, and sufficient condition in the production of agonistic behavior.

The care and ingenuity with which these investigations have been carried out are worthy of the greatest admiration. From these investigations it is clear that there are areas of the brain that are involved in or are associated with aggressive behavior. But this is far from being the same thing as saying that the neurological structures comprising these areas of the brain are innately organized to function as aggressive behavior, that, in short, all that is required is the appropriate stimulus to trigger off the mechanisms that will result in aggressive behavior. I believe such claims to constitute a gross oversimplification. Certainly such circuitry is readily establishable in particular areas of the brain, but this is a very different thing from saying that there exist areas of the human brain which cause humans to behave aggressively, that the individual, regardless of his own previous and present experience, is genetically "programmed" or "wired" for aggressive behavior.

Stimulation Experiments

In the matter of eliciting aggressive behavior by brain stimulation, we have briefly to consider the typical findings and also what they mean.

Stimulation of the amygdala in cats results in attack behavior. The physiological signs of rage, as well as erection of the hair, elevation of blood pressure, increased respiration also occur. What is striking about the behavior is that it is directed. A cat will attack a rat in a cage and even stalk it. The behavior is not automatic or inflexible. In monkeys, this effect is even more striking. Unlike cats, monkeys are social creatures. Stimulation elicits attack behavior only if a safe object is present. A rhesus monkey will not attack a social superior, but it will attack an inferior or stuffed toy tiger. Stimulation that will elicit aggressive behavior of a dominant monkey toward a subordinate or submissive one will altogether fail to induce such behavior in the same animal in the presence of a newly introduced dominant animal. Indeed, the formerly dominant monkey now exhibits all the signs of submissive behavior. The animal simply does not react in an automatic manner, but evaluates the situation and responds with the appropriate behavior. In humans, stimulation in certain areas produces feelings of anxiety, depression, anger, fright, and horror, but it does not elicit attack. One woman reported she wanted to slap the experimenter, but she did not do so. A further complication in human beings is that they are influenced by what they think the experimenter expects of them. The findings on human temporal lobe epilepsy are relevant here because the epileptic is a sort of inadvertent stimulation subject. Too much electrical activity is going on in specific areas of the brain at one time and this resembles what happens to a subject whose brain is stimulated electrically by an experimenter.

It has been traditionally believed that temporal lobe epilepsy is frequently accompanied by aggressive behavior. Recent studies, however, of large numbers of epileptics, as Dr. Allan F. Mirsky and Nancy Harman of Boston University have shown, indicate that such aggressive behavior "is sufficiently rare to be considered either a curiosity or, perhaps, a non-existent phenomenon." And as the authors go on to emphasize, the production of aggressive attack behavior by brain stimulation in experimental animals does not present a good model for what goes on in the human brain.

The laboratory findings show that in experimental animals fear, rage, and attack can be evoked in many, but not in all, subjects by stimulation of specific locations in the brain. And this is possible because stimulation bypasses the normal sensory channels and directly activates parts of the brain that would be activated if the individual actually were in a frightening, unpleasant, or dangerous situation. However, the reason why stimulation can elicit these responses is that the individual has had such experiences in the past—that is, he or she has been in frightening, unpleasant, or dangerous situations—and these particular areas of the brain were activated on those occasions. Subsequently one can fool the individual into thinking that the same environmental events are present by electrically stimulating the regions of the brain that were active on those earlier occasions. However, it is important to note that even when one taps right into the system of stimulation, the resulting behavior is by no means automatic. The cat attacks the first thing it sees. It makes the "logical" inference that if it is experiencing fright or anger, and possibly even pain, whatever it sees near it is responsible, and it acts accordingly. The monkey may draw the same inference, but its decision to attack or not is based on the social status of the individual who is present. A human carries this process further. First, there may be recognition of the fact that the individual who is present is not necessarily responsible for the unpleasant sensations; and, second, even if that individual is seen to be responsible—for example, the experimenter who turned on the current—even then, social constraints prevent a direct attack. It is clear, then, that definite parts of the brain are involved in aggression, and it is equally clear that stimulation of these areas does not result in automatic, thoughtless aggression divorced from the animal's past experience. Stimulation of these areas of the brain evokes aggression only if the right stimuli are present. Dr. Pierre Gloor of the Montreal Neurological Institute of McGill University has argued that brain stimulation in the so-called fight and flight areas makes the animal defensive. Apparent separation of these effects in electrical stimulation experiments may be, he suggests, an artifact due to the artificial nature of the situation.

Defense is probably the fundamental brain program. Whether the animal fights or flees will depend upon processing information at a higher level—i.e., the cerebral cortex. The animal's decision about what to do will depend upon possible escape routes, size of enemy, and the like. Drs. E. S. Valenstein, V. C. Cox, and J. W. Kakolewski also have criticized the artificial nature of stimulation experiments. They point out that stimulation elicits several drives at once, but that usually the experimental situation is rigged in such a way that the animal does not have a variety of behavioral options. Although they were concerned mostly with experiments on the elicitation of eating following brain stimulation, their arguments apply to experiments on aggression. Perhaps if the stimulated animal had the choice of fleeing or attacking, it would choose to flee. Typically, however, in such experiments, the animal is restrained, immobilized in a chair or caged in a limited space or the like. Drs. J. L. Brown and R. W. Hunsperger, however, claim that in their experiments with cats, who as we have already stated are not particularly social animals, brain stimulation elicited attack, in rigid stereotyped behavior which occurs regardless of environment, age, sex, and temperament, even if no appropriate object is present, and even if the animal is blind.

Brain stimulation effects are not completely understood, and certain conclusions from experimental findings, especially on primates, are rather more than open to question. Some findings are frankly puzzling. For example, in an experiment by Dr. Rod Plotnik of San Diego State University and his coworkers the most dominant monkey never made aggressive responses following pain-producing stimulation, although other monkeys did so. If stimulation produces an automatic response, one would expect the effect to be most readily elicited in an animal that is easily provoked to aggression.

The Relation Between Brain Stimulation
and Aggression Questioned

In an extensive and illuminating survey of the evidence Dr. Plotnik, one of the most active investigators engaged in brain stimulation experiments, has arrived at the following startling conclusion: "To date, there are no experiments in which electrical or chemical stimulation has elicited aggressive responses in animals that have been prevented from learning these responses. Therefore, *neurological* evidence for innate (unlearned) aggressive circuitry is lacking in lower as well as in higher species." Plotnik draws attention to the fact that while there appear to exist neural circuits for predation in such animals as rats and cats, most investigators do not regard predation as aggressive behavior in the commonly understood sense of the term, that even if predation were to be regarded as one kind of aggression it is misleading to conclude that there is evidence for the existence of innate neural circuits for aggression. "Thus," Plotnik concludes, "for one of the underlying questions of whether there is any neurological evidence from brain stimulation for the existence of innate aggressive circuits, the answer is 'no.' If an author reports that such evidence exists, then he or she has included predation under aggression."

The fact that brain stimulation may produce aggression in some subjects may mean, Plotnik suggests, that aggression has been elicited as a result of exciting neurons involved in pain or noxious sensations, and that it is these noxious sensations that elicited the aggression. When an electric current is applied to a monkey's skin the animal will attack another monkey. When the same current is applied to the monkey's brain the animal will attack another monkey. Few would say that there is a trigger for aggression in the monkey's skin. Is there any reason for saying that such a trigger exists in the monkey's brain? In skin stimulation the aggression is quite clearly secondary to the noxious stimulus —that is, it is pain-mediated aggression. Plotnik believes that much of the aggression that has been attributed to the direct action of brain stimulation is in fact secondary or pain-mediated aggression.

The two cases of "primary" aggression in humans resulting from brain stimulation, one in a violent girl, and the other in a schizophrenic female patient, were so inadequately studied that, as Plotnik emphasizes, they cannot be depended on as satisfactory examples of primary aggression.

Delgado and Plotnik *et al.* have emphasized how limited are the conclusions that can be drawn from brain stimulation experiments. In this area of research Delgado urges that if we are ever to arrive at dependable results it is desirable (1) to test animals in social situations as well as alone; (2) to compare the responses of stimulated animals to dominant and subordinate animals; (3) to distinguish between aggression produced as a direct result of brain stimulation and aggression produced indirectly as pain-mediated aggression; (4) to establish a baseline during control sessions so that data obtained during brain stimulation sessions can be meaningfully evaluated; (5) to establish reliability, i.e., show that if one keeps on stimulating the same site over a period of months, one always elicits aggression from that site; and (6) to use more than one test.

Genetic and Environmental Influences

There can be little doubt that in humans as in other animals specific neural fiber systems and nuclei or groups of nerve cells are prefunctionally developed in the brain to serve specific functions, but that to a much greater extent than in other animals these prefunctional elements may be later organized or not by subsequent experience. In short, that in humans the neural elements associated with aggression do not determine the development of aggressive behavior, but that in humans, at least, it is to a large extent experience that functionally organizes specific neural fiber systems and nuclei and determines whether or not they will function in aggressive behavior. This is not to imply anything so foolish as the claim that genetic influences do not exist or are uninfluential in contributing to the expression of aggressive behavior, or that in some cases genetic factors may not largely influence such behavior. But it *is* to imply that, in the generality of human beings, genetic influences alone cannot be responsible for aggressive behavior, and that in most cases such behavior is largely dependent on interaction with environmental factors.

Professor R. W. Sperry of the California Institute of Technology at Pasadena has written that it is now possible to see how behavioral nerve circuits of extreme intricacy and precision can be inherited and organized prefunctionally solely by mechanisms of embryonic growth and differentiation. He believes that "the way now clears for the much abused concept of instinct to make its belated if somewhat qualified comeback."

If these statements are meant to apply to humans, and it would appear that they are, then they represent the kind of biological reductionism which overlooks the important fact of humanity's evolutionary and individual plasticity. Since aggression is involved Professor Sperry's remarks strike me as not unreminiscent of the speculations of the Alexandrian theologian Origen (A.D. *c.* 185-*c.* 254) on the prenatal sins of souls. This kind of neurological reductionism has about it the sulphurous odor of predestination. The fact is that Sperry's remarks concerning the developmental patterning of neural connections are based largely on experiments involving large neurons with long axons (Golgi type I), which, as Sperry acknowledges, differentiate quite early in development. By contrast, the small interneurons with small processes (Golgi type II), which are everywhere in the nervous system, are still differentiating in adolescence, and, Sperry feels, it is a reasonable conjecture that "the plastic changes imposed by function are located not in the long-axon systems but in the Cajal [Golgi] type I neurons." This is not correct, for such changes also affect type I neurons. Since small interneurons occur in large numbers in the regions of the brain which have been associated with aggressive reactions, it would appear most probable that plasticity is a characteristic of the regions involved, and that inflexibility is not a characteristic of any of the functions of these cerebral areas. Yet this is not the impression that Sperry seeks to communicate. Other workers in neurobiology have shown that in many mammals certain types of nerve cells (hippocampal and especially cortical pyramidal cells) continue to proliferate well after birth, and show all the stages of growth, migration, and differentiation.

The fact that the brain is still in process of growth and development for a considerable period after birth should remove all doubt that early experience does indeed influence and modify nerve cells and the synaptic connections they are able to establish with numerous other nerve cells, and thus affect any preexisting patterns.

Sperry feels that none of these findings alters the fact that in the past there has been a widespread underestimation of the importance of genetic determinants in the development of the brain. This may, indeed, well be so, but in no way changes the fact that genetic influences, which are undoubtedly at work, do not determine anything. When Sperry writes that "it is easy to think of a persisting pressure for diffuse growth of new connections among late maturing microneurons that become ordered secondarily through functional reinforcement and/or disuse atrophy," the available evidence overwhelmingly supports that statement. He then goes on to add: "One must remember, however, that it is yet to be demonstrated that the changes in circuit morphology effected by experience consist of more than an enhancement, maintenance, or neglect of connections that already are basically patterned by selective growth." This is perfectly true—firstly, because it is extremely difficult to make such a demonstration and, secondly, because much more is involved than mere changes in circuit morphology. Anatomy is important, but so is chemistry. Undoubtedly fine changes in the structure of the nerve cells in the brain occur as a consequence of different kinds of experience, and the evidence is now abundant that complex chemical changes are induced in the brain as a result of experience. Drs. E. L. Bennett, biochemist, Marian C. Diamond, anatomist, and David Krech, psychologist, all at the University of California at Berkeley, working together as a team have found that rats of the same genetic strain brought up in an enriched environment have heavier, larger brains, with increased weight of cortical tissue, and an increase in acetylcholinesterase. Acetylcholine is the chemical transmitter substance that facilitates the passage of impulses across synapses—that is, the locus at which a nervous impulse passes from the transmitting axon of one neuron to the receiving dendrite of another. An index of such activity in the brain is the amount present in it of the enzyme acetylcholinesterase, which serves to inactivate the acetylcholine at the synapses and restore it to its resting state. Research of this kind constitutes a highly important and significant beginning, which will undoubtedly be greatly intensified in future years. There can, however, be little doubt today that differences in the chemistry of the brain can be induced by various kinds of experiences, and that these can significantly influence the development of the individual's behavior from prenatal life well into postnatal life. Our point here is that purely descriptive accounts of morphological changes in the brain are quite inadequate to explain what takes place within it, and is certainly quite insufficient as an explanation of its development. The creation of neural mechanisms in the service of behavior is not simply a matter of an anatomical unfolding, like a coded tape upon which the message is written which the organism will automatically translate into behavior. More in keeping with the observable facts, the growth of the brain is a matter of increase in complexity, that is, development, in which the organic changes induced by experience are incorporated. No one has expressed this better than George Ellett Coghill in the final words of his classic book *Anatomy and the Problem of Behaviour,* published in 1929.

> If, then, it is conceded that growth is one of the means by which the nervous system performs its function in behaviour, it must be granted, contrary to the doctrine of certain behaviourists, that man is more than the sum of his reflexes, instincts and immediate reactions of all sorts. He is all these plus his creative potential for the future. Even the embryo of *Amblystoma punctatum* [the experimental axolotl of Coghill's experiments] is, mechanistically considered, more than the sum of its reflexes or immediate behaviour possibilities. The real measure of the individual, accordingly, whether lower animal or man, must include the element of growth as a creative power. Man is, indeed, a mechanism, but he is a mechanism which, within his limitations of life, sensitivity and growth, is creating and operating himself.

There are orders of freedom for development, even at the embryonic level, for which investigators like Sperry do not allow. The development of the organism is certainly coded by genes, but those genes are themselves subject to the influences of the environments in which they find themselves. It is that process of interaction which gives us development, and a living, labile organism.

The So-called Reptilian Brain

Dr. Paul D. MacLean, of the Laboratory of Neurophysiology of the National Institute of Mental Health, argues that the two oldest parts of the human brain, the so-called reptilian and old-mammalian, are quite similar to those of animals, and that therefore it is quite permissible to apply behavioral observations made on animals to human affairs. A similar view is taken by Professors Vernon H. Mark and Frank R. Ervin in their book *Violence and the Brain*. Mac-Lean writes: "On the basis of the behavioral observations of ethologists, it might be inferred that the reptilian brain 'programs' certain stereotyped behavior according to instructions based on ancestral learning and ancestral memories. In other words, it seems to play a primary role in instinctually determined functions such as establishing territory, finding shelter, hunting, homing, mating, breeding, forming social hierarchies, selecting leaders and the like." "The most explosive issue, of course," Dr. MacLean adds, "is the problem of controlling man's reptilian intolerance and reptilian struggle for territory, while at the same time finding a means of regulating our soaring population."

The behavioral observations of ethologists, however, provide no support whatever for Dr. MacLean's remarkable inferences. Nor does there exist any evidence for "ancestral memories." Ideas of this kind, including "racial memories," the "archetypes" of the Swiss psychoanalyst Carl G. Jung, have long been discredited among scientists. Nor does there exist any evidence, experimental or otherwise, that the so-called reptilian brain instinctually determines any of the functions which Dr. MacLean attributes to it.

And are reptiles really "intolerant"? Do they really "struggle" for territory? There are more than five thousand different kinds of reptiles, including the crocodiles, lizards, snakes, tuatara, and turtles, and they run the full gamut of behavior from aggressive to nonaggressive and from terri-torial to nonterritorial. In view of these facts one cannot legitimately generalize for the class as a whole either "intol-erance" or territoriality. And even if all reptiles were "in-tolerant" and "struggled" for territory, is it at all likely that any form of stereotyped behavior which may have character-ized our remote reptilian ancestors would still remain as the foundations for human behavior today? Or that the se-lection of leaders by human beings has the remotest connec-tion with what reptiles may have done 200 or more million years ago? It seems to us extremely unlikely for the reason, among others, that there has been an enormous amount of genetic change during that long period of secular time since the origin of the mammals from a reptilian stock. It there-fore seems highly improbable that whatever functions may be associated with the so-called reptilian brain are of the na-ture described by Dr. MacLean. As Schneirla has pointed out, new adaptive levels were achieved in evolution not simply by increase in complexity of existing structures af-fecting function but through qualitative changes as well. From primitive vertebrate to reptile-like mammalian an-cestor basic changes occurred in the conduction system with significant consequences for behavioral organization and for new behavior. It may be reasonably inferred from devel-opmental trends during the evolutionary process that the result was not so much that mechanisms of lower levels were repeated at higher levels as that they underwent modification in relation to the new context. It is probable, then, that the "old brain" was not merely retained in a more complex form, but that it was progressively repatterned correlatively with the cortex. "In mammals," Schneirla concludes, "as compared with invertebrates, not only are structural mechanisms much more versatile in their functional relationships, but limitations of action by specific structures relax increasingly, widening the breadth and plasticity of behavior in its bearing on species adaptation."

The evolutionary trend of the brain has been toward progressive development of the cortex and forebrain; the term "cephalization" is employed to describe this trend; what cephalization denotes is cerebral plasticity. The developed forebrain and cortex allow for greater flexibility of function through greater associative capacity. As the neurologists Professors Harvey B. Sarnat and Martin G. Netsky point out, the ability to regress and exclusively use phylogenetically old centers is lost. An opossum with a lesion of the visual area of the cortex, for example, may still retain useful vision if the optic portion of the brain known as the tectum remains intact, whereas a similar lesion in humans causes blindness. Unilateral destruction of the motor cortex or corticospinal tract in the rat results in transient locomotor impairment; a similar lesion in humans leads to permanent spastic hemiplegia. In different classes of vertebrates similar functions are accomplished through different structures, such as association in the corpus striatum of birds and in the neocortex of mammals. It is this kind of plasticity, as Sarnat and Netsky state, "which makes generalizations about function based on the study of one species highly speculative when applied to another."

Dr. MacLean tells us that "the reptilian brain appears to

have inadequate machinery for learning to cope with new situations." That may well be in reptiles, but it is a statement of more than doubtful validity when extrapolated to humans—the most educable of creatures. In the evolution of the brain few structures have ever been totally discarded. What has occurred is that as new ones have developed the old ones have been reduced in importance and relative size, although many of the connections and pathways remain. It is, however, quite unsound to draw the inference, on the basis of such facts, that because similar brain structures exist in reptiles and in humans, our behavior must inevitably be reptile-like. As Professor Steven Rose has put it, "It is like arguing that we think by smelling because the cerebral hemispheres developed from the olfactory lobes."

It does not follow that if similar brain structures are present both in reptiles and in humans they operate in the same way and serve similar functions. The "new brain" or cortex simply isn't plastered onto the old brain, but interacts with and influences the way in which subcortical structures function. The brain does not act in segments or bits and pieces. It tends to act as a whole. The new brain has largely taken over the functions once exclusively performed by the old brain. What the so-called reptilian or old mammalian brain may be doing is generally under the scrutiny of and capable of being controlled by the new brain, the cortex. Schneirla has effectively criticized the practice of extrapolating from the study of lower level neural systems to their imposition upon higher functional levels. In organisms considered "lowest" in the psychological sense, organic structure tends to have a rather "directly determining" efficacy for behavior; whereas the patterns of behavior in the "higher" organisms' varying stages of development and intervening part-processes must be considered. This interpretation of the facts has recently been reinforced by a survey of comparative primate neuroanatomical development in relation to aggression by Drs. Orlando J. Andy and Heinz Stephan. These investigators found that brain structures related to aggressive behavior in the different families of primates were characterized by different rates of development and enlargement. On the basis of these different rates it was possible to recognize three distinctive groups:

Group 1, characterized by structures which showed the least development in primate evolution, namely, the midbrain structures (mesencephalon and diencephalon) characteristic of the prosimian lemurlike primates.

Group 2, structures consisting of the hippocampus, septum, and amygdala, characteristic of the monkeys, in which the rate of enlargement tended to be greater than in the first group.

Group 3, in which the greatest rate of enlargement occurs in the neocortex (and striatum, i.e., the basal organization of cells situated between the thalamus and the central white matter of the hemisphere) of apes and humans. Indeed, the rate of progression of the neocortex in relation to the striatum went from fifteen times in the prosimians to an index of 156 times in man.

Electrical or chemical stimulation of Group 1 areas—that is, the phylogenetically least progressive structures—easily elicited the most integrated aggressive behavior. In contrast, stimulation of the Group 2 areas elicited only fragments or attenuated forms of aggression. Stimulation of Group 3 areas, representing the most progressive group (the apes and humans), failed to elicit aggression, but when the neocortex was removed aggression tended to be facilitated, thus strongly indicating the inhibitory effect of the cortex upon any tendencies toward aggression. The authors conclude that the progressively increased control of the aggressive state, as the primate evolved, was predominantly due to the increased growth of the cortex.

Dr. MacLean puts it this way: "Although . . . man shares with other mammals the same type of primitive neural mechanisms for survival through violent action, he has at the same time the largest brain development for their intellectual control" (p. 25). But again, as Dr. MacLean notes in an earlier paragraph of the same paper, "Among animals . . . it is usually not death from combat that reduces population density to tolerable levels. Rather, nature appears to have ruled that aggression should take its toll indirectly through wasting disease and loss of fertility."

In passing it may be observed that "nature" doesn't rule anything, and that aggressive behavior only rarely leads to disease and loss of fertility. Certainly, disease and loss of fertility serve to control population density in animals, but these are factors which are usually operative quite apart from any form of aggressive behavior, direct or indirect. It is only under certain conditions that intraspecific aggression will stress the members of a population sufficiently to affect reproduction by reducing copulation frequency and/or inducing abortions, but this is the exception rather than the rule. Aggression or the threat of aggression probably constitutes one factor which sometimes serves to space animals so that there is enough food and cover.

Mr. Ardrey finds Dr. MacLean's observations most convincing in that, among other things, they have shown, according to Mr. Ardrey, "just what went wrong in the brain explosion of the mid-Pleistocene." Even more strikingly illustrative of the dangers of accepting uncritically MacLean's observations is an interesting book by Brian Crozier entitled *A Theory of Conflict* (1975). Mr. Crozier, who is director of the Institute for the Study of Conflict in London writes: "If Paul MacLean . . . is right in his illuminating theory of the evolutionary brain, much of the work and many of the hopes of the sociologists and socialists, and even of traditional moralists and theologians, are shown to be misplaced and futile." "It is our tragedy to have three brains cohabiting within the same cranial box. When Man behaves like an animal, as alas he does so frequently, this is literally true, for at that point one or both of the earlier animal brains takes over. The mob, as Ardrey percipiently puts it, reverts to the reptilian brain. . . ."

Preceding both Ardrey and Crozier, Arthur Koestler in his book *The Ghost in the Machine* (1967), basing his ideas on MacLean's work, concluded that our "schizophysiology" resulting from the dissonant functioning of the phylogenetically old and new cortex represents an evolutionary "mistake" built into our species. Such an explanation, he suggests, "would provide a physiological basis for the paranoid streak running through human history, and would point the direction of the search for a cure."

We question the validity of the inferences Dr. MacLean has drawn from the data of the ethologists as seen through the prism of his own neurological speculations, while at the same time fully endorsing the necessity of continuing and, indeed, intensifying research in both ethology and neurology. We would, however, urge caution in the interpretation of the findings obtained through these disciplines, and even greater caution in their application to the interpretation of human behavior.

A More Reasonable Perspective

The correlation of aggressive behavior with specific areas of the brain is by no means a simple one-to-one relationship, as many investigators seem to have believed. This has been underscored by the experimental findings of Drs. J. L. Brown and R. W. Hunsperger. These investigators found that reactions to electrical stimulation of the midbrain, the hypothalamus, and the amygdala in cats were dependent upon the location of the electrode in the brain, the intensity of the stimulating current, and the sociophysical environment. Attack and escape behaviors were found to be located in overlapping areas of the brain. As Drs. Charles Boelkins and John W. Heiser have remarked, "It seems that all too often laboratory investigators are prone to forget that the spectrum of threat, attack, and withdrawal behaviors (known collectively as agonistic behaviors) are adaptive *social* behaviors, and that their evolution has occurred in the context of a species-general social interaction."

José M. R. Delgado, until recently professor of physiology at Yale University School of Medicine, and now head of the Neurological Laboratory of the Medical Faculty at the Universidad Autonoma, Madrid, concludes on the basis of his own experimental studies that "individual identity and personal behavior are not properties of the brain which will unfold automatically through neuronal maturation, but are acquired functions which must be learned and therefore depend essentially on the reception of sensory inputs." That while violence and aggression are patterns of behavioral responses that may be related to specific areas of the brain, the expression of such responses "depends essentially on previous sensory inputs and experience." The most essential element in the development of aggression, as Delgado points out, is the personal reception and processing of environmental information through the various mechanisms of the brain. The activation of these specific areas of the brain by the processed information will induce the behavioral responses characteristic of aggression or violence.

It is not the brain's output of aggression or the specific areas of the brain associated with aggression that require investigation, as much as the interactional effects of the environmental inputs into the brain which serve to organize and activate those areas into trigger-ready systems that are primed to fire upon the slightest provocation.

Referring to MacLean's view that behavioral problems are caused by the animalistic tendencies of the "reptilian" and "old mammalian" brains, Delgado remarks that if such assessments of cerebral evolution are correct, then we have no choice but to struggle through life disguised as "modern men" and burdened with our share of reptilian and old mammalian brains. In a seminal passage which deserves to be quoted in full Delgado writes:

> I would like to propose a more optimistic view giving less functional importance to the genetic past and a more prominent role to sensory inputs and cultural information which, especially at an early age, are decisive for the determination of many anatomical, chemical, electrical, and functional properties of cerebral neurons. According to this view, most of our present individual and social behavior problems do not depend on biological heritage or neurophysiological precasting. The problem is not our animalistic tendencies or that our brain has not evolved sufficiently for the requirements of our present age, but rather that we do not feed appropriate sensory information or provide suitable social and emotional settings at the crucial ages for imprinting. It is not that there is a natural aggressive instinct in man to kill man. . . . The basis for human hostility is mainly cultural or environmental, and as proved by history, aggressive tendencies may be decisively modified by education. One of the tasks for future scientists is the experimental study of these prob-

lems, recognizing that environmental stimuli may
radically affect the physical and chemical development
of every organ including the brain.

Coming from a leading student of the neurophysiology of
aggression, these words of Professor Delgado bear an espe-
cial weight. There is much else, along similar lines, that has
been said by other investigators.

Delgado rejects the idea of the immutability of values
and the fatalistic determination of destiny to which the innate aggressionists subscribe. "Instead of accepting natural
fate," he writes, "we gain greater freedom by using intelligence. . . . Ideological systems and behavioral reactivity
are only relative human creations that can be improved and
modified by the feedback of reason. . . . Even if political
ideas, cultural values, and behavioral reactivity vary, the
basic physical, intellectual, and emotional needs of men are
the same, and they must have similar neurophysiological
mechanisms. Hate and destruction are not functional
properties of the brain, but elements introduced through
sensory inputs; they originate not within the person, but in
the environment."

It would be quite impossible to give an account of all the
findings of the neurosciences in connection with the problem of aggression. The best brief summary of it with which
I am acquainted is by Professors David N. Daniels and Marshall P. Gilula, both of the Department of Psychiatry of the
Stanford University School of Medicine. The findings of the
neurosciences, they write, "strongly suggest that basic
neurophysiological processes and neuroanatomical structures exist which permit the development and expression of
aggression and delimit the forms it may take. But the actual
expression of aggression is not an inherent, genetically programmed instinct or drive resulting from a disturbance in

internal homeostasis, such as occurs in hunger, thirst, and probably sex. That is, there is no known internal physiological state that requires aggression to restore equilibrium. Aggression is basic to survival but not as a drive toward discharge of an internal need state. Aggressive behaviors depend upon environmental factors that the undergirding biological mechanisms make easy to learn. Thus, aggression is basic, but we are not preprogrammed to aggress. We are not fated to an instinct of violence that must be discharged periodically as an inevitable part of man's makeup."

It should, perhaps, be explained that when Daniels and Gilula speak of aggression as basic to survival they are, at that particular point in their discourse, using the term "aggression" in the sense of assertive, intrusive, stimulus-seeking and dominance behaviors, while at the same time referring to aggression designed to inflict injury as being noninstinctive and not inherent.

The XYY Anomaly

As an evidence of the alleged genetic determinance of aggression in some men, a chromosomal anomaly discovered in 1965 has been cited. This is the XYY anomaly. As is well known, sometimes when chromosomes divide, instead of each passing to opposite poles and into separate cells, they stay together, so that both chromosomes pass into one cell. When a sperm carrying such a nondisjoined YY chromosome fertilizes a normal single X chromosome ovum, the result is an XYY fertilized cell (zygote), from which a male develops who carries in all body cells an extra Y chromosome. Investigations conducted in maximum security prisons revealed that 3.5 percent of the prisoners who had committed crimes of violence were XYY, and a large proportion of them were over six feet in height. Soon the anomaly came to be called "the XYY syndrome," as if it were a disease, or a genetic condition exhibiting a group of specific traits. Immediately all sorts of premature and unwarranted conclusions were drawn. The extra Y chromosome was considered to be a cause of the violence for which these men were incarcerated. Since the XYY anomaly is now known to occur in about 1 out of every 1000 males at birth, it constitutes one of the more common forms of chromosomal anomaly. Moreover, since a very small proportion of XYY males find their way into institutions for violent offenses, it is clear that an extra Y chromosome is not a "violent" chromosome. The XYY chromosome occurs in behaviorally perfectly normal males, and we now know that while aggressive behavior may occur in some XYY incarcerates, most of them have in fact committed crimes against property rather than against persons. Furthermore, XYY individuals often tend to be very mild characters.

The early and rather premature attribution of aggressive behavior to the possession of an extra Y chromosome appears now to be an example of the fallacy of *post hoc, ergo propter hoc*. In fact, the history of the XYY anomaly constitutes an object-lesson in how not to draw conclusions about causation from conditions that happen to be associated. Individuals who happen to be tall, in the fertile soil of a predisposing environment, may develop antisocial behavior, not because there is anything in their genetic constitution that drives them to such behavior but because the environment in which they happen to find themselves encourages such behavior. Such tall boys may also be teased and taunted by their peers and others, and impelled either to withdrawal or to aggressive behavior. Under the pressures of unfavorable social conditions, as juveniles, adolescents, or adults, such males may find themselves selectively nurtured

in environments encouraging physical aggression as a means
of adaptation.

Experience and Development

The implication of the innate aggressionists that the
genes rigidly determine the behavior of the individual is
not justified by the evidence. Under a variety of novel developmental conditions all animals will behave differently
from their usual patterns. All will not behave in what are
often considered to be their "normal" innate forms of behavior. For example, lions raised as pets in domestic environments will be neither aggressive nor capable of hunting. In fact, such animals are at a complete loss to know
what to do when put out to fend for themselves in their
"natural" environments. Clearly, the potentialities for living under "natural" conditions, for hunting, and for aggression are present in the lion, but they have to be organized
by training and experience into a learned form of behavior.
As functional traits they are simply not situated in the
genes, as the innate aggressionists maintain.

Anyone who has seen the Canadian Film Board film *The
Call of the Wild* will know that wolves, too, have to be
taught quite early how to hunt, otherwise they will not do
so. When taken into the wild after being raised domesti-
cally they will observe caribou and other animals with lack-
adaisical interest, but even though they are hungry it will
not occur to any of them to disturb the caribou.

At the 28 December 1971 meeting of the American Association for the Advancement of Science, Dr. Allen Deets
of the University of Pittsburgh and Dr. Harry Harlow of
the University of Wisconsin reported that rhesus monkeys
isolated from approximately 6 months of age to 18 months

become extremely violent when exposed to other monkeys, especially defenseless infants. The investigators concluded that contrary to the expectations of some theorists, the capacity for violent behavior, at least in monkeys, is innate. It is the ability to control aggressive tendencies, they suggested, that must be learned.

"Cultural evolution has clearly outstripped biological evolution in shaping the nature of human social organizations," Dr. Deets said. "But this does not mean that man has escaped his biological heritage as a primate. As part of this heritage, we believe that innate factors influence the nature of human aggression and that the same maturational sequencing of affection, fear, and aggression occurs in human [growth and development]."

The evidence, according to Deets and Harlow, shows that aggression in the rhesus monkey is an unlearned, innately determined behavior. In fact, their experiment shows nothing of the sort. What it shows is that if rhesus monkeys are deprived of contact with their mothers, together with the support, affection, and stimulation they would normally receive from them and from others, they will suffer massive privations and frustrations, which will gradually produce behavior of a distinctively disharmonic kind. The truth is that six-month isolates are frightened rather than aggressive when they are out of isolation and are forced to deal with new situations for which their early experience did not prepare them. They are only aggressive when other animals try to interact with them. Social isolation is a very traumatizing experience, especially for the young primate. The condition of isolation is, to put it mildly, disorderingly unsatisfying, and the fear induced by the approaches of other animals causes them to react defensively, not so much against the others as in defense of themselves. The defense is not against physical attack, for such animals will react in much the same aggressive ways toward their own infants, again in what appears to be the defense of their own crippled identity.

Whatever the correct interpretation of the genesis of their aggressive behavior may be, it would seem evident that the very considerable frustrations that these animals experienced in the isolated situation were the principal factors in leading to the development of aggressive behavior.

So much, then, for these animals' "innate" aggression. Dr. Deets tells us that "as part of this heritage, we believe that innate factors influence the nature of human aggression." The word to be underscored in that passage is "influence." Dr. Deets does not say "determine." With his quoted statement there can be not the least disagreement—innate factors probably influence every human behavior, and aggression is no exception—but that is a very different thing from claiming that learning plays no role in the expression of that behavior, for the truth is that learning plays a determinative role in virtually every form of behavior, and this is probably true, in varying degrees, of all animals.

The spurious dissociation of "heredity" and "environment" is not dead yet. It seems clear, however, that the errors committed by the reductionist hereditarians and environmentalists, though shared equally between them, in the final analysis make the former position rather more dangerous than the latter.

Anyone who has read the genetic literature over the years will frequently have encountered the phrase that such and such a gene "determines" such and such a trait. In many cases this is intended as no more than a piece of scientific shorthand. But one cannot always be sure. The truth is, of course, that genes do not determine traits. What genes do is to influence the physiological or developmental expression of a trait, structural, functional, or behavioral. Furthermore, genes are themselves influenced in their structure, functions, and behavior by the environments—which in-clude other genes—in which they undergo development. In short, all traits represent the expression of the interaction of genes with environments. Behavior is no exception to this rule, for we know that without learning all animals thus far observed exhibit behavioral defects proportional to the defi-cit in learning they have suffered.

When monkey or human infants who have been failed in their expectations of love react with writhing movements, crying, or withdrawal, or apathy, or regurgitation from both ends of the alimentary tract, and the like, these behaviors constitute evidence not of order, programming, or wiring but of disorder in the organism.

It is fallacious to speak of the organism as "programmed" or "wired" to react to the frustration of its expected satis-factions with such predetermined behaviors, even though similar deprivation behavior appears to be universal under such conditions in most animals. The evidence, on the other hand, indicates that all organisms, when they are failed in the satisfaction of certain needs, especially the dependency needs, the need for love,* draw upon the same organic re-

---

* Love, a term often used, but seldom by scientists in their scientific role, is rarely defined. A short definition might be: behavior calculated to confer survival benefits in a creatively enlarging manner upon the other. For the dependent infant it consists in the satisfaction of its basic needs as well as such perceptual needs as touch, vision, hearing, and the vestibular, oral, and gastrointestinal experiences, to name the more obvious ones. Even more im-portant than these is the communication of the feeling of deep involvement in the welfare of the other, that the infant can depend upon you for the support, sustenance, and stimulation it requires for that feeling of security so essential to healthy development. Harlow's isolation-reared monkeys were massively deprived of such experiences and subjected instead to an ex-treme form of sensory deprivation: no sights, no sounds, nothing to cling to, and so on. Since it is usually the biological mother who provides the satis-faction of the infant's needs, we speak of her behavior as "maternal love." But it doesn't have to be the biological mother; any mother surrogate will do as long as the adequate satisfactions of the infant's needs are provided.

sources for making their needs known. These resources are not areas, centers, limbic systems, amygdalae, hypothalami, or pathways for aggression, but a miscellany of resources, psychological, cerebral, hormonal, and chemical, available to the organism that can be quickly mobilized for the purpose, among other things, of compelling attention to its needs. Whether the infant develops an aggressive component in its behavior will to a large extent depend on the manner in which it has been socialized and on the models society has provided.* It is in this manner that it comes about that some societies, like the Tasaday, tend to be made up of wholly unaggressive individuals, while among the members of other societies the expression of aggressive behavior may run the gamut of all possible degrees of development.

It is not that the brain is "wired" for aggression, but that neural elements located in certain parts of the brain can be readily organized by experience to function in behavior we call aggressive. Such behavior is the resultant of the interaction between the specific neural potentials and experience. In brief, the evidence indicates that there exist specific areas of the brain in which the appropriate neural circuitry must be experientially organized in order to function in the service of many different behaviors. The evidence suggests that just as certain areas of the brain are organized by experience to function, say, in the service of speech, so certain areas of the brain can be organized to function in the service of aggression. It is clearly the brain that does the mobilizing, and it is equally clear that it is not a matter of random selection by the brain of what neural arrangements are employed in making aggressive responses. In the func-

---

* See Albert Bandura, *Aggression: A Social Learning Analysis.* Englewood Cliffs, N. J. , Prentice-Hall, 1975; Ashley Montagu, *On Being Human.* Rev. ed. New York, Hawthorn Books, 1966; Ashley Montagu, *The Direction of Human Development,* 2nd ed., New York, Hawthorn Books, 1970.

tioning of the brain as a whole the experimental findings
show that certain parts of the brain are usually involved in
the elicitation and control of aggressive behavior. But this
does not mean that many other parts of the brain, which
have no connection whatever with aggressive behavior, are
not also involved. They clearly are, for what the experimental findings unequivocally show is the enormous modifi-
ability of overt patterns of aggression by experience or
learning. Clear as this is for other animals, it is even more
so for human beings, especially since there is no convincing
evidence in them of any neural arrangements determining
fixed—that is, instinctual—motor acts of aggression. There is,
however, clearly something in the human brain which,
under the appropriate conditions, can be readily mobilized
to function and be expressed in aggressive behavior. This
something undoubtedly consists of complex arrangements
of nerve cells and their interrelations, almost certainly in
association with certain chemical states, situated in certain
circumscribed parts of the brain. It is misleading to speak
of such parts of the brain as "centers," "circuits," or
"wiring," because the false impression is conveyed that
there exist complex structures in the brain which have but
to be stimulated to result in aggressive behavior. The cellular arrangements are there, but they are not rigidly fixed
or determined to follow along predestinate grooves, as it
were, to eventuate in aggressive behavior. There is no phylogenetic neural programming, as many have claimed, for aggression in man, but what do exist are neural arrangements
which can be experientially organized to function in anything from complete control of any tendency toward aggressive behavior to the most impulsive and destructive forms
of aggression.

Whether or not aggressive behavior, as well as its kind

and nature, will be elicited by any stimulus will depend upon what has been previously organized by social experience into the central nervous system.

Some light has been thrown on these matters by Professors Victor H. Dennenberg and M. X. Zarrow of the University of Connecticut. In a series of ingenious experiments these investigators found that when newborn mice were given to a lactating rat mother who readily accepted, nursed, and cared for them, the rat-reared mice were heavier than the mouse-reared control mice. They were also less active in the open-field 32-inch square box, and preferred to spend time near a rat rather than a mouse. The most dramatic finding was that rat-reared mice would *not* fight when placed in a standard fighting-box situation. This was in contrast to the incidence of 44 percent of fights among mice reared by mouse mothers. In addition to the mothering study, Dennenberg and Zarrow investigated the effects of peer group interaction. Some of the mice were reared without littermates while others were reared in the typical litter situation. This was done using mice reared by mouse mothers, and mice raised by rat mothers. With the rat mother it was possible for mice to have rat siblings as well. After weaning, mice were reared in isolation, with other male mice, or with rats. When put in the fighting box it was again found that rat-reared mice did not fight. Mice reared alone with mice mothers were more likely to be aggressive than mice raised with littermates. Lack of peers, then, up to the stage of weaning increased aggressiveness.

Among the mice reared by mouse mothers peer group interaction after weaning had the opposite effect. Mice reared with mice peers after weaning were more likely to fight than mice reared in isolation or with rat peers after weaning.

For rat-reared mice, peer group relationships had no

effect upon aggression. Regardless of whether they were raised in isolation or with peers either before or after weaning, these mice did not fight. This experiment, therefore, conclusively proved that it was the rat mother who was the causal agent in bringing about reduction in fighting.

This experiment suggested that it would be possible to eliminate or reduce aggression in rats as well as in mice. To test this hypothesis the following experiment was set up: At weaning 20 rat-mouse pairs were kept together for 36 days. The mice were then removed and the rats were placed in the rat colony room until they were 90 days old. At this stage the experimental rats and an equivalent group of 40 control rats (who had never been exposed to mice) were tested for mouse-killing. None of the experimental rats killed mice, whereas 45 percent of the control rats killed mice.

As the experimenters point out, the control rats in their behavior met all the requirements that Lorenz has specified as the indispensable conditions for instinctive behavior. They killed mice. The experimental rats did not. Dennenberg and Zarrow conclude:

> Obviously, we must therefore reject any hypothesis that states that aggression is a genetically determined, instinctive response that cannot be modified by experience. The social context within which the animal develops is critically important in determining his later aggressive behavior. This is not to suggest that genetic factors are not important. It is obvious that they are. What we are saying is that both the genetic background and the environment in which these genes grow and develop must be considered *jointly* if we are to advance our understanding of behavior patterns. They go on to add: The fact that an organism has genes that may ulti-

mately contribute to aggressive behavior does not
mean that these genes will necessarily have to express
themselves in that manner. We feel that appropriate
rearing conditions can have a marked effect in modify-
ing presumably inborn aggressive tendencies, and that
they may even keep the tendencies from being expressed.

There exists a great body of similar experimental findings
and observations which fully support the findings of Dennenberg and Zarrow. Certainly the evidence for humanity
thoroughly substantiates these investigators' underscoring
of the role played by environment in learning aggression or
nonaggression. How else could one account for the nonaggressiveness of the peoples discussed earlier in this volume?
Whatever predispositions the members of these societies
may have had toward aggression, they have successfully
learned not to develop them. Contrary to Lorenz, their
members exhibit no "spontaneous" urge toward aggression.
They do, however, like all human beings, exhibit a spontaneous urge toward cooperation. Contrary to the entrenched
beliefs of many people, the evidence unequivocally indicates
that in the evolution of all animal forms, and most particularly in the human species, cooperative behavior has been a
far more influential factor than aggressive behavior, that,
indeed, cooperative behavior has competitively been the selectively most successful form of behavior in all animal
groups.

In our experience it is the striving of the infant and child
to become human that is so impressive—human in the sense
of humane, gentle, loving, and cooperative.

To suggest that human beings are already "programmed"
at birth or "wired" for aggression is to render confusion
worse confounded, to fail to understand the clear evidence

and the pivotally most consequential fact about the nature of humans. The predominant fact about human nature is not that we become what we are predestined to be, but that we truly become, as human beings, whatever, within our genetic limitations, we learn to be. That is the important statement about the nature of humans.

9

The Philosophy of Real Estate and
the Biologically Just Decision

The Alleged "Instinct of Territory"

At least as old as the alleged "instinct of aggression," according to Robert Ardrey, is the "instinct of territory." The "instinct of territory" is defined by Ardrey as "an inherent drive to gain and defend an exclusive territory."

And, according to him, in defense of territory "the instinct of aggression" plays a major role. It is this viewpoint that Mr. Ardrey develops in his book *The Territorial Imperative*, published in 1966, and significantly subtitled *A Personal Inquiry into the Animal Origins of Property and Nations*. Man, Ardrey argues, has an innate compulsion to gain and defend territory, preserve, or property. And since the "sense of trespass" is so evident in the intruder, he wonders whether "there does not exist, more profound than simple learning, some universal recognition of territorial rights." His personal inquiry leads him to the conclusion that such a profound recognition does exist, and that the territorial nature of man is genetic and ineradicable. It is Ardrey's thesis that man is as much a territorial animal as is a mockingbird. We defend the title to our land, the sover-

eignty of our country, in response to drives no different, no
less ineradicable, than those that motivate other animals.
The innumerable territorial expressions of man are simply
human responses to an imperative lying with equal force on
mockingbirds and men. And if this is so, says Ardrey, we
must begin to think of a radical revision of our human nature. In fact, says he, so almighty a force is this territorial
drive that in power it exceeds even the sexual drive. "How
many men have you known in your lifetime," asks Ardrey,
"who died for their country? And how many for a woman?"
It is a rough test, he admits, but it is clearly to him one that
clinches the argument. It is the kind of logic that characterizes most of Ardrey's arguments. A part of our evolutionary
nature, and fixed in our genetic endowment because of its
survival value, Ardrey tells us, the territorial imperative is
no less essential to the continuing existence of contemporary
humans than it was to our early protohuman ancestors millions of years ago.

Instinct, Again

Instinct exists, Ardrey insists, and we cannot neglect it simply because we do not know where it lives. It exists and it
makes use of learning just as a furnace sucks in air. The scientist is a good example of the workings of the instinct of
territory, we are told, for no matter how humanitarian his
motives, in time of war he will have no hesitation in making
available the most sophisticated achievements of his discipline for the defense of his country. "All apparent conscience, all cultural instruction and religious teaching concerning the immorality of killing vanish before the higher
command to defend his country, and the scientist makes
available to the art of murder the most intricate secrets of
his trade. In the language of this inquiry we should say that

he fills out from the particularity of his learning the generality of that open instinct, the territorial imperative" (p. 28).

Ardrey defines an instinct as "the genetically determined pattern which informs an animal how to act in a given situation" (p. 29). It was the territorial instinct, apparently, that caused the makers of the atom bomb to embark upon its development, even though they were opposed to its ultimate use. He quotes Margaret Mead and myself as exemplars of the opposite view that, as Margaret Mead says, human beings are "dependent neither on instinct nor on genetically transmitted specific capabilities but on learned ways of life that accumulated slowly through endless borrowing, readaptation, and innovation." And he quotes me as saying, in my introduction to *Culture and the Evolution of Man,* "It is principally through cultural pressures that primate nature, in the case of man, has been changed into human nature. It must be emphasized that this change has been brought about not—among other things—by the suppression of primate instinctual drives, but by their gradual supplantation by an adaptively more effective means of meeting the challenges of the environment, namely, by enhancing the development of intelligence. . . . In the course of human evolution the power of instinctual drives has gradually withered away, until man has virtually lost all his instincts. If there remain any residues of instincts in man, they are, possibly, the automatic reaction to a sudden loud noise, and in the remaining instance to a sudden withdrawal of support; for the rest, man has no instincts."

Mr. Ardrey finds this reminiscent of John Broadus Watson's behavioristic psychology. He correctly quotes me as having said that "everything human beings do as human beings they have had to learn from other human beings." Neither my reference to man's instinctless nature nor to his having to learn everything he comes to know and do as a human being from other human beings has anything to do with what John Broadus Watson may or may not have thought about the nature of man. Watson's view that man is "an assembled organic machine ready to run," and that at birth human infants, regardless of their heredity, are as equal as Fords turned out on the assembly line, is undiluted nonsense. Equally absurd is Watson's claim that the infant simply represents a system of unorganized units of unlearned behavior, which the environment acts upon to organize into a system of habits, one person differing from another only as these habit systems differ.

Watson's behaviorist views have been largely discredited, and belong mainly in the Academy of Scientific Curiosities. The very title of the other book from which Ardrey quotes me, *The Biosocial Nature of Man,* implies that in my view man is a product both of his biology and of his social experience. But apparently I did not make myself clear enough. When I wrote that man must learn everything he comes to know and do as a human being, I meant, and mean, just that. But what that statement has been misinterpreted to mean is that everything man does he has to learn. This is clearly not so, and is not what I wrote nor what I meant. The operative words are *as a human being.* I mean and repeat that those behaviors that distinguish *Homo sapiens* as a human being, those behaviors that distinguish him from all other animals, he has to learn from other human beings. This does not for a moment imply that there do not exist unique biological potentialities in man for such behaviors. What the statement does imply is that man lacks any genetically determined patterns that cause him to exhibit such behaviors. The evidence does not support the view that such genetic determinants exist for either aggressive or territorial behavior.

In the case of aggressive behavior the evidence indicates that there certainly exist biological arrangements in the brain which are capable of being readily organized to function in various forms of aggressive activity, but equally certainly such areas of the brain are not genetically determined to function in the form of aggression unless they are mobilized to do so by external stimulation, normally of quite complex kinds.

Capacity, Experience, Learning, and Ability

Homo sapiens learns to speak, and does so because humans have an innate capacity to develop that ability when exposed to the appropriate experiences. But unless they are exposed to the necessary learning experiences they will not speak. Humans do not possess an "instinct" which causes them to break out into the appropriate chopped-up segments of sound upon being spoken to. For the greater part of its first postnatal year the human infant has "no language, but a cry" and the ability to babble. It takes the human infant a considerable amount of time before it begins to utter its first words, and this is usually achieved at about the age of fourteen months. During that period it has already done a considerable amount of learning, and it is upon that learning that its ability to speak depends. An ability is a trained capacity. Apes do not possess the capacity for speech, and therefore cannot be trained to speak. Learning is the increase in the strength of any act as a result of training—that is, through repetition. No matter how often speech is repeated or how long the training, a chimpanzee cannot learn to speak because it simply lacks the biological capacity to do so. It is therefore unequivocally clear that in humans speech is the product of the interaction between two things; one is represented by the biological potentialities genetically inherited by every normal child, and the other the social environment of speech, to which the child is exposed from an early age. The *ability* to speak is not genetically determined. What is genetically determined is the *capacity* for speech. Given that capacity the child will learn to speak only if it is exposed to at least one other human being who speaks to it. It is not a matter of the appropriate stimulus eliciting the proper response, for speech is not preformed in the human brain.

Noam Chomsky has suggested that there is good reason to believe that innate mechanisms exist in the human brain that pre-set the child for the acquisition of knowledge of a language which enables it to acquire the restricted form of grammar involved. But Chomsky nowhere claims that this is an instinct. In this connection he writes: "It is no doubt true that there are innate tendencies in the human psychic constitution that lead to aggressiveness under specific social and cultural conditions. But there is little reason to suppose that these tendencies are so dominant as to leave us forever tottering on the brink of a Hobbesian war of all against all." Chomsky explicitly states that he does not want what he is saying to be confused with the attempts of others to revive a theory of human instinct.

While all animals are capable of aggressive behavior, humans are the only creatures who are capable of speech. It is reasonably clear that the two forms of behavior are of very different evolutionary antiquity and character. Nevertheless, I am devoting so much space to the discussion of the development of speech because it presents a clear illustration of the manner in which a capacity is transformed into an ability, the manner in which a potentiality is developed by the environment. Clearly, the capacity for speech is inherited, but the ability to speak is learned. Similarly, in humans, at least, the capacity for aggression is inherited, but the ability to be aggressive has to be learned. In *Homo sapiens* aggression as such is no more an inherited trait than is speech.

This seeming divagation from the discussion of territoriality has been designed to put in proper perspective Ardrey's claim that territoriality is instinctive in man, an ineradicable imperative. For as Ardrey has correctly stated, "The concept of instinct lies at the centre of the contemporary controversy."

Nonterritoriality in Animals

If neither aggression nor speech is an instinct or an imperative, it would seem even less likely that territorial behavior in man represents such a "force." The truth is that not only does territorial behavior in man fail to satisfy Ardrey's own criteria for instinctive behavior, but so does the behavior of many animals in relation to territory fail to do so. There are many animals that show not the slightest tendency toward territorial behavior. To name but a few among mammals: the California ground squirrel, adult male long-tailed field mice, she-wolves, the red fox, the Iowan prairie spotted skunk, the northern plains red fox, the zebra, Grant's gazelle, wild dogs, the Bahamian rodent or hutia, cheetahs, mountain goats, deer, wallabies, rhesus monkeys, langur monkeys, baboons, and in the Hominoidea, the superfamily to which man belongs, together with the orang, the chimpanzee, and the gorilla. After surveying the evidence, Professor François Bourlière of the University of Paris concludes: "It would seem that territorial behavior is far from being as important in mammals as in birds, and very often it is limited to the temporary defense of the nest or of certain parts of the home range." It is not surprising, therefore, that Ardrey draws almost all his examples of territoriality from birds. Since among birds there is a great deal of diver-

sity in territorial behavior, one finds that even among closely
related species one may be territorial while the other is not.
Apparently Mr. Ardrey fails to recognize also the difference
between "territory," "home range," "core area," "area of
dominance," and "personal space." A territory is a defended
area; the home range is the whole area in which the animal
lives—usually shared with other animals. "Core area" refers
to an intensively and exclusively occupied area within a
home range or territory. "Area of dominance" refers to a do-
minion from which submissive individuals are not excluded.
"Personal space" refers to the "on sight" defensive reaction
to another animal. In larger animals the last is a form of behavior more common than territorial behavior, but it is
often confused with territoriality. A territory is recognized
by the marked change in behavior of its owner at its border:
"Within the territory the owner is confident and aggressive,
outside it he is timid and aggressive towards strangers." Ardrey makes no distinction between any of these forms of
behavior.

When Mr. Ardrey—with obvious disappointment—has to
mention the nonterritoriality of the great apes, it is in reference alone to the chimpanzee that he does so. The orang and
gorilla, both nonterritorial animals, receive no mention.
"The chimp is the only primate," writes Ardrey, "who has
achieved the arcadian existence of primal innocence which
we once believed was the paradise that man had somehow
lost" (p. 222). To the extent that the life of the chimpanzee
in its natural habitat is justly describable as arcadian, to that
extent also is that of the gorilla and orang. However that
may be, with reference to the chimpanzee Ardrey goes on to
say, "I presume, that we must reckon on some degree of innate amity in the primate potential; but as I have indicated,
it is a very small candle on a very dark night."

This suggests that most primates are for the most part unamiable, aggressive, and territorial. The fact is so few primate species have been studied that we really don't know. But from the observations that have been made we have reason to believe that in these traits primates are at least as variable as members of most other orders of mammals. While some may exhibit territorial behavior, when studied at close range under natural conditions it is frequently found that both their alleged territoriality and aggressiveness have been greatly exaggerated. Dr. Brian C. Bates of the University of Oregon has reviewed recent field studies of territorial behavior in primates, and has found that such cases are exceptional, notwithstanding the fact that many investigators have looked for evidence of aggression between primate groups in defense of a geographical boundary. "Even in the exceptional cases," he concludes, "the belligerent groups very rarely go beyond various types of threat or antagonistic display." Overt fighting, as he points out, occurs only in unusual circumstances, as during prolonged and severe water shortages resulting in friction among baboons at water holes, or conflicts among rhesus macaques living in severely overcrowded conditions in Indian cities.

Different groups of primates are kept apart at geographical boundaries, not by overt aggression or fighting but by the daily routine of the group in its own range, by rigid social behavior, and, in others, by loud vocalizations.

The attempt to link aggressive with territorial behavior simply does not wash. The truth is that most primate groups seem to come into contact relatively infrequently. There is great specific and intraspecific variability in the behavior of such groups upon meeting. In general the tendency is either one of mutual avoidance or withdrawal of one from another. Ardrey cites the chimpanzee as "an evolutionary failure" because amiability "offers small promise for chimpanzee survival." The baboon, however, according to Ardrey, is "an outrageous success" because of "baboon tyranny, with its gang of thugs at the top."

Ardrey's prejudicial language distorts the facts. "Gang?" "Thugs?" Does Mr. Ardrey really believe that these are the proper terms which appropriately describe the dominant animals of the baboon group? These animals do not constitute a "gang" nor is their behavior that of "thugs," for by their individual qualities they have established themselves in roles of leadership which they exercise in defense of the group. However, with his loaded language Ardrey wishes to make a point, without due respect for the facts.

Ardrey tells us that the baboon troop "maintains a territory . . . and defends that territory against others of its kind. As a society it demonstrates all those hostile traits normal to the individual proprietor." But Professors Irven DeVore and K. R. L. Hall, who studied several populations of baboons in Africa, write that although they never saw any indication of defended territories, this does not imply that groups did not move about without reference to fixed boundaries. Nevertheless, even in areas of high population density, different groups were observed to be in close daily contact without displays of intergroup aggression, and this was true not only of different groups of baboons but also of baboons and vervet monkeys at the same waterhole. Similarly, Crook, in his field study of the gelada baboon (*Theropithecus gelada*) of the high mountains of central and northern Ethiopia, found that herds "show no defensive behavior of any kind in relation to other geladas and a male's aggressive behavior occurs in relation to his 'harem' only."

Dr. Geza Teleki, who for a year daily observed the interactive behavior of wild chimpanzees with nonhuman primates living in the Gombe Forest (Gombe National Park) in Tanzania, was greatly impressed with the mutually tolerant coexistence of these creatures. The fundamental tolerance and "consistent[ly] friendly interactions" between anubis baboons (*Papio anubis*) especially, even within the context of repeated killing and eating of young baboons by chimpanzees, and the absence of any really harmful fighting between them over food or anything else, within the common habitat shared by all the animals, are facts which play havoc with innate aggressionist theories.

If baboons are more numerous than apes, and such seems to be the case, it is not because they are more aggressive, but probably because baboon ways of life are conducive to larger social groupings than those of apes.

Dr. Hans Kummer of the University of Zurich, who studied hamadryas baboons (*Papio hamadryas*) in the field, found them to be not altogether unamiable characters, even though they may engage in a good deal of ritual and quite harmless "fighting." Baboons, like most other "wild" animals, have had a bad press. Yet, it is very strange that the man Ardrey admires so much, the late Eugene Marais, in his book *My Friends, the Baboons,* wrote of the chacma baboon (*Papio ursinus*) as a not unamiable, thoroughly unpredictable creature who romped and played with the native children with obvious enjoyment. Ardrey was also responsible for the publication of Marais's *The Soul of the Ape,* in which the author continued his sympathetic account of the chacma baboon.

Another reason why baboons are more numerous than apes may be that some of their habitats have not suffered the misfortune of being invaded by men armed with lethal weapons. Furthermore, as forest-dwellers, the apes were probably never more numerous than were prehistoric men. In any event, if the nonterritorial baboons are an evolutionary success, so are the apes. If the continued existence of the apes is menaced, it is not because they are evolutionary failures but because they are threatened with extinction by the ruthlessness of misguided men. At any rate, the equating of large numbers with evolutionary success is a fallacy. The measure of evolutionary success is survival, differential fertility, quality, *not* quantity. Thus far the apes have managed to survive for many millions of years in small enclaves, and if humans continue to increase at their present rate, even though the living apes are today numbered only in the hundreds and humans in the billions, they may yet outsurvive man, their most deadly predator and conscienceless enemy.

To repeat, the diminishing number of apes is due not to their nonterritoriality, nor to their nonaggressiveness, but to the simple fact that during the last hundred years and more their habitats have been increasingly invaded and they have been mercilessly slaughtered in large numbers by men against whom they have no defense. As recently as 1971 Dian Fossey reported the wholesale slaughter of mountain gorillas just south of her own study area. "The bodies of five animals were found scattered about in an arc of some 75 yards. They had been mauled by dogs, pierced by spears, and battered by stones, apparently just for the excitement of the hunt."

The variability in territorial behavior among animals is, as one would expect, considerable. The "defended areas" concept of territoriality simply has no real counterpart among many animals, who occupy territories which they do not defend. Indeed, the diversity of territorial behavior is so great among animals that the very definition of that behavior is questionable. Even among birds, as Professor John T. Emlen, Jr., has stated, "it is a purely speculative assumption that any particular area carries any special significance to the bird as an object to be defended."

Professor Peter H. Klopfer remarks that discussions of territoriality such as that of Ardrey "rest on abysmal ignorance of the diversity of territoriality in general and the implication of this diversity. . . . In short, there are neither factual nor theoretical bases for assertions regarding the role of ancestral territorial 'impulses' in the structuring (or fracturing) of human social behavior." And as he goes on to say, territoriality "probably represents not a single adaptation but a host of different adaptations serving different purposes for different animals. This fact alone precludes the facile extrapolation to man and a biological justification of property rights."

Environmental Conditions and Territoriality

To equate the territorial behavior of some animals with the holding of property by humans constitutes yet another example of the fallacy of the unequal equation. As Professor S. A. Barnett has pointed out, territorial behavior in animals depends on systems of signals common to the whole of each species, with responses to these signals standardized. Learning plays a small part in the development of these behaviors. In humans, on the contrary, the rules governing property are culturally determined and are learned; there is no pattern of signals common to the whole species. Hence, the diversity in different societies of such rules, and the variety of conditions encountered in which aggression in defense of property is permitted. Furthermore, territoriality, in those species that display it, seems to insure some sort of regulation of density. In humans it does not.

Even within the same populations alterations in daily life will produce changes in territorial, feeding behavior, and social relations. Indeed, whether territorial behavior shall be exhibited or not depends largely upon environmental conditions. For example, crowded together in zoos, hamadryas baboons become extremely "territorial," but under natural conditions hamadryas baboons are nonterritorial.

The ayu, a salmonid fish, is territorial in shallow brooks but moves in schools in deep pools. Most illuminating in this connection is a piece of little-known history involving United States fish hatcheries. For many years it was taken for granted that bass reared in breeding ponds of the U.S. Department of Fisheries were instinctively both territorial and cannibal, until 1932, when Dr. T. H. Langlois noticed that the few ponds in which cannibalism did not occur were wide and shallow and contained little vegetation. Langlois found that when bass were put into weedy ponds they tended to become separated by the vegetation and failed to form large social groups. Some of the fish took up lodgings in secluded spots and began to prey on the smaller bass. Any small outsider unlucky enough to stray into these restricted territories got eaten. The cannibalism did not stop when other food was thrown into the pond, for apparently the predators were unable to see the food owing to the thickness of the vegetation. Langlois's solution was to remove the vegetation from the ponds before stocking them with young bass. With the removal of the vegetation the large bass were able to see the food when it was thrown into the pond, so that they made for this immediately, ceased their cannibalism, and dined amicably together with their fellows of all sizes. With everyone well fed and everyone acquainted with everyone else, no one tried to eat anyone. In some ponds it was possible to bring about cessation of cannibalism by introducing bass from other ponds that had learned to be dependent on the external food supply. These fish appeared to influence other bass to imitate their example. But in some instances the introduced bass seemed to adopt the habits of the bass in the pond and quit taking the offered food made available from outside. In other cases individual bass with established territories were induced to relinquish them. This was done by motivating a school of fish that had learned to follow the shadow of the person who fed them to swim repeatedly over the area which an individual bass was attempting to protect. In these cases the individuals gave up their territories and joined the group.

Another case in point is the house mouse, which may become territorial under concentrated population pressures but ceases to be so when population drops below a certain level.

Monkeys provide interesting examples of territorial differences under different ecological conditions. In the Amboseli Reserve of Kenya, East Africa, vervet monkeys (*Cercopithecus aethiops johnstoni*) may be aggressively territorial, and in Uganda, where they are crowded on Lolui Island, they are also aggressively territorial. But a few miles away, at Chobe, the same species live peaceably with little or no fighting and no evidence of territoriality. In open country where the home ranges are large, as among most cercopithecine monkeys, these animals are nonterritorial. Forest cercopithecines with small home ranges tend to be territorial. A similar relationship exists between size of home range and territorial behavior in Indian hanuman langurs (*Presbytis entellus*).

Examples could be multiplied, and they would serve to reinforce the fact that far from being an innate fixed behavior pattern, a genetically determined ineradicable trait, territorial behavior is not a fixed action pattern at all but a form of behavior very much dependent on the context of the situation—that is, on the influences of the environment. Ecological and social factors appear to be the conditions determining whether a population does or does not exhibit territorial behavior. This is the conclusion of most field investigators.

The Nature and Function of Aggression in
Territorial Behavior

That there exist genetically structured parts of the brain which can be readily organized to function, in response to the appropriate stimuli, as aggression, there can be not the least doubt. There can, equally, be no doubt that a genetically determined appetite for aggressive behavior does not exist in the higher mammals and humans. Wallace Craig pointed out many years ago that it is aversive behavior rather than appetitive behavior that is observed in many acts of aggression. Such aggressive behavior Craig described as an "aversion." Craig wrote: "Fundamentally among animals fighting is not sought nor valued for its own sake; it is resorted to rather as a means of defending the agent's interest. . . . Even when an animal does fight he aims not to destroy the enemy but only to get rid of his presence and interference." Even the physical appearance of the animal is often useful in securing the desired result without the necessity of fighting. Thus, many animals are made conspicuous by some special characteristics such as a vividly marked or, for the particular occasion, specially enlargeable part of the body, which serves to convey the message to other animals to keep their proper distance. This may also be done by vocal as well as by visual display. As Crook says, "Much of the aggression in territorial defense consists of threatening display or ritualized fighting whereby spacing is achieved with little damage done to the protagonists." Clearly, the purpose of such display or ritualized aggression is not aggression, but the achievement of the animal's object without physically harmful aggression.

Under different types of competitive conditions, for food, females, space, dominance relationships, and so on, many kinds of territorial responses are exhibited by animals. These responses, however, are not the product of genetically determined influences, but for the most part are the product of socially acquired norms.

While density may in some nonhuman primates in itself constitute a cause of aggressive and territorial behavior, in other populations density in relation to environmental resources will determine whether there will be either aggressive behavior or territoriality, either one or the other or both. Forest-dwellers and those living in environments where cover and food are abundant are likely to be both nonterritorial and less aggressive than those living outside forests in which cover and food are comparatively poor, although nonterritoriality also occurs in such groups. Clearly a principal adaptive function of aggression in such groups is the control of habitat utilization. Different environmental conditions will call for different forms of aggression or non-aggression in the defense or nondefense of territory.

Humans and Territory

Before intensive research began in the field, it was apparently an easy matter to determine whether a people was territorial. They occupied a specific piece of land which they called their own, and would defend it against all intruders. That proved that they were territorial. But as soon as the subject came under systematic scrutiny it was found that the matter is not quite so simple. Indeed, the more intensive and careful the studies, the more complex the subject of territory has become. Really detailed studies of the territorial behavior of humans are still relatively few, but those we do have show how very oversimplified the earlier anthropological descriptions of territory were.

The tendency to generalize from findings on other pri-

mates to humans was also a characteristic of the earlier literature. For example, the pioneer in field studies of the
primates, Dr. Clarence R. Carpenter, in his field study of
the gibbon, wrote: "It would seem that the possession and
defense of territory which is found so widely in the vertebrates, including the subhuman and human primates, may
be a fundamental biological need." Even at that time, in
1940, this was a rather surprising statement, coming as it
did from a field worker who six years earlier had reported
on the fluid territorial behavior of the howler monkey
(*Alouatta palliata*). While howler monkeys possess three-
dimensional territories, there is considerable overlapping,
and the ranges of some groups may also be identical, while
the shifting and extension of territorial ranges are constantly occurring in particular groups. No mention was
made by Carpenter of any defense of territory as an exclusive preserve. But the idea of territorial defense among animals, and especially among humans, as a well-nigh universal
phenomenon was so widespread, it seemed "only natural"
that territorial defense should be "a fundamental biological
need."

It is also, therefore, not surprising that Mr. Ardrey, who
is greatly indebted to Carpenter for much of his thinking
about territory, should have come to write about it in similar terms. Ardrey defines territory as follows: "A territory is
an area of space, whether of water or earth or air, which an
animal or group of animals defends as an exclusive preserve.
The word is also used to describe the inward compulsion in
animate beings to possess and defend such a space. A territorial species of animals, therefore, is one in which all males,
and sometimes females too, bear an inherent drive to gain
and defend an exclusive property."

We have already seen that Ardrey considers this inherent
drive to be genetic and ineradicable, and we have also seen

that there is some evidence which shows that this is certainly not the case in many animals, from fish to nonhuman primates. Ardrey's fundamental errors are two: the first is the assumption that with few exceptions animals are territorial; and the second is that if that is so then therefore, as a consequence of their animal ancestry, humans must also be territorial.

We have also established that territoriality varies greatly among animals, and that it would be inaccurate to attribute either a genetic determinance or ineradicability to such behavior, especially in mammals. In man what we encounter is the full range of variability, from the fierce territoriality of many New Guinea peoples to the complete nonterritoriality of the Eskimo, the Hadza of Tanzania, not to mention the Comanche and Shoshoni Indians of North America. Some peoples are territorial, some only partially so, while others are thoroughly nonterritorial. No evidence is observed of that "spontaneity of instinct" postulated by Lorenz and asserted to be equally innate by such writers as Ardrey, Desmond Morris, Anthony Storr, Eibl-Eibesfeldt, and others. On the contrary, territoriality in many animals, and especially in humans, shows every evidence of being a "socioecologic" response or adaptation to specific environmental conditions, *not* an instinctive reaction.

Only too often it has been carelessly assumed that "territory," "aggression," and "defense" present a natural linkage. Nothing could be farther from the truth. As Professor Richard Lee has pointed out, culturally defined boundaries do not necessarily imply sanctions against trespass. The same social and ecologic effect can be achieved by rules for accommodating people across boundaries as when there are no boundaries at all. All hunting peoples have institutionalized means for moving from group to group, "so if we find boundaries in a given case, we should not commit the frequent error of assuming that they enclose a defended and exclusive territory." Furthermore, many territorial human groups are not particularly aggressive or defensive about their territory; such, for example, are the Tungus and Yurok of Siberia, the Kwakiutl of the Pacific Northwest coast of America, the Ituri Pygmies of the Congo, the Western Aranda of Central Australia, the Kiadilt of Bentinck Island, and the Tiwi, both of Northern Australia. The !Kung Bushmen of the Dobe area of Botswana share their range amicably with the Herero and Tswana pastoralists. Boundaries here and in Australia were never so rigid as to make it difficult for members of one tribe to avail themselves of the resources of the others' territory. This was especially true in times of drought or famine, as also in the case of an individual fleeing his own group. The obligation of hospitality seems to have been virtually universal among the Australian aborigines.

Radcliffe-Brown has stated: "Acts of trespass against this exclusive right of a horde to its territory seem to have been very rare in the social life of the aborigines, but it appears to have been generally held that anyone committing such a trespass could justifiably be killed." This statement has been shown to be quite incorrect by the findings of later investigators. The fact is that all fieldworkers who have investigated the matter since 1930 have reported the unrestricted movement of foodseekers over broad regions that included totemic sites and many patriclans (clans in which an individual belongs to the father's clan). Dr. L. R. Hiatt of the Department of Anthropology of the University of Sydney, in summarizing the findings for Australia, concludes: "The evidence is clearly against the existence in aboriginal clansmen of an instinct to occupy and defend territory. But it points to a strong impulse to establish and maintain territorial ownership." This impulse grows principally out of emotional attachment to a land in which the individual is born and lives his or her life. It has nothing whatever to do with instinct.

Indeed, Dr. James N. Anderson of the Department of Anthropology at the University of California at Berkeley, in summarizing the evidence for hunting peoples, concludes that "exclusive territoriality with territorial defense by a mixed group of people is rare at best."

Finally, perhaps our leading authority on the subject, the late Professor Julian Steward of the Department of Anthropology at the University of Illinois, wrote: "There have been many contentions that primitive bands own territories or resources and fight to protect them. Although I cannot assert that this is never the case, it is probably very uncommon. . . . Defense of the territories of patrilineal bands has also been claimed, but this too is open to question."

I have chosen to spend a good deal of time discussing the alleged territorial behavior of foodgathering-hunting peoples because their way of life more closely approximates that of early humans than does that of any other known peoples; their mode of life can therefore suggest what territorial behavior may have been like among our early ancestors. We have seen from the reports surveyed that not only is there no evidence for an instinct of territoriality among gatherer-hunters, but that territorial behavior in the sense of fighting to defend a territory is quite rare among such peoples, and that it is only with the growth of farming and urbanism that we witness the development of territoriality. With the advent of agriculture and the possibility of settling permanently in one place, the earliest village communities came into being, not much more than 12,000 years ago. Agriculture, the control of the reproduction of plants for use as food, necessitates a sedentary settlement, and such a settlement, to which the control of the reproduction of animals is added, leads to the eventual demarcation of the boundaries of the place, which then becomes identified with its inhabitants, who regard it as their village, their "home." It is from such villages that the first towns grew and developed. Raiding, *not* by "hostile" bands, *not* from "instinctual aggressiveness," but for the purpose of acquiring the products of the target village, and later the goods and valuables of the town attacked, would serve to consolidate the feeling of belonging to a particular place, which one would be ready to protect and defend against all marauders.

The emotional attachment which human beings develop for their "homeland" is customarily reinforced by the institutionalization of private and public allegiances to the "land" of one's birth, loyalty to the community, and the equivalents of such modern institutional devices as flag-waving, pledges of allegiance to the flag, "my country, right or wrong," and all the other shibboleths of patriotism. "Fatherlands," "Motherlands," or "Homelands" become emotional involvements endowed with all the complexity and beliefs that the tribalist zealously brings to the support of such emotions. All such sentiments are identified with a particular territory. It may be a territory as large as the USSR or as small as Monaco, but however extended or circumscribed its boundaries, the attachment to the homeland will remain something woven into the fabric of one's being all the days of one's life. The weaving is done out of the elements of the individual's experience; it is culturally conditioned by the training received from all those social, political, religious, secular, and educational sources that work upon the member of the tribe. These are all cultural forces and have nothing whatever to do with biological imperatives.

Territorialists may, of course, argue that the absence of territoriality in some peoples does not necessarily mean that they lack an instinct, or imperative, or force, or whatever other name the territorialists choose to call it. It may simply be that the instinct is being controlled or overlaid or displaced or sublimated or redirected into other activities. For this would-be argument I can find no support in the available evidence.

Mr. Ardrey's preoccupation with our long hunting past, which, according to him, "placed selective advantage on those who took pleasure in the violent way," is belied by the evidence of ethnology, of prehistory, and the lives of contemporary gatherer-hunter peoples. Human hunters do not hunt because they take pleasure in violence but because, like the Gombe Forest chimpanzees, they take pleasure in eating meat. Teleki points out that the Gombe chimpanzees spend a considerable amount of energy in obtaining fresh meat when other foods are regularly obtainable with much less effort. Furthermore, "the meat is usually eaten and shared in a leisurely manner more suggestive of pleasure than basic hunger alone." The pleasure was not derived from the satisfaction of some innate urge to violence, but quite clearly from the delight these occasional hunters took in eating every part of their prey.

The evidence of ethology relating to the territorial behavior of mammals, and especially nonhuman primates, strongly supports the view that territorial behavior, at least in the "higher" mammals, is learned. It is possible that in some birds such behavior may be instinctive, but there is no continuity between the instinctive territorial behavior of birds, upon which Mr. Ardrey relies for his arguments, and the learned social behavior of humans. Human beings acquire socially conditioned incentives to defend socially defined homelands or territories against socially defined "enemies." The identification with a particular territory may become emotionally so deeply embedded that it results in a motivational complex which can be easily aroused to the highest pitch of enthusiasm, at the sound, for example, of some otherwise banal piece of music like the national anthem or a more rousing song like any one of those associated with the various services of the armed forces. As the Ukrainian proverb (quoted by Lorenz) has it, "When the banner is unfurled, all reason is in the trumpet." "To the humble seeker of biological truth," Lorenz tells us, "there cannot be the slightest doubt that human militant enthusiasm evolved out of a communal defense response of our prehuman ancestors." Without this "most powerfully motivating instinct," says Lorenz, not art nor science nor any of the great endeavors of man would have come into being. And whether this form of "communal aggression" is made to serve these endeavors, or whether this powerful "instinct" makes him go to war "in some abject silly cause," depends almost entirely on the conditioning and/or imprinting he has undergone during certain susceptible periods of his life.

So here we have a supposed "instinct" which, according to Lorenz, has evolved out of a communal defense response of our prehuman ancestors. This, according to him, is the most powerful of motivating "instincts," that can drive men to fight in whatever cause they are conditioned or alternatively to the creation of art or the development of science.

And who were these prehuman ancestors? Lorenz doesn't say. Presumably they were the australopithecines or, if not the australopithecines, perhaps some earlier or later prehuman, more humanlike form? But, as we have seen, the evidence is entirely against such ideas. There is every reason to believe that prehuman populations were very small, widely dispersed, and, like the baboons and living great apes, had no more need for communal defense against their own species or in most cases even against neighboring species than do nonhuman primates today.

Ardrey believes that "our attachment to property is of an

ancient biological order," and that our failure to recognize this has led to all kinds of social and political derangements. The failures of Geneva, of foreign policies, the Arab-Israeli conflict, Pearl Harbor, the Cuban crisis, and much else, are all discussed in terms of territoriality.

The resemblances between animal and human territorial behavior are analogical and superficial. The fact that our nearest relations, the chimpanzee and gorilla, are nonterritorial should serve to render more than questionable any basis for a territorial instinct in humans.

Not only is there no ground for believing that a territorial instinct constitutes the basis or cause of human aggression, but the evidence abundantly indicates that even among other animals there is no necessary connection between territorial behavior and aggression. For example, it has been found that among certain cichlid fish nonterritorial males fight more than territorial males. Some birds are territorial only during the breeding season, some for the purpose of feeding, others during mating, roosting, and so on. Among human societies one cannot help wondering why it is that such countries as Switzerland, Iceland, Ceylon, Costa Rica, the principalities of Monaco and Luxembourg, all of which have distinct territories, are so unaggressive as never to have cast an envious eye upon the property or territories of other peoples or have had to defend themselves against them, whereas the larger industrial nations have behaved quite otherwise. And how does it happen that England, which was once the foremost of the imperialist nations, has not only ceased to be so but has deliberately relinquished all future dreams of territorial conquest and even, some say, of defense? Can it be that the "territorial instinct" in the English has suffered a sudden mutation to nonterritoriality or simply atrophied? Or is it possible that for social and political reasons the Labour government resolved to return to their rightful owners the lands which their forebears had forcibly taken? Does being a small country or principality do something to the territorial instinct which prevents it from exploding into an attack upon another country or principality? And is it necessary to appeal to a fantasied territorial instinct to account for the fierce competition for foreign markets during the eighteenth and nineteenth centuries and later, which led to the annexation and exploitation of foreign lands by the Great Powers?

To attach an interest in the acquisition of real estate to an instinct is simply to misread the clear evidence of history. Juvenile gangs will fight on our streets for "territory," and so will gangsters. Outraged citizens will "fight" to preserve their right to preserve trees and parklands threatened by developers; conscientious objectors will "fight" to preserve their right not to kill their fellow men, while pacifists will attend peace meetings in order to "fight" for the preservation of peace. Mr. Ardrey, presumably, would nod in agreement and claim that these were merely examples of the "open instinct" of territoriality expressing itself in different forms. "Open instincts" are described by Mr. Ardrey as those which in order to complete their innate patterns must gain information from individual experience. "Closed instincts" are those which dispense with experience. Here Mr. Ardrey confuses us, for in discussing "the territorial imperative" throughout the greater part of his book he does so in terms of the definition offered early in it, namely, as a fixed action pattern, "the genetically determined pattern which informs an animal as to how to act in a given situation" (p. 29)—that is, as a "closed instinct." But when he enters upon the discussion of such matters as patriotism, modern international treaties, war, street fights, and the like, "closed" instincts become "open" ones. So that what we are really left with is a powerful drive ("instinct") which, so the theory has it, is activated by stimuli of every kind relating to territory. The stimulation will then result in protective or aggressive behavior calculated to bring about the desired result. The desired result may range all the way from standing at attention with or without the palm of the hand resting on the chest somewhere in the vicinity of the heart, to firing deadly weapons at an unseen socially designated "enemy," to the writing of plays or the solving of mathematical problems. But this kind of "explanation" is rendered more than dubious since it attributes to "instinct" a generalized plasticity which is wholly opposed to the customarily accepted definition of an instinct as a fixed action pattern which causes the organism to react to a given stimulus with a predetermined behavior.

The fact, of course, is that the appeal to "instinct" as an explanation of territorial behavior in humans is both unparsimonious and wholly gratuitous, since what it offers to explicate is much more efficiently explained by the general educability of the human organism.

Like present-day gatherer-hunter peoples, prehistoric humans were mobile and nomadic, seeking food over extensive areas of land, the low energy foods consumed making it necessary for them to be more or less constantly on the move. Territories, as Klopfer points out, were no more likely to be of use to them than they are to similarly feeding goats and gazelles. And with Klopfer we may conclude: "whatever the origins of defense of property in man they are unlikely to lie in primordial and unalterable habits ordained by selection imposed on his ancestors."

10

War and Violence

Territory and War

"We must face the fact," writes Lorenz, "that militant enthusiasm has evolved from the hackle-raising and chin-protruding communal defense instinct of our prehuman ancestors and that the key stimulus situations which release it still bear the earmarks of this origin."

Robert Ardrey tells us that the "territorial drive, as one ancient, animal foundation for the form of human misconduct known as war, is so obvious as to demand small attention. . . . But the drive to defend and maintain territory can be regarded not as a cause but only as a condition of war." "Human warfare comes about only when the defensive instinct of a determined territorial proprietor is challenged by the predatory compulsions of an equally determined territorial neighbor."

"The principal cause of modern warfare," Ardrey informs us, "arises from the failure of an intruding power correctly to estimate the defensive resources of a territorial defender." In other words, if Hitler had known he would lose the war, there would have been no second world war, a claim entirely disproven by the historic facts. To oversimplify the matter greatly, Hitler made war because he was a psychopathic monster, suffering among other things from delusions of grandeur, and not on the basis of an erroneous estimate of the war's outcome. Commenting on this "nursery-floor view" of human affairs, Professor Edmund Leach remarks, "This is the Hobbesian notion that if there were no policemen each of us would immediately set about murdering everyone else in sight, and it is total rubbish."

Niko Tinbergen, in his inaugural address as professor of animal behavior at Oxford University, delivered in February 1968, stated that man has developed similarities to wolves, lions, and hyenas, and that as a social, hunting primate he must originally have been organized on the principle of group territories. Territorialism, Tinbergen believes, is one of our ancestral traits. "In order to understand what makes us go to war," he writes, "we have to recognize that man behaves like a group-territorial species." What causes war, according to Tinbergen, is the upsetting of the balance between aggression and fear, and this upsetting is due to a number of the consequences of cultural evolution. These are: the outpacing of man's limited behavior adjustability by the culturally determined changes in his social environment, the enormous increase in the pressures of population, the advent of long-distance communication, mobility, intergroup contacts, and the exposure to continuous external provocation of aggression. These alone would not explain man's increased tendency to kill his fellow man; such conditions would merely lead to continuous threat behavior. What upsets the balance between aggression and fear is the brainwashing into all-out fighting that our warriors are made to undergo, the use of long-range weapons, and hence, the removal of appeasement and distress signals of opponents which would stop our warriors short of killing. It is these last three factors alone that Tinbergen considers as sufficient to explain how we have become such unhinged killers. Tinbergen believes that Lorenz is right when he claims that the elimination, through education, of the internal urge to fight will turn out to be very difficult, if not impossible.

Desmond Morris, a student of Tinbergen's, had earlier developed these views of his teacher in his widely read book *The Naked Ape,* and later in *The Human Zoo.* Under natural conditions, Morris points out, the goal of aggression is domination, not destruction, but this goal has become blurred in the case of man "because of the vicious combination of attack remoteness and group co-operativeness." Men fight now to support their comrades rather than to dominate the enemy, "and their inherent susceptibility to direct appeasement is given little chance to express itself. This unfortunate development may yet prove to be our undoing and lead to the rapid extinction of the species."

Lorenz, like Tinbergen and Morris, believes that human cultural evolution has been so rapid that we have not had time to develop those inhibitions which would have served to restrain our aggressive drives. It seems never to have occurred to these writers that possibly humans have never developed such inhibitions because they really have no biologically determined aggressive drives, that the aggression exhibited is largely culturally conditioned, that the only forms of inhibition humans have found it necessary to develop are also cultural, and that as an instinctless creature the human requires no inbuilt biological behavioral controls.

In his book *Human Aggression* Anthony Storr, an English psychiatrist, tells us: "It is obvious that man could never have attained his present dominance, nor even have survived as a species, unless he possessed a large endowment of aggressiveness." Since Dr. Storr uses the terms "aggression"

and "aggressiveness" in so many different senses it is difficult to say whether or not he means that humans owe their
present dominance, even their survival, to warfare. In any
event, he agrees with Lorenz, Tinbergen, and Morris that
humans lack strong inhibitions against killing their own
species because they are ill-equipped with natural weapons.
"If men had tusks or horns they would be less, rather than
more, likely to kill one another. The artificial weapon is too
cerebral a device for nature to have provided adequate safeguards against it" (p. 112). In passing it may be remarked
that nature—to employ Dr. Storr's phrasing—would most
probably have done nothing of the sort, since with the
equipment Dr. Storr describes it would have been easy to
produce power imbalances completely altering the cost-
benefit ratio in regard to aggression. Such aggression could
have been very destructive of human groups.

Adaptability, Inhibition, and Control

Lorenz and Ardrey, as we have seen, claim that man has
aggressively employed weapons from the very beginning of
his attainment of human status, that, in fact, he owes his
emergence as a human being to his use of artificial weap-
onry. That would be a matter of some five million years or
longer, a more than sufficient time for "nature" to have provided the necessary safeguards countering the continued
use of weapons against his fellow man. When the innate aggressionists speak of man's cultural development having outpaced his limited behavioral adjustability to the environment they forget a most important fact—namely, that man
has evolved as the most malleable, flexible, and educable
of all creatures for the reason that he has constantly been
making those adaptively successful behavioral responses to
the challenges of the environment which, under the pres-

sures of natural selection, have enabled him to make himself what he has become. Furthermore, were the function of that organ through which all these changes are principally expressed—the human brain—to be characterized by one word, that word would be "inhibition." The human brain is the organ of inhibition. It is the organ of deliberation and of choice. As Delgado has said, to behave is to choose one pattern among many. The human brain is the organ that permits voluntary rather than biologically predetermined inhibition. What, however, the innate aggressionists have in mind when they speak of inhibition is the biologically determined variety they attribute to other animals in response to appeasement behavior.

I am not convinced that either appeasement behavior or the response to it is innately determined. It seems to me much more likely that in mammals, at any rate, such appeasement behavior is to an appreciable extent learned. But however that may be, a considerable number of human societies have cultivated inhibition of aggressive response in their members. The gatherer-hunters discussed earlier in Chapter 6 as examples of peoples who have the expression of aggression well under control were the Australian aborigines, the Bushmen of the Kalahari Desert, the Eskimos, the Pygmies of the Ituri forest, the Hadza of Tanzania, the Lepchas of Sikkim, the Birhor of southern India, the Semang of Malaya and the Punan of Borneo (both peoples who until recently were exclusively gatherer-hunters), and the Tasaday of Mindanao who, until their discovery, were exclusively foodgatherers. To these may be added the Comanche and western Shoshoni Indians, the Papago and the Pueblo Indians, the Ifaluk of the Pacific, and a good many other peoples. The Israeli and Arab nations have become formidable military powers not out of militant enthusiasm or a desire to react to the stimulus of threat or attack, but because their

governments and citizens have been forced to protect themselves against the artificially created militant enthusiasm of
their respective enemies. Arabs as a whole and Israelis in
particular despise and deplore any form of violence. But in
a world of tension, threat, and violence they have no choice
other than to resort to arms. In the case of the Israelis it is
their dearly purchased right to existence as a persecuted people rather than territory that they seek to defend. This in
no way implies that it is some archaic territorial instinct that
fuels their resistance to attack, or that they are unable to
inhibit the driving power of such a putative instinct, when
they respond to attacks upon them. The Israelis would like
nothing better than to live at peace with their neighbors,
and to be of help to them, and, indeed, to turn the sword
into a plowshare. They would prefer nothing more than to
practice total inhibition of all hostile responses to threatening behavior. But their hostile neighbors do not stop at
threats, and the Israelis know this, and so they have no alternative other than to be prepared for whatever onslaught
from whatever side it may come. Indeed, if one needed an
example of inhibition of aggressive behavior in the face of
real threats to a people's continued existence, a more striking example could hardly be found than that presented by
the Israelis.

The point I am endeavoring to make is that inbuilt, innate inhibitions against any form of behavior are quite un-
necessary in malleable creatures such as humans, who can be
trained or train themselves to the most rigorous and consistent forms of inhibition. That this has always been the
case may be dependably inferred from the fact that, for
example, so powerful a drive as the desire for sexual intercourse has been successfully inhibited by countless numbers
of human beings in the face of the most powerful tempta-
tions. The Nambikwara, of Brazil, for example, after the

birth of a child abstain from sexual intercourse until the
child is weaned—that is, until about its third year. This deliberate spacing of children is made as a response to their
nomadic existence and the meager resources of the environment. The vows that monks and nuns have taken for generations constitute impressive examples of the power of voluntary inhibition of which human beings are capable.

It is not for lack, then, of the capacity for inhibition that
many societies show such a frightful record of killing, for
most peoples have developed such inhibitions, but rather
that in the matter of sanctioned killing of the enemy in time
of war most societies of the civilized world have actively discouraged any inhibitory reservations the individual might
have. Indeed, in such societies those are most highly rewarded who behave as if they have no inhibitions about killing the enemy. The hero is he who kills or makes it possible
to kill the greatest number of the enemy. Virtually all our
institutions, traditions, and public media conspire to ele-
vate and sanctify the uninhibited killing of the enemy as the
most noble of moral obligations in the service of one's
country. Those who refuse to participate in such killing,
either by conscientious objection, or by evading the draft,
by desertion, or by any other means, are condemned, jailed,
or otherwise penalized. The rewards and encouragements
for sanctioned killing are everywhere so constantly emphasized that even were humans to possess innate inhibitions
against killing the defeated "enemy," they would be so overlaid with positively reinforced rewards for killing that such
inhibitions would hardly have a chance to express themselves. But since humans naturally lack any drive to kill
their fellow humans—or to kill anything, for the matter of
that—they need no innate inhibition to inhibit what they
do not possess. Since, however, they are capable of learning
to kill other animals as well as their own kind, such social

inhibitions are required in order to limit and control their behavior. Hence, every society has instituted rules and regulations relating to such conduct, and these are gradually absorbed by the growing member of society.

So the answer to the innate aggressionists is that humans have no innate inhibitions against killing, nor do they possess any innate mechanism for responding to appeasement gestures, not because cultural has outrun biological development, but simply because humans have no innate tendencies directed toward killing. And although they are at least as capable of learning to develop such inhibitions as other animals, in many human societies they are encouraged to regard the killing of the enemy as a sacred and patriotic duty. It is absurd, therefore, to cite the lack of inhibition in such societies against sanctioned killing as a reason for that killing, or an explanation of it. Where, as in those human societies in which the prohibitions against intragroup killing become part of the socialization process, human beings do not kill each other. The small proportion who commit such killings are generally abnormal persons who have suffered significant failures of need satisfaction, especially of maternal love, during the socialization process.

The Unwarlike Nature of Many Peoples

The fact that modern societies with all their resources must devote so much time and energy to the cultivation and development of aggressive and "warlike virtues" in their citizens suggests that such allegedly instinctual drives toward war do not exist. If wars were due to the arousal of instinctive drives, nations would not have to resort to conscription and the draft in order to raise armies. Dr. Richard G. van Gelder, chairman of the Department of Mammalogy at the American Museum of Natural History, has remarked in this

The Nature of Human Aggression

connection, "There is no more reason to believe that man fights wars because fish or beavers are territorial than to think that man can fly because bats have wings."

Blithely made assumptions, such as Tinbergen's that since humans were originally small hunting primates they must therefore have been organized on the principle of group territories, are typical of the overgeneralizations of the innate aggressionists. We have seen in the preceding chapter that our closest relations, the gorilla and chimpanzee, are non-territorial.

Dr. Storr tells us that anthropologists report "a few cases of people amongst whom aggressive behavior and war are relatively rare." Most of these people, he goes on to say, "seem to be living under the dominance of neighboring societies who are more aggressive than themselves, and have simply adopted a form of submissive adaptation in the face of perpetual threat."

Again, this is a typical innate aggressionist statement, and there is no truth in it. It has already been made clear that there are many unaggressive peoples, and with very few exceptions these do not live under the domination of anyone but themselves. Nor are the peoples "few" in number who do not engage in war. It may be taken as the general rule that peoples who are not politically organized are also not given to war, and gatherer-hunter societies lack political organization. Such political functions as are carried out in these societies are performed partially or wholly by institutions such as religious or kinship organizations, and these exist primarily for ritual purposes and the regulation of initiation, marriage, and inheritance. As Beals and Hoijer put it, "Bands, tribes, and confederacies appear to represent the most frequent types of political organization found among nonliterate peoples, and it is of interest to note that these political forms are perhaps universal among peoples who

have never developed warfare for conquest. The warfare
that does exist in such societies is generally a matter of petty
raiding for small economic gain or for purposes of vengeance
or prestige." The possession of others' territory, political or
economic exploitation or subjugation, is never the end of
petty raiding—raiding which is in no way comparable with
the warfare waged by politically more sophisticated peoples.
Warfare, in the sense of an armed attack by one group
against another for the purposes of conquest and exploitation, does not occur among any of the gatherer-hunter peoples. Horse-raiding and vengeance parties have been known
to occur among American Indians of the Plains. These
groups were usually very small, a few men in the case of a
vengeance party, eight or ten in the horse-raiding party. In
the vengeance party the object was to kill a member of the
offender's tribe. Raiding for horses was often sanctioned and
encouraged in a vision, and as for the killing of the member
of another tribe, the mission was considered completed
when a killing occurred.

Most of the peoples of the Arctic, Subarctic, Great Basin,
northeast Mexico, and probably Baja California, lacked anything resembling true warfare before European contact.
They had no permanent military organization, special fighting regalia, or associated public ceremonies.

Freud, like Dr. Storr, also found it difficult to believe that
there existed any unaggressive unwarlike people on this
earth. In his famous answer to Einstein's question, "Is there
any way of delivering mankind from the menace of war?"
he wrote: "In some happy corners of the earth, they say,
where nature brings forth abundantly whatever man desires,
there flourish races whose lives go gently by, unknowing of
aggression and constraint. This I can hardly credit."

Unfortunately, one of the hazards attendant on addiction
to one's own theories is that it tends to make one insensible

to the facts. The evidence for the existence of such unaggressive peoples was available in Freud's day, had he taken the trouble to seek it out. It is a pity that he did not do so. He preferred, instead, to disbelieve in the existence of such peoples, presumably because he would have found it difficult to reconcile them with his theories. Nevertheless, such peoples exist to this present day, and they can be neither denied nor explained away.

The important fact for us to recognize is that at the level of the non-politically organized gatherer-hunter stage of human development the coefficient of aggressiveness is relatively low, and with the exception of the Andaman Islanders, the Ona and the Yaghan of Tierra del Fuego, and three or four other gatherer-hunting groups, the organized attack of one group against another in anything resembling warfare is a rarity.

The late Verrier Elwin, the distinguished Anglo-Indian anthropologist, in his book on the Baiga, a hunting-cultivating people of the Satpura Mountains in Central India, tells how during the Second World War an old Baiga woman grew concerned for the welfare of Elwin's English countrymen. "This," she said, "is how God equalizes things. Our sons and daughters die young, of hunger or disease or the attacks of wild beasts. The sons and daughters of the English could grow old in comfort and happiness. But God sends madness upon them, and they destroy each other, and so in the end their great knowledge and their religion are useless and we are all the same." Alas.

One day a party of Baigas, anxious to help their English friend's countrymen, came to Elwin with a bundle of bows and arrows which they wanted him to forward to the British government to aid in the war. When Elwin explained to them that modern battles were no longer fought with such weapons they were much perturbed. "But if they use guns," they said, "people will really get killed." The gentle, unaggressive Baiga could be roused to sympathy for the cause of their white friend's people, but they themselves could not imagine anyone seriously attempting to kill anyone. The only aggression they understood was sympathetic magic against some other person.

The purely pastoral Todas who live on the undulating plateau of the Niligri Hills in southern India, make no use of weapons of any kind. Only on ceremonial occasions do clubs and bows and arrows make their appearance, but these ceremonial objects are never used against anyone, for the Todas live in peace among themselves and with their neighbors. Writing of them in 1906, the English anthropologist W. H. R. Rivers described them as "grave and dignified, and yet thoroughly cheerful and well-disposed toward all." The Todas devote themselves almost entirely to the care of their buffaloes together with the dairying and the complicated rituals which have grown up in association with them. Living as they do in many different villages, and in fairly close proximity to half a dozen different tribes, they manage to coexist in complete amity with each other.

Clearly, both the Baiga and the Todas conform to the general principle that where political organization is wanting or elementary the people are likely to be unaggressive and unwarlike. As Hobhouse, Wheeler, and Ginsberg stated in their classic study of 1915, *The Material Culture and Social Institutions of the Simpler Peoples,* the idea that early societies were, and simpler societies are, in a constant state of warfare is a gross exaggeration. Their survey of over 300 societies led them to conclude that "relations between neighbouring communities are in general friendly, but they are apt to be interrupted by charges of murder owing to the belief in witchcraft, and feuds result which may take a more or less organised form."

Another completely unaggressive, weaponless, unwarlike people are the reindeer-herding Lapps. Their gentleness has been a matter of history for several hundred years, yet, somehow, in the discussion of unaggressive unwarlike peoples they have, in common with a good many other peoples, been overlooked. But everyone who has lived among them has commented enthusiastically on their peaceableness and gentle character. We seem to have a selective capacity for overlooking the obvious. Even though the Lapps are a Christianized people and live in Europe, writers like Dr. Storr appear to be unaware of their existence, for had he known of them one can hardly imagine his writing of them as among those rare unwarlike peoples who live under the domination of neighboring societies who are more aggressive than themselves. The Lapps live under the domination of no one; even though the Finns, the Swedes, and the Norwegians are their neighbors, they maintain the integrity of their own way of life.

It has already been mentioned that the peoples of the Arctic and Subarctic before European contact were, with few exceptions, not given to warfare. From the Aleuts to the Zeshaks there are more than 500 populations in Siberia alone—most of them unstudied. But from what we do know of them aggressive behavior seems to have varied from frequent to rare. Keith Otterbein in his cross-cultural study of war found that of the sample of thirty uncentralized political societies he surveyed six engaged in warfare, i.e., 20 percent.

The existence of so many different peoples at all levels of cultural development, gatherer-hunters, pastoral, agricultural, urban, and industrial, who are or were unwarlike, certainly renders very dubious the claims of the innate aggressionists for the existence of a powerful drive toward war.

The simple fact appears to be that stateless societies do not as a rule indulge in war, and that it usually takes organization of a society into a political state before those conditions that lead to genuine warfare come into play. These conditions may be conflict of interest, material or ideal, actual or traditional, economic objectives, territorial expansion (or its prevention), nationalism, the prevention of ideological conquest imagined or real, and the like.

The existence of nonaggressive and unwarlike peoples does not, of course, disprove the possible existence of predispositions to aggression or warfare. What the existence of such peoples does prove is that aggressive behavior and warfare are not ineluctable accompaniments of the human condition, that do what we will they must and will find expression.

In the light of the facts we have thus far considered it seems hardly necessary to appeal to any innate drive which can be meaningfully attached to such artificial purposes. If some humans behave "very much like a group territorial species," as indeed they sometimes appear to do, it is not due, it may be suggested, to genetics, but to frenetics, to tribalism closely identified with an emotional attachment to a particular territory.

The Causes of War

Modern wars are not made by nations or peoples, nor are they made by men in a state of aggression welling over with an instinct of territory. Wars are usually made by a few individuals in positions of great power, "great leaders," "thoughtful" and "respected" statesmen generally advised by "the best and the brightest," almost always with calm and deliberation, and the pretense if not the conviction of complete moral rectitude. Generals, removed far from the battlefront, give orders for the annihilation of the "enemy" with no more aggressiveness or emotion than when they order the gardener at home to mow the lawn a little closer. The "fighting" man shoots at or drops his bombs on an "enemy" he hardly ever sees, and from whom his emotional disengagement could scarcely be more remote. He is engaged in "hostilities" in which there is no emotional enmity, and in "aggressive" behavior in which there is no feeling of aggression. His behavior is not instinctively but state-directed toward the enemy. Such aggression falls into the class that Professor Karl E. Scheibe of the Department of Psychology at Wesleyan University has called "legitimized aggression." Such "aggression" is justified and legitimized by a collectivity, whether state, political party, a cause, or a self-appointed prophet, and is acted out by individuals for reasons that are self-transcending rather than self-assertive. Neither physiological processes, instincts, nor learning paradigms are involved in such "aggression," and it is virtually empty of cultural content. Enemies are indicated and the subjects are called upon to show their loyalty. The potentiation of legitimized aggression is like the arming of a weapon, while the assignment of the enemy, of evil, is like pointing it at a specific target. "An order is given and the harm is done."

Jean Rostand, the French biologist, has put it very well. "In war," he said, "man is much more a sheep than a wolf. He follows, he obeys. War is servility, rather—a certain fanaticism and credulity—but not aggressiveness."

Bernard Brodie, professor of political science at the University of California at Los Angeles, has pointed out that war is a rather poor outlet for human aggression or rage. It is too dangerous and too costly, and the enemy is too impersonal and remote. Aggression and rage are more suitably immediately expended on visible, tangible persons close at hand. Furthermore, the intervention of enormous, over-organizing policy-directed bureaucracies, is not very satisfactory for getting any kind of a job done. Aggression seeks immediate relief against a target. War machines succeed in rendering weak or wanting any aggressiveness that may have been present. The truth is—and this is perhaps the greatest of all paradoxes—motivationally, war represents one of the least aggressive forms of man's behavior. A state is not a natural creation but an artificial entity, and it is as such artificial entities that states wage war, with artificial weapons from artificial motives for artificial purposes, conducted for artificial ends. It was confidence in "reeking tube and iron shard" that led Germany from peace and security into two world wars, and resulted in those holocausts and disasters for which the world will long continue to pay the devastating cost. It was the superpatriotism of such militarists as General Friedrich von Bernhardi whipped up in his notorious book *Germany and the Next War,* published in 1911, and read throughout the civilized world with fascination and more than a certain grudging admiration, that formulated Germany's program for the first World War. It was Bernhardi who, as a young officer, was the first to enter Paris at the head of a unit of Uhlans, after the fall of France in 1871. He was quite evidently an upright and honest man who seems to have been convinced by his own rectitude that what he believed must therefore be true, and since virtually every German from the Kaiser to the simplest citizen thoroughly agreed with him, there could be no doubt of the truth of his claims. In his book Bernhardi expressed and fortified the German will to war. He wrote the book, he declared, to protest against "the aspirations for peace, which seem to dominate our age and threaten to poison the soul of the German people." "War," he declared, "is a biological necessity, as necessary as the struggle of the elements in Nature. It gives a biologically just decision, since its decisions rest on the very nature of things." "The whole idea" of arbitration "represents a presumptuous encroachment on the natural laws of development," for "what is right is decided by the arbitrament of war." And to cap it all Darwin is invoked as well as "the plant and animal world," in support of this "universal law of Nature."

These ideas had an immense appeal, not only for the German militarists but also for their counterparts and industrialists everywhere, just as do the ideas today of Lorenz, Ardrey, Morris, and the other innate aggressionists. Perhaps none of these writers subscribes to Bernhardi's idea that the arbitrament of war is alone capable of giving the only biologically just decision between nations, but they do agree with the general that the drive toward war is a natural one, and that in the past, at any rate, it played an adaptively valuable role in human evolution. The evidence discussed in this book, on the contrary, suggests that up to some twelve thousand years ago war played an insignificant role, if any, in human evolution. Since the Neolithic, when the first village communities came into being, war, if anything, has become increasingly dysgenic and humanly socially destructive. It now threatens the very survival of all life on earth. Plunged as we are into crises before we are aware that there are problems, we cast about for ready solutions. In order to save us from the final Armageddon the innate aggressionists have offered a variety of dubious solutions.

The Redirection of Aggression

Tinbergen suggests employing aggression as the motive force for useful activities, not by eliminating it but by taking the sting out of it. Scientific research, he believes, offers the best opportunities for deflecting and sublimating aggression. "The whole population should be made to feel that it participates in the struggle." Hence, the scientist's duty to inform the public of what is being done, of the relevance and importance of scientific work.

If there are any behavioral scientists who are suffering from a surfeit of unexpended aggression or are in need of redirecting or deflecting it, one can think of a far more immediately effective use for it than trying to learn what we can from animal studies. One could, for example, devote oneself to improving the social conditions which make it possible for men to be sent to war. The "all-out attack on the enemy within" that Tinbergen recommends, "our unknown selves," is rather a strange way of putting things. If man is an "unknown self" how can what is unknown be identified with "the enemy within"? It cannot. But Tinbergen clearly assumes that the "enemy within" is man's putative innate agressiveness. So our scientists' aggression must be used for an all-out "attack" upon what we can do about either controlling or deflecting this aggressiveness. This seems to me to put us squarely into the land of Topsy-Turvydom. Is the scientist's consuming curiosity and devotion to his work to be equated with "aggression"? And is "the enemy within" really to be identified with either "the unknown" or with an "innate urge to fight"? "The question is," said Alice, "whether you *can* make words mean so many different things."

What chance is there that "the whole population" can be persuaded to feel that it participates in the struggle to find "ways and means for keeping our intergroup aggression in check"? What chance is there that even a small proportion of the population could be so involved? And would it not be more practical to involve the citizen in more immediately promising activities at a very wide range of levels, in one or more of which he or she could join, designed to bring about those social changes which would serve to eliminate or reduce aggression, whether individual or collective, from the human scene?

The danger of such recommendations as the innate aggressionists make for the control of aggression is that they tend to divert attention from the real causes of aggression and war, and thus to waste time, talent, energy, and money on projects which will in no way serve to enlighten us concerning the nature of those causes, while the conditions they are designed to control worsen exponentially.

Lorenz tells us that "a simple and effective way of discharging aggression in an innocuous manner is to redirect it at a substitute object." Sport, which Lorenz believes contains elements of contest rendering it akin to serious fighting, has as its main function today the cathartic discharge of aggressive urge. More important, it educates man to conscious and responsible control of his own fighting behavior. Transgressions in sport are quickly punished. The demands for fairness and chivalry, according to Lorenz, must be respected even in the face of the strongest aggression-eliciting stimuli. The most important function of sport, however,. is to serve as a safety valve for the dangerous pressures of collective military enthusiasm. So Lorenz recommends sporting contests of every kind between nations as outlets for their collective militant enthusiasm. The suggestion is that such contests would promote personal acquaintance between the people of different nations, and they would therefore unite in enthusiasm for a common cause people who would otherwise have little in common.

Dr. Storr agrees with Lorenz on the efficacy of sports in the redirection of aggression, and goes on to suggest that annual competitions between nations could take the form of competing to see which one could produce the most efficient mental hospital, the safest car, the best-designed house for a worker, and so on, through an endless range of possibilities.

The idea that competitive sports can serve to deflect aggression into more useful and less damaging channels than warfare is subject to testing. If there is any truth in the idea then societies that are peaceful should indulge, according to the Drive Discharge theory, in a good many competitive sports which serve to drain off the assumed otherwise dangerous aggression. Conversely, warlike societies should be lacking in such competitive sports. Societies tend to be internally consistent in their attitudes and behaviors manifested in different activities. This being so we would expect to find, according to the Culture Pattern Model (that aggressive behavior is primarily learned), that combative sports are more likely to occur in warlike societies than in peaceful ones. Rather than alternatives to war, such combative sports would represent the embodiments of the same theme or outlook on war. These possibilities have been investigated by Dr. Richard D. Sipes of the Department of Anthropology of the State University of New York at Buffalo. In his study entitled "War, Sports and Aggression: An Empirical Test of Two Rival Theories," Dr. Sipes used two test strategies: a cross-cultural correlation study and a developmental (diachronic) case study of the United States. A careful statistical analysis of 130 different societies revealed that, in the cross-cultural study, there were only four exceptions to the rule "that where we find warlike behavior we typically find combative sports and where war is relatively rare combative sports tend to be absent." The hypothesis is, therefore, refuted that combative sports constitute alternatives to war as discharge channels of accumulated aggressive tension. "It casts strong doubt on the idea that there is such a thing as accumulable aggressive tension. . . . It clearly supports the validity of the Culture Pattern Model (that aggressive behavior is primarily learned), and

as clearly tends to discredit the Drive Discharge Model,"
(p. 71), namely, that aggressive sports tend to reduce aggressive tension.

In the years since the turn of the century the United States has been engaged in 28 military actions, an average of 1 every 2.7 years. According to innate aggressionist theory, the combative sports are more likely and the noncombative sports less likely to discharge accumulated tension successfully. If this were, in fact, the case we should, according to the Drive Discharge theory, expect an inverse relationship to be found between combative sports (hunting and football) and military activity, and no, or a smaller, inverse relationship between noncombative (betting and baseball) sports and military activity. On the other hand, the Culture Pattern Model would lead one to expect either no or a direct relationship between combative sports and military activity, and no or a smaller direct relationship between noncombative and military activity. Dr. Sipes's findings tended strongly to support the Culture Pattern Model. "We need not postulate," Dr. Sipes concludes, "an innate propensity in the individual toward violent aggression and killing nor speculate on the mechanics involved in natural selection for warlike or combative killing behavior in humans when it is not found in animals. The tendency for a group of men to engage in war can be more parsimoniously and satisfactorily explained as being carried in their society's culture than in the individual men's genes" (pp. 79-80).

Dr. Sipes also draws attention to the fact that the prevalence of combative sports throughout a large part of the world does not require resort to individual hunting patterns, aggression, the need to excel, or the like. Such sports form components of a combative culture theme, integral parts of a combative culture pattern, and wherever one finds a warlike society there one will find combative sports. The internal consistencies shown in the behavioral patterns of such societies render cultural explanations of these behaviors rather more cogent than the appeal to "innate" propensities. There is much other evidence which shows that sporting contests, far from siphoning off or deflecting or sublimating aggression, tend, in fact, to reinforce it and even to exacerbate it.

Even though the borders between Canada and the United States remain open and undefended, Canadian and U.S. hockey teams when in competition seldom manage to avoid getting into a fight. "War on ice," as ice hockey has come to be called, is expected by the spectators to involve fighting. When, in Czechoslovakia, in March 1969 the Czechs defeated the Russians in hockey, the supporters of the opposing teams battled one another. Such conflicts have occurred with increasing frequency and violence in recent years in England, Mexico, Uruguay, Italy, Chile, and a number of other countries. In 1964, in Peru, a referee disallowed a goal during an Olympic soccer match, whereupon the supporters of the penalized team rioted, and before the melee was over a hundred people were dead and 500 injured, while numerous buildings were destroyed. During a soccer match between El Salvador and Honduras in 1969 each side claimed the other had used unfair tactics. This led not only to a riot but to a three-day war between the two nations, during which 1,000 people died. Fights at competitions between Blacks and Whites during high school sports in the United States do not speak highly for sports as a means of reducing or deflecting aggressive tensions. Nor, unfortunately, does the violence which has occurred at sporting events in many other countries tend to support the notion that sports offer any kind of a solution to the problem of individual, national, or international aggression. Even when a team wins its supporters are often so aroused they seem to be only too eager to exhibit their pleasure in responding to the aggressive behavior of the supporters of the other side. Crook has pointed out that the wanton destruction of train interiors by British football fans on their way to a game played away from "home" would suggest that the whole context of such games does not contribute to a lessening of tension. And certainly it is becoming increasingly evident that the organization of major sporting events can no longer take place without the institution of effective rules of management and crowd control.

Aggressive behavior at sporting events, if anything, often seems to elicit similar behavior from the spectators. This is especially frequently seen at boxing and wrestling matches, when many of the spectators appear to be not merely vicariously but actively engaged in worsting their man's opponent. There are a great many studies in this particular connection which show that it is not so much tension reduction that is achieved on these occasions as reinforcement of aggression. Those who find this kind of "sporting" aggression rewarding are not likely to undergo any long-lasting reduction in their aggression, but will continue to be at least as aggressive as they ever were, if their aggression is not, in fact, augmented.

The idea that sports and aggressive games will siphon off aggression is taken for granted by many writers on the subject. For example, the American psychiatrist William Menninger has written that "competitive games provide an unusually satisfactory outlet for the instinctive aggressive drive." As we have seen, the facts are quite contrary to this belief, a belief, however, which continues to rank among our more familiar popular superstitions. Berkowitz has carefully investigated the alleged relationship and can find no evidence for it, and so have several other investigators, with the same results.

There is, as we have seen, good reason to believe that
competitive sports often evoke and worsen the aggressiveness of the competitors. This is as true of children as it is of
adults. The evidence from many studies both on children
and adults shows that far from producing a cathartic reduction of aggression, the expression of aggressive behavior
tends either to maintain or increase it. Surely, if one wishes
to train children in cooperation it is more sensible to do so
in games that are cooperative rather than those that are
competitive. Indeed, the National Commission on the
Causes and Prevention of Violence deplored the reigning
competitive attitudes of winning at all costs, and emphasized
the desirability of cultivating and producing a graceful
loser. There are few among us who seem to understand that
the true winner in a race is often the one who comes in last.

What seems evident is that if it is assumed that sports constitute proper occasions for the expenditure of aggression,
then they will only serve to encourage and perpetuate aggression, rather than diminish it or result in its redirection.

Recently Lorenz has somewhat modified his views, and
now expresses "strong doubts whether watching aggressive
behavior even in the guise of sport has any cathartic effect at
all." His doubts, however, do not appear to extend to active
participation in sports.

It appears, then, that the recommendations of the innate
aggressionists for the control of aggression are unsound and
impracticable on several counts. First, aggressive behavior
is not ineradicable; since its expression is learned, no matter
how firmly based the "wiring" of that behavior may be in
the brain, it can be prevented or controlled by not being
taught, and untaught when learned. Second, whatever aggression is, it is not an energy or a fluid which tends to overflow after it has reached a certain level or pressure, and
third, therefore, it cannot be siphoned off or sublimated in

activities such as sports or some other display of energetics. If, then, we are to find a solution to the problem of human aggression, it must lie rather in careful and detailed research into the conditions of human experience that influence the development or nondevelopment of aggressive behavior.

11
Ideological Consequences

Homo sapiens *the Flawed Species?*

According to the innate aggressionists the reader belongs to a flawed species, and therefore needs to adjust his vision to a new image of humankind: not the creature of loving-kindness, humanity, and dignity that many of us have been led to believe is an attainable condition of humankind, but a creature of murderous proclivities for whose innate force some less dangerous outlet must be found.

Are we, with our knowledge and vision of humanity's possibilities, who at the very inception of our species and of our own lives greeted the dawn like cocks, to salute it now like capons in indolent acceptance of a fate that many find congenial because it makes life easier for them? Because it offers a view of human nature demanding less work than that requiring us to shape ourselves?

The flaw, we have seen, is not in our genes but in the environments which men have created, and which they identify with reality, for their creations are real things, both artifactual and social, yet nonetheless as artificial as a tool or an abstraction.

Earlier in this book we discussed the peculiar appeal of the theory of innate aggression. It might have been supposed that the idea of man as an instinctive killer would have been found repellent by most people and vigorously rejected. The very opposite has in fact occurred. The view of man's nature our Victorian forebears so engagingly characterized as "innate depravity" has enjoyed the widest appeal, serving as it does both an explanatory and a redemptive function. We readily embrace the view that it is nature, not ourselves, that is to be blamed for the sinfulness within us, for the violence of our species. We experience the illumination with feelings of relief and gratitude, for we are absolved of all responsibility for belonging to so delinquent a species.

We have already mentioned some of the evidences of the bandwagon effect of this view of human nature according to the gospel of the innate aggressionists. This is to be seen in art, the novel, and especially in the seemingly motiveless malignity of recent films. The belief of the makers of these films is that human nature dictates a cruel or brutal resolution to every conflict, perhaps every contact, between humans. The writings of Mr. Ardrey and everyday "observation" are cited in support of these beliefs. As we have seen in the preceding chapters, Ardrey and the kind of "observation" upon which his disciples depend are both rather slender reeds upon which to lean for support. Observation of the sometimes violent behavior of animals and of men, no matter how extensive it may be, tells us nothing of the origins or causes of that behavior. Nor do naïve explanations of human behavior dressed up in the language of ethology contribute anything but seemingly plausible but essentially antirational obfuscations of the nature of human nature.

Scientism and Human Nature

Study of the behavior of other animals, especially under natural conditions, can teach us a great deal about the behavior of human beings, but only if we always remember that they are very different creatures from ourselves, that we are human. It takes a great deal of knowledge and much skill in interpretation to bring the findings of ethology to bear upon the analysis of human behavior. The study of the origins and evolution of human behavior is an extremely complex one, much more complex than, say, neurophysiology or plasma physics. Yet no one who lacked specific training in these subjects would dare write or deliver an opinion involving some technical aspect of these fields. Nonetheless, when it comes to human nature, since we are all so very much in the midst of it, we are—most of us—instant authorities on the subject, in spite of the fact that human nature is one of the most difficult to understand of all the phenomena on this earth.

It is, of course, good and desirable that we should be interested in understanding our own behavior and that of other human beings in all its fascinating variety, but we do ourselves a disservice when we take it for granted that it is easily explicable by an appeal to what other animals do. When we do that we tend to oversimplify and to settle for easy explanations. Not only lay persons do this; scientists are also capable of the same error, especially when they step out of their own field onto unfamiliar ground. In such circumstances when they happen to become enamored of a particular theory they have been known to exhibit an omniscience, dogmatic absolutism, and mystic privilege they would never claim within the confines of their own fields.

Unfortunately, in such conditions we have the "halo effect" in operation. One may be an ethologist like Konrad Lorenz or Desmond Morris, or one may be a playwright like Robert Ardrey, and each of them will see the meaning of the world according to the kingdom that is within him. Lorenz is really a moralist interested in the problem of evil, as is clear, among other things, from the German title of *On Aggression,* namely, *Das Sogennante Böse*—that is, "The So-Called Evil"—and his later book, *Civilized Man's Eight Deadly Sins* (1974). To be as deeply interested in morals and in evil as Lorenz is, is of course commendable. What is questionable is whether animal ethology, at least at this stage of its development, has anything to contribute toward the understanding of either morals or evil in humans, which it seems to me, are essentially cultural and metaphysical problems. Even though their effects may be biological, it only serves to confuse the issue to approach them as biological problems.

But to return to the scientism of scientists. Ideological distortions of science can be insidiously seductive. When pillars of the scientific establishment venture pronouncements outside their own fields of competence, they may be said to function as so many flying buttresses, giving support to all sorts of rickety and precarious edifices. Even in their own fields, and especially in one so complex as animal behavior, scientists often fall into prejudiced fudgings and anthropomorphisms of which they themselves seem to be unaware, as when they read human emotions into other animals and then extrapolate from such glosses to quite unjustifiable conclusions about the nature of man. "My dear Graylag Goose, Ada, several times a widow," who was recognizable by "the grief-marked expression of her eyes."

"How charming," we say, "and how touching," failing to perceive that the magician, in this case Professor Lorenz, has pulled off yet another of his favorite anthropomorphic tricks, and has slipped, unseen, human marriage, mourning, and grief under the feathers of his Graylag Goose. This is a kind of prestidigitation that would scarcely be of much moment were it not for the fact that such ideas are often taken seriously, especially when the behavior of animals is made to do service as an explanation for human behavior. This is what the innate aggressionists have in fact done, and, un- critically accepted, the ideological consequences of their views could prove very damaging indeed. In response we might almost take our stand with Coriolanus, and declare:

> I'll never
> Be such a gosling to obey instinct; but stand
> As if a man were author of himself,
> And knew no other kin.
> *Coriolanus,* act v, scene iii.

Social and Political Consequences

The ideas of the innate aggressionists are capable of creating a climate of opinion that could lead to the most unfortunate social and political action. To give point to this statement let me quote from a communication by a physician to the *Journal of the American Medical Association.* "Ardrey," he writes, "may have something important to say regarding the directions we are taking in providing for health care. He presents a strong argument for three basic biological needs of all creatures, including man: (1) identification or status, (2) stimulation or excitement, and in a poor third position, security. When security is accentuated as in the provision of total health care, man is denied the means of obtaining stimulation and excitement, and turns in abnormal direc- tions such as to drugs, violence, or rebellion." And the writer concludes: "A further study of what Ardrey has to say to medicine as well as to society in general is vitally important."

Identification or status, stimulation, and excitement, all of which are abundant in America, are all right, but, according to this physician, the poorly positioned security can be overdone when it becomes a main object of life, and stimulation and excitement as a result are diminished. Hence, stimulation and excitement are likely to be sought in drugs, violence, and rebellion. So much, then, for the welfare state. The Scandinavian welfare states have for many years provided their people with complete security, from the cradle to the grave. A principal complaint heard in these societies is that stimulation and excitement are, indeed, diminished, the people are anything but rebellious, and while the suicide rate long before the advent of the welfare state was always high, violence rates of every kind are comparatively low, and drugs are not a problem since alcohol has been the traditional anodyne.

Our American physician's argument is clearly aimed against National Medicine, for as the president of the American Medical Association put it in his Inaugural Address in 1967, "We are faced with the concept of health care as a right rather than a privilege." If one can bring support to that view of the claim of the citizen to the care of his health from such an authority as Robert Ardrey, he may indeed have something "vitally important" to say to many physicians.

On an earlier page, it will be recalled, we read an English physician and writer, Dr. John Rowan Wilson, commenting approvingly on Ardrey's *The Territorial Imperative*, observing that racial prejudice and distrust of the foreigner may be the factors that hold societies together; that perhaps we ought to give up the attempt to understand and love our

neighbors, and instead keep to ourselves, "barking across
our fences now and then, and baring our fangs in ritualized
aggression."

It is to such dismal conclusions that the writings of the
innate aggressionists lead. Let us cultivate our gardens, and
be sure to erect our fences securely around them, not only
to keep our neighbors out but also to let them know every
so often by the proper display of teeth that we are ready to
defend our territory against all foreign invaders, "particularly those of a noticeably different culture and physical appearance." As for brotherly love, equality, and other such
"platitudes," they are strictly for those whom Ardrey calls
"romantics," and, we may suppose, similar unrealistic
dreamers of dreams, the "Christian Scientists of Sociology,"
as Tiger and Fox call them, the "egalitarians," as Lorenz
labels them. According to them the party of humanity is
strictly for the transcendentalists. But the truth as revealed to
the innate aggressionists is for realists who are willing to accept the facts. It is in such a guise that the new barbarism may
descend upon us.

The political overtones of much of the innate aggressionists' writings is fairly obvious. Here is a typical passage
from *On Aggression,* in which Lorenz writes: "The hostile
neighboring tribe, once the target at which to discharge
phylogenetically programmed aggression, has now withdrawn to an ideal distance, hidden behind a curtain, if possible of iron. Among the many phylogenetically adopted
norms of human social behavior, there is hardly one that
does not need to be controlled and kept on leash by responsible morality."

The reference to an "iron" curtain is, presumably, not
undeliberate, and "a responsible morality," supposedly enforced by the state, must be devised to keep the phylogenetically adopted norms in leash.

Contemporary innate aggressionism differs from Social Darwinism only in that it draws upon newer material for support, and is less open in declaring its advocacy of reactionary ideas and totalitarian politics. As Dr. Patrick Bateson, lecturer in zoology at Cambridge University, has pointed out, the innate aggressionists "are not so much making a plea for certain kinds of investigation as prescribing courses of action for society at large."

It is, of course, very comforting to "the true believers" to be told that what some have claimed to be remediable social ills are, in fact, inherent in the very nature of things; that it is not the social system that produces the aggressiveness we see all about us, but that man's destructiveness and cruelty are part of his nature. Hence, it is a naïve "romantic fallacy," Mr. Ardrey derisively tells us, to expect that social changes which would better the lot of millions of frustrated and unfulfilled human beings would in any way help to reduce the inherent aggressiveness of men. This, in the language of the day, is a cop-out. There are only two irremediable human conditions, as has long been recognized, one is aging and the other is death, and I am not so sure about the former. In any event, as for the disruptive conditions of human life there is nothing about them that cannot be remedied. It is a myth to talk about the irremediable human condition. That condition where it needs remedying can be ameliorated by attending to the social ills to which human beings are subjected so that they may live in dignity and enjoy the autonomy and power for good of their own personalities, in freedom and fulfillment. It is our social conditions, *not* our genetic condition, that require the focus of our attention.

Neither Mr. Ardrey nor Professor Lorenz has left any doubt concerning the political implications of their beliefs, even though they have not been as explicit as one might have expected. Just as it was a socio-political view of the relations of men in society that Darwin adopted from Malthus and translated into a biological theory of the evolution of all living forms, so, too, we have reason to believe that the ethological theories of Ardrey and Lorenz relating to man's aggressiveness have grown out of their political predilections. This is the kind of human tendency from which hardly any theorizing human being is ever exempt, and least of all the present writer. None of us is possessed of the absolute truth. Such truth is the privilege of only one class of human beings, absolute fools. For a scientist certainty has nothing to do with absolutes. Certainty for a scientist constitutes the highest degree of probability that attaches to a particular judgment at a particular time level. The method of science is, in a word, verification, the continuous checking, testing, and examining of hypotheses. As Mark Twain put it, "Supposing is good, but finding out is better."

The ideas of the innate aggressionists find their way into strange places. For example, in a book on the attitudes of Americans toward the wilderness during the last three and a half centuries. Roderick Nash, professor of history at the University of California at Santa Barbara, in the second edition of his book *Wilderness and the American Mind* (1973), tells how his views concerning wilderness came to be completely changed as a consequence of his becoming acquainted with the writings of the innate aggressionists. In the new edition of his book he now takes the view that "the explanation of man's conduct and attitudes lies not in the five-thousand-year veneer we call 'history,'" as he had formerly believed, "but in the mind-boggling millennia that went before." On the basis of this new illumination Professor Nash constructs a whole new theory which seeks to explain man's attitudes toward the wilderness, the main components of these attitudes being fear and hatred. Behold, the new history!

Prejudices have a way of becoming hypotheses and by easy stages growing from theories into "facts." A fact is a verified hypothesis, but verification is itself capable of being prejudiced. Of this there are many examples, even among the most distinguished scientists. The methods of verification employed by such scientists as Richard Owen, the great English palaeontologist, and Louis Agassiz, his American contemporary, for example, did nothing to alter their steadfast refusal to accept Darwin's theory of evolution. Francis Galton and Karl Pearson, the two founding fathers of modern statistical methods, committed the most egregious scientific solecisms in the firm belief that their statistical methods of verification could solve virtually any problem of human and social biology. Hence, the importance of independent verification by others.

Both Mr. Ardrey and Professor Lorenz imply that most behavioral scientists are engaged in a conspiracy to perpetuate various "false" ideas concerning human nature. Ardrey refers to the "party line." "All scientists," he writes, "must accept the responsibility of hiding from public view, so that scientific infallibility may be preserved, the picture that so many know so well. It is the picture of cultural anthropology, behaviorist psychology, and environmentalist sociology like three drunken friends leaning against a lamppost in the enchantment of euphoria, all convinced that they are holding up the eternal light when in truth they hold up nothing but each other."

One anthropologist, Robin Fox, professor of anthropology at Rutgers University, in a review in *The New Republic* quotes this passage with complete approval, and describes it as "beautiful!" Standards of what is beautiful seem to differ, even among anthropologists.

On an earlier page in the same book, *The Social Contract,* Mr. Ardrey writes "that the three sciences central to human understanding—psychology, anthropology, and sociology—successfully and continually lie to themselves, lie to each other, lie to their students, and lie to the public at large, must constitute a paramount wonder of a scientific century. Were their conditions generally known, they would be classified as public drunks."

These remarks effectively speak for themselves.

Prediction and the Self-fulfilling Prophecy

It is the demand for hypotheses of predictive value, Mr. Ardrey tells us, that has inspired his inquiries, so that once we know what the nature of man is we can predict and prescribe the course his future development should take. It follows from his and Lorenz's viewpoints that certain controls will have to be imposed on people if their aggressiveness is to be kept within reasonable bounds.

Here it should be pointed out that for predictive or any other purposes the claim that man is innately aggressive partakes of the nature of a self-fulfilling prophecy. If we are convinced that we are innately aggressive we will begin to see ourselves as such, and begin to act out the role that is expected of us. It is true that we ought to attempt to control our aggressiveness, but we shall always be able to excuse recidivism on the basis of theories such as "spontaneity" and "instinct." Our tendency to accept violence as a normal form of behavior is made all the more tolerable, if not acceptable, when we are told that it is man's nature to be violent, a bequest from his prehistoric ancestors. As Vincent Ruggiero,

professor of English at the State University of New York at
Delhi, has remarked, there is a point at which speculation
becomes creation. The view that man is innately aggressive
has reached that point, and it is a view that for considerable
numbers has shaped their conception of human nature. It
happens to be an image of man that constitutes a sorry par-
ody of his unique evolutionary history. According to the innate aggressionists, man experienced an evolutionary Fall
with the invention of weapons. And, indeed, as we have
seen, they assert that man owes his origin as man to the invention of weapons. But there was no invention of weapons
nor was there an evolutionary Fall with the advent of man.
The invention of weapons (as distinct from implements)
and the Fall came millions of years after the origination of
man, apparently during the Neolithic period, some 15,000
or so years ago—possibly somewhat earlier, but principally associated with the development of agriculture and the growth
of village life.

Humanity Makes Itself

It should be evident that no matter what the lives of our
prehistoric ancestors may have been, their ways of life do
not in the least place any constraints upon us or in any way
require us to conform to any of their patterns of behavior.
In spite of what the innate aggressionists believe, we are not
programmed to proceed like so many automata in predestinate grooves. Our view of human nature, the image we have
of ourselves, exercises a determinative effect upon our conduct and our society. It is, therefore, important always to remember that humanity has made and remade itself again
and again, and that what it has done in the past it can do
and will be capable of doing in the future. As Patrick Bateson has said, "If we think of ourselves as aggressive, as

hoarders of property, and as incorrigibly class-conscious, that's how we'll stay. If, on the other hand, we see ourselves as gentle, co-operative and equal in status, maybe we'll become a little more like that."

Men and societies have made themselves according to the image they have had of themselves, and they have changed in accordance with the changing image they have developed. History is replete with such instances, the most recent of which is the British. As the leading imperialist nation of the world Britain voluntarily shed itself of its empire and dependencies even though it meant a stupendous decline in its power and the subsequent development of foreseeable economic problems at home. Going back to earlier times, the boisterous joy of life of the English in Elizabethan days and the lusty libertinism of the Restoration Englishman contrast sharply with the prudery of the Victorian Age. The Englishman's image of himself in the sixteenth century was very different from that he held of himself in the seventeenth century, and still more different in the nineteenth century. The Scandinavian peoples constitute another example. From the violent sea-raiders they once were they have become among the most peaceful peoples of the earth. The Japanese are a very different people from what they were before their contact with Commodore Perry, and so we might go on for many other peoples, especially in recent times, who have changed according to the new image they have developed of themselves.

Territoriality, Racism, and Inequality

Among the most dangerous of the ideological consequences of the innate aggressionists' views is the plausibility with which they make acceptable an image of man that could readily lead to a political and social totalitarianism. As John

Hurrell Crook has said, "The fact that a given viewpoint is academically unsound may not lessen the impact nor prevent it finding expression in the social attitudes and political views of the less disciplined." Crook goes on to remark that many of the views, especially those purveyed by Robert Ardrey, suggest that it would be a biologically quite natural event were territorially defended racial enclaves to be established in the United States and elsewhere. Views much the same as Ardrey's have been expressed by Lorenz. Both attack the "egalitarians" and the notion of equality. "The inequality of races," says Ardrey, "if it exists, must be systematic. It must rest on discernible factors in the differing natural selection placed on the hodge-podge of human mosaics to which we give the term 'race.'"

It is to be regretted that nowhere does Ardrey make reference to the fact that Professor Theodosius Dobzhansky and I, in a paper entitled "Natural Selection and the Mental Capacities of Mankind," published in *Science* as long ago as June 1947, examined the whole matter from the evolutionary, genetic, and anthropological standpoints. In that paper we concluded that since the challenges of the environment everywhere were much the same, favoring plasticity rather than fixity of response, the effect of natural selection in man has probably been to render genetic differences in personality traits, as between individuals and particularly as between races, relatively unimportant compared with their observable plasticity. As Professor George Gaylord Simpson put it, "When human races were evolving it is certain that increase in mental ability was advantageous to *all* of them. It would, then, have tended over the generations to have spread among all of them in approximately equal degrees. For any one race to lag definitely behind another in over-all genetic adaptation, the two would have to be genetically isolated over a very large number of generations. They would, in fact, have to become distinct species; but human races are all interlocking parts of just one species."

Similar views have been expressed by a number of other scientists. Such views, which Mr. Ardrey prefers to ignore, are shared by most geneticists, evolutionary biologists, and anthropologists, but not by Ardrey, and certainly not by Professor Lorenz. The latter attacks a straw man of his own creation which he calls the "pseudodemocratic doctrine," namely, the view that all men are born biologically equal. It would be of great interest if Lorenz would name a single scientist who ever made such a claim. The alleged "egalitarian" viewpoint, Lorenz says, is completely antibiological. And so it would be if anyone ever made it. The truth is that the "egalitarians" of whom I have any knowledge know that human beings vary considerably in their biological endowment, and that no two are ever the same—not even so-called identical twins—but that whatever their physical and mental variability all human beings are or should be born with equal rights to personal fulfillment and political freedom. In misrepresenting the views of "egalitarians" Lorenz makes it easy for the reader to interpret his remarks as an attack upon the idea of racial equality. By completely ignoring the work of a whole generation of geneticists like Herman Muller, J. B. S. Haldane, Sewall Wright, Julian Huxley, Theodosius Dobzhansky, Bentley Glass, L. L. Cavalli-Sforza, W. F. Bodmer, and many others, Ardrey and Lorenz leave the impression that the subject of race is a domain of investigation in which nothing but emotion and political bias prevail. While it is true that the subject of race has often been discussed in an atmosphere in which both emotion and political prejudice have played a dominant role, this does not mean that there is not also a great deal of solid scientific evidence which has led workers in this field to the conclusion that whatever differences may exist between races they are not of a kind which require any inequality of treatment.

The danger of such views as Lorenz and Ardrey have popularized is that they tend to divert attention from the real causes of inequality between members of different races and cast into contempt and disrepute the attempts to equalize the conditions of life and the full enjoyment of social and political rights of all human beings within what could one day become once again the family of humanity. Views such as those expressed by Lorenz and Ardrey could quite easily be exploited by a nationalist racist ideology such as the inhuman apartheid doctrine in practice in South Africa and in Ian Smith's Rhodesia, as well as enlisted to serve and reinforce the endemic racism of the United States.

The innate aggressionists do not seek to justify war—in fact, they agree with most of the human race in deploring it—but by attributing it to instinctive drives they make it appear inevitable and inescapable. Finally, with their instinctivist approach they divert attention from the conditions and causes of war to which we should be actively attending. As I have already mentioned in an earlier chapter of this book, there are some teachers of political science who have expressed the hope that Ardrey's *The Territorial Imperative* will be widely read, "especially in Washington, D.C." There can be little doubt that the writings of the innate aggressionists have not gone unnoticed there, for they provide a more than acceptable rationalization for the policies of the Pentagon and related agencies of government.

In all the areas mentioned, as well as numerous others unmentioned, such as child-rearing, education, social services, the very structure of society itself, the effects of the innate aggressionists' views would undoubtedly be reactionary. Fortunately, as we have seen in the preceding pages, these views are quite unsound. Human beings are not puppets designed to be manipulated by a phylogenetically triune brain which impels them toward acts of cruelty and destructiveness. It is true that human beings have in the millions been turned into something resembling puppets, but this has been achieved not by a system of phylogenetic programming, but by a system of social programming, through social ideologies transmitted through the family, the schools, and the state. When every allowance has been made for biological and individual genetic factors in influencing the behavior of human beings, it must be recognized that by virtue of their unique educability they are, at least in the matter of aggression and cooperation, capable of becoming whatever they are trained to be. Our tasks for the future should be to train the child for cooperation, and to discourage *every kind* of aggressive behavior. We have evidence in small societies and among ourselves in particular families that such training is feasible and that it works. This, at least, is an ideology that would be worth giving a practical trial.

A genuinely healthy society is maintained and sustained not by the competitive struggle for existence to achieve a factitious success, but by a striving for that human cooperativeness which is the true dignity of man, and the respect that humans owe to each other.

12

Conclusions

The "New" Image of Man

The writings of the innate aggressionists leave one with the impression that man is little more than a mechanism driven by innate instincts ineradicably inherited from ancestral "killer" apes. It is a dreary picture they have painted, and were it true the future of the species would, indeed, be dark and unpromising. In the preceding pages I have endeavored to examine the views of these writers in the light of the scientific evidence, and I hope I have succeeded in showing that on every one of the fundamental claims they have made concerning man's allegedly instinctive aggressive drives they are demonstrably wrong. This is important, and constitutes something more than a mere exercise in scientific polemics, for what is involved here is not simply the understanding of the nature of man but also the image of man that grows out of that understanding. It is, therefore, most urgent that we do not falsely base our image of man upon unsound foundations even though we may not fully understand what the sound ones may be, for the image we hold of man, of ourselves, is the image that will largely influence our individual and collective behavior toward ourselves and toward our fellow man. The aftermath of two world wars, the unspeakable horrors of the Hitlerian holocaust, not to mention the more recent involvement of the United States in Indochina, have understandably left most people with a strong conviction of man's innate depravity. Man is, we customarily say, the most aggressive creature on this earth, and the most destructive. But "man" is not any of the terrible things that have been attributed to him; it is only some men who are. The cruelties of such men and the sadistic pleasures they take in inflicting torture and pain on their fellow human beings, not to mention countless other creatures, are facts, but they are the crimes committed by a minority of men— *not* by the majority. To indict the whole species for the terrible excesses committed by a few is as erroneous as it is unjust. Even if it were true that all men are cruel and destructive, that in itself would not prove that they are innately so. Learning could account for the universal noxiousness. But since cruelty and destruction are far from universal in the human species, and there are examples of several peoples who are characteristically unaggressive, whatever the causes of their unaggressiveness they give the lie to the blanket stigmatization of the whole species.

Environmental Influences of Behavioral Expression

We think the evidence overwhelmingly indicates that it is the social environments of humans that largely determine how their genes, whatever their propensities may be, will express themselves. We have seen that there is good reason to believe that during almost the whole of man's evolutionary history he lived in peace and cooperation with his fellow man.

As societies evolved technologically they usually became

progressively more violent and vastly more efficient in their destructiveness. Civilized man everywhere today lives under the threat of annihilation by weapons infinitely more powerful than any that have been previously available. The power of persuasion over force, of which Plato wrote more than two millennia ago, and which he defined as civilization, seems to have been worsted in the debate with the argument of force.

War, the "Beast," and the "Savage"

In the six thousand years of recorded history there have been many wars between peoples—no one knows exactly how many. Periods of uninterrupted peace have not been many. Since 1945 the nations of the world have almost doubled, from 68 to 129, each with its national destiny to achieve, its own border to defend, its own power of decision, and—thanks to the cold war and the resulting supplies of weapons and military training—its own armed forces. Today there are more military men acting as political leaders than at any time in the twentieth century. The bloody conflicts between Catholics and Protestants in Northern Ireland, between Cypriots and Greeks on Cyprus, between West and East Pakistanis, Nigerians and Biafrans, North and South Vietnamese, to name but a few of the most recent conflicts, abundantly testify to the institutionalization of violence.

The frightening and increasing violence in our cities, with murder, aggravated assault, and forcible rape the most rapidly increasing of crimes—all seems to lend support to the view that man must universally be driven to his acts of aggression by some deep-seated internal force. It is certainly a very obvious and simple conclusion to draw from the evidence. Darwin drew it and so did Freud, and so have many thinkers before and since. Darwin, in *The Origin of Species,* spoke of "the warfare of nature," and since man was a part of nature, it was to be expected that man, too, would be a warlike creature. Freud, in *Civilization and Its Discontents* (1930), spoke of men as wolves to their fellow men, whose aggressiveness "manifests itself spontaneously and reveals men as savage beasts to whom the thought of sparing their own kind is alien." On every point—on his Hobbesian view of nature, on wolves, on the spontaneity of aggression, on savages, and on beasts—Freud is wrong, profoundly and abysmally wrong. There is no warfare of nature. If there is a law of nature, it is in the balance between cooperation and conflict leading to stable cooperative societies. But in an Age of Conflict this is not the viewing glass through which nature is likely to be looked at. The social context from which we judge events, our particular and special ideologies, color our judgments. Animals make no war, nor are they in a constant state of conflict; rarely do they kill their own kind. In fact, compared with man most animals are natural pacifists. When they fight among themselves seldom is it to inflict injury, and rarely do their fights end in death. Their aggressive behavior is primarily a way of competition rather than destruction. Wolves, contrary to Freud and popular belief, do not attack other wolves. Aggressiveness in men and other animals is not spontaneous, but must have some external stimulus before it can be activated. Beasts are not savage, and "savages" are seldom as savage as they are accused of being. In an age of escalating violence it has become fashionable to blame our animal relatives for many of the distressing things we do to each other. Animals make good scapegoats. They can bring no suits for libel, neither can they protest against the loads of mythology with which they have been traditionally saddled. Hence the myth of the beast from which we are said to derive the animal within us, the animal that causes us to behave like a "beast." The "beast," with all its accumulated pejorative connotations, helps to explain for us the source of human aggressiveness and cruelty. But since man is the only mass killer of his own kind, the innate aggressionists, not being able to saddle the rest of the animal kingdom with that particular blemish, must nevertheless find a biological solution to that problem. Their solution is that man shares with the rest of the animal kingdom an instinct of aggression, but that whereas other animals have developed biologically determined appeasement gestures or ritualizations—that is to say, behaviors designed to communicate emotional states, which quickly terminate the aggressive behavior in the dominant animal— man, because his cultural development has outpaced his capacity to develop such biological inhibitory behaviors, lacks them and therefore continues to be the killer he always was.

The wholly unwarranted assumption that man has always been a killer of his own kind is based on the view that from the moment his early ancestors took to toolmaking they used those tools as weapons not only against other animals but also against fellow men. Since he never developed those ritual forms of behavior which serve to inhibit killing, man, so the theory goes, has remained a killer throughout his history.

Having examined these views from every possible approach, we have seen that they will not stand up to critical examination. The idea, therefore, that man is an innate killer may be rejected as wholly unsound.

Distortion and Misfocus

It is a characteristic of the innate aggressionists that, for the most part, they abjure the study of the relevant anthropological literature, and even the ethological data that fail to

Conclusions

305

support their theories. As Professor Roger N. Johnson has said, "Instinct theorists have chosen to ignore the bulk of the scientific literature on aggression, either by choice or out of ignorance. One need only glance at the reference section of a book like *On Aggression* (Lorenz, 1966) to see that the evidence cited is very limited. It is not even a good sample of the scientific literature on animal aggression." Professor J. P. Scott, reflecting on the anomaly of a biologist publishing a book which leaves out of consideration most of the scientific discoveries of the last fifty years, attributed the omission to the fact that Lorenz is a very narrow specialist who knows a great deal about the behavior of birds, but who "evidently reads very little other than material which is directly related to his own specialty." Erich Fromm comments on the fact that while Lorenz may be a competent observer of lower animals it seems clear to him that his knowledge of man does not go beyond that of the average person, nor that he has "refined it either by systematic observation or by sufficient acquaintance with the literature." Indeed, as we have already remarked, when specialists step outside the boundaries of their own fields their opinions on other subjects, no matter how glittering the halo they have acquired in their own realm, are not likely to be of much more worth than those of others who deliver themselves on matters outside their own expertise. As Professor Dennis Chitty has remarked, "Gratifying as it is to have their work acclaimed, zoologists would nevertheless be wiser to put their own house in order before allowing conclusions whose truth is at present arguable even within their proper contexts to act as props for still more arguable interpretations of human conduct." It is a consummation devoutly to be wished.

When Robert Ardrey puts on the title pages of his books that they represent "a personal inquiry," that is, at least, candid. But he, too, completely neglects any consideration

306   *The Nature of Human Aggression*

of the evidence or criticisms of his ideas which would nullify the validity of his "personal" views.

The argument by analogy, the extrapolations from animals to humans, the one-sided interpretations, and usually misinterpretations, of the facts as they relate to humans, the misapplied and quite irrelevant anecdotes, together with the tendentiousness of their arguments, all combine to make the writings of the innate aggressionists undependable and misleading. Since the works of these writers are all composed with skill and persuasiveness, and, indeed, make most beguiling and stimulating reading, they have served to draw attention to some of the most urgent of human problems confronting man today. Where more dependable writers have failed, the innate aggressionists have succeeded in enlisting the attention of a wide readership. And it is because they have misfocused that attention on erroneous explanations of the origin of human aggression, and the consequences to which that misfocus could lead, that it has been felt necessary to put the facts in proper perspective. This we have attempted to do in this book.

In addition to outmoded attempts to explain human behavior by the resort to "instinct" or "innate" determinants, perhaps the worst and most egregious error committed by the innate aggressionists is their elementary failure to understand the meaning of our humanity. As Crook has put it, "The new genre of popular biological exposition neglects the humanity of man." Our genius is our humanity—and at the same time it is our greatest danger. Any attempt to explain human behavior without taking that humanity into account is like attempting to explain *Hamlet* by omitting the Prince of Denmark from the play. It is the quality of humanity that distinguishes *Homo sapiens* from all other creatures. And by humanity we mean not merely our capacity for being humane, kind, and compassionate, but also the combination of traits that renders it possible for humans to make those adjustments to the challenges of the environment of which they alone, as human beings, are capable.

The Plasticity of Human Behavior

When we look over the enormous range and variety of behavioral adjustments that humans have been called upon to make to the great variety of challenges with which they have been confronted, we cannot help but be impressed by humanity's inventiveness and ingenuity. But necessary as those behavioral traits were for physical survival, what was clearly more essential for the survival of both the individual and the group was the dependence of humans on each other. Such dependence is the indispensable condition for the survival of any society. When for any reason the members of a society become concerned exclusively with their own selfish interests, so alienated from the rest of the group that they lose all sense of involvement in them, and live entirely for themselves, such a society is doomed to extinction. The Ik, to whom reference was made on an earlier page, represent such a people.

Robert Ardrey writes of Turnbull's description of this people: "I cannot think what social scientists will do about this book, since it attacks their central assumption: Man is by nature good, or at least neutral, and what vices or aggressions he may demonstrate are distortions in his nature brought on by social forces." The answer, as we have seen, is that in the case of the starving Ik it was precisely those social forces, the power of which Mr. Ardrey denies, that within three generations turned them into the monstrous creatures they became. Why the Ik fell into this Hobbesian way of life rather than that followed by other gatherer-hunter groups who, when faced with starvation, as for ex-

ample the Eskimo and American Indian, choose to sacrifice
themselves so that others might live, would be a matter for
further inquiry. But certainly the easy "explanation" which
so appeals to an innate aggressionist like Ardrey is abundantly refuted by the evidence of innumerable peoples who
under prolonged stress maintained their dignity as human
beings and rejected all temptation to fail each other. That
there have been some cases of failure does not prove that
humans are innately concerned only for themselves, any
more than the history and frequency of violent behavior in
humans proves that aggressiveness is innate.

Genes and Environment

That human beings inherit genes which influence human
behavior is a fact. It is also a fact that genes for basic forms
of human behavior such as aggression, love, and altruism are
the products of a long evolutionary history, and that in any
serious examination of the nature of such forms of human
behavior the evolutionary history of the species and its relations must be taken into account. In the development of human behavior evolutionary pressures have been at work
over a long period of time, but they are evolutionary pressures that have been influenced by a unique social environment, a wholly new zone of adaptation, namely, that of
culture.

As a consequence of cultural selective pressures humanity
has greatly influenced the genetic substrates of its own behavioral development. This does not mean that humans
have been altogether freed from the influences of genes
which similarly affect the behavior of other animals, but it
does mean that in humans behavior is far less under the direction of genes than is that of other animals. Furthermore,

that the educability, lack of fixity, and remarkable flexibility of the human genetic constitution is such that humans are able, as a consequence of their socialization, to canalize the behavioral expression of genetic influences in all sorts of ways, creative as well as destructive.

To a greater or lesser extent learning and what is learned are genetically influenced, but learning and what is learned are also influenced to a very large extent by the human environment. To repeat once more, to some extent behavior is always the expression of the interaction between genetic tendencies and environmental influences.

The behavioral species trait of *Homo sapiens,* namely, educability, makes it possible for human beings to mold genetic behavior tendencies in a variety of different ways. Since the expression of genes is a function of the environment, genes are subject to human control. In humans that control can be considerable. Humans differ behaviorally from other animals in their possession of a genetic constitution which is much more amenable to the influences of the cultural environment. This does not, of course, mean that genetic substrates for behavior play an insignificant role in influencing certain human behaviors, but it does mean that such genetic factors do not determine the development of such behaviors.

What we can legitimately conclude when the full range of human behavior is considered, from the most loving to the most murderous, is that humans are creatures potentially capable of any form of behavior, depending largely upon the socialization, the conditioning, which they have undergone from infancy. This is not to deny in any way that some genetic contribution, direct or indirect, is involved in virtually every form of human behavior. But what it does deny is that that behavior is genetically determined. The conditioning environment interacts with the genetic potentials and the resulting behavior is the expression of that interaction. But whatever the nature of that interaction, it is the essentially human environment which will serve to turn the infant *Homo* into *Homo humanus,* into a human being. Without his potentialities for becoming so, humans could not, of course, be transformed into such creatures. Nor could they, with all those potentialities, be molded into human beings without the prolonged conditioning of a humanizing environment. So it should not be surprising that human beings become what they are as social beings largely as a consequence of the organizing or disorganizing influences of the environment acting upon the unique potentials of the individual. One can never quite separate the genetic from the cultural contribution to the development of the person as a human being. However, it is seldom difficult to determine that in the development of most social behaviors of the individual social factors have been the most influential. The culture of which the individual is a member may not be determined by genes, but the social behavior of the individual, though principally influenced by cultural conditioning, is to some extent also influenced by genes. What weight in any particular behavior is to be apportioned to genes and what to cultural conditioning, in any particular individual or any particular population, can only be decided, and then only approximately, by detailed study. But clearly cultures differ from each other not because of genes but because of the differences in the history of the experiences they have undergone. There are racists and others who would explain such differences as being due to genetic factors, but most scientists do not subscribe to such a view.

As Professor Paul E. Simonds of the University of Oregon has said, "The genetics of behavior tends not so much to determine behavior patterns as to set limits and define directions; in other words, it is a genetics of tendencies."

The Precariousness and Value of Human Life

In the course of humanity's immense and unique journey, unparalleled by any other creature, our species has acquitted itself well. Much of the time its chances of survival were not very high. From its very origin through all the days of its existence the challenges of the environment have been formidable. For a savanna-dwelling nomadic species, wandering in small bands from one source of food to another, with one child at a birth at intervals of several years, with high infant mortality, and an average longevity of about thirty-three years, this hairless, big-brained biped nevertheless managed to overcome all obstacles and threats to its continued existence, until it has become the most widespread and dominant species on earth.

Not that life was unduly hard, for it was far from that most of the time, but because life being itself precarious it was proportionately greatly valued and respected. No baby, if we may legitimately reason from the practices prevalent among recent gatherer-hunters, with the slightest abnormality was allowed to survive, a practice that would seem further to have contributed to the precarious balance of a population attempting to maintain itself. The custom was probably based on the traditional knowledge that a defective child would grow into a defective individual who would only serve to make life more difficult for the band and for itself in the struggle for existence. The sanctity of life was held to be something greater than life itself, a birthright in which the child had the right to be born and grow up free of physical and mental handicap. The deep affection which

gatherer-hunter peoples have for their children, and the
complete delightfulness of the children, have been repeatedly remarked by all who have come to know them. Because
they value and respect their children, and mothers nurse
their young for several years, a natural spacing takes place
between the birth of children, so that each is able to receive
the full attention of its parents. It is laughter and play that
one hears and sees among children most of the time, not
quarreling and fighting. And while quarrels and fights may
occur among adults, these tend, as we have seen, to be occasional and seldom serious.

I am attempting to state the facts without glossing over
any of the unpleasant ones in the lives of gatherer-hunters,
and presumably of our prehistoric ancestors. They do occasionally quarrel; they do sometimes fight; they even on occasion have been known to kill members of their own group.
But such occasions are for the most part comparatively rare.
Gatherer-hunters, being human, know that to be human is
to be in danger, that in order to survive their humanity
must be brought to bear upon the solution of the problems
with which they are daily confronted, not alone in interaction with their own kind but with the whole of nature, in-
animate as well as animate. Hence, the gatherer-hunters live
in amity with each other, with the living creatures around
them, and with the world that sustains them all. It is not an
unfriendly world, a world in which the allegedly hostile
forces of nature are pitted against the puny human. Nature
is not hostile, nor do gatherer-hunters consider it so. Even
though they may occasionally be exposed to thirst and famine, their view of nature is that it is bountiful, the great nur-
turer, the Great Mother, the sustainer and supporter of life,
in which all things are interrelated and, hence, involved in
each other.

Cooperation

By the measure of such a view of life there is no room for killing or the resolution of interpersonal conflict by resort to violence. It may occur, but it seldom does. We may be impressed by the primitiveness of primitive humans, by the gatherer-hunter Bushmen or Australian aborigines, but what impresses us beyond all else is their natural dignity, their humanity, and how essentially peaceful and unaggressive they usually are. We stand and marvel at the ingenuity with which they have adapted themselves to their environment, the skill with which they have fashioned their tools and implements, the cultures they have developed. But what we come most to admire when we get to know them is the image which they have of themselves, and the name reflecting this, by which they often call themselves, defining them as human beings. And even more admirable than this is the image that we can now see them presenting during the long continuum of human history, as the creatures who managed to survive, not because they were killers but because they were cooperators. Not because they cooperated to kill, but because they cooperated to nurture and to nourish. Speaking of aboriginal peoples whose subsistence-economy is fishing-hunting, agriculture, or stock-herding, Paul Radin wrote: "If one were asked to state briefly and succinctly what are the outstanding positive features of aboriginal civilizations, I, for one, would have no hesitation in answering that there are three: the respect for the individual, irrespective of age or sex; the amazing degree of social and political integration achieved by them; and the existence there of a concept of personal security which transcends all governmental forms and all tribal and group interests and conflicts." Those are the opening words of Paul Radin's *The World of Primitive Man*. In his final chapter he writes: "Happiness, love and affection, humility and modesty, kindness and forbearance, play a dominant role in their civilizations. To attain them is, in fact, the goal of every individual's life."

In the broad and illuminating spectrum of writing by anthropologists and others who have lived among "primitive" peoples, allowing for all the exceptions, it is the humanity, the dignity, and the quality of the individual that is repeatedly emphasized. Of course, as human beings, they are capable of the full range of human emotion and conduct, but in the interest of the group the individual is trained in the control of both, opportunities being provided on ceremonial occasions for the ritualized expression of emotion and sometimes aggressive behavior. The structure of the human brain may simulate the successive geological strata of the earth, and the neocortex, the gray matter with which we think, may overlie and be rooted in a primitive midbrain which contains remnants of a brain organization from our remote reptilian origins, but it is gravely to be doubted whether it is justifiable to speak of this old brain, the archepallium, as if it contained functional behavioral remnants of our "bestial" past which, do what we will, must find expression in aggressive behavior. There is no "center" or region of the brain which compels us to be aggressive, nor is there anything in our genes which renders aggression inevitable, but there are areas of the brain and there are genes that can readily be organized by the appropriate experience to produce aggressive behavior. In other words, the brain contains elements which, under certain kinds of stimulation, can be quickly mobilized to function in aggressive behavior—not as a result of "wiring," "programming," or "blueprinting," but rather as a consequence of the socially induced integration of cellular arrangements in the brain. The functioning of such cellular arrangements is very much more under conscious control in humans than it is in other animals, as is the experience which tends to produce aggressive behavior. There have been many societies and many individuals who have managed to reduce that kind of experience to a minimum, so that aggression in such societies and in such individuals is seldom observed. The sources of strength upon which such societies and their members in every society have drawn are present in ourselves. What they have achieved it is within our power as human beings also to achieve. The world we have made as civilized beings we have not made very well, but that fact does not foreclose the possibility of remaking it as it ought to be. It is not that the Golden Age lies in the buried past of our ancestors' Arcadian existence. Not in the least. The possibility of a Golden Age lies in the future, when humans will have learned to live as if to live and love were one. There is no Promised Land: only the promises we carry within ourselves. Meanwhile, we can begin by becoming once again involved in each other's welfare, and undeceive ourselves of those false prophets who seek to convince us that we are a scarred species, branded with the mark of Cain, driven by archaic impulses to violence and destruction.

Potentialities and Educability

Humans are neither naked apes nor fallen angels riven by that original sin, that great power of blackness, which Calvinistic commentators and their modern compeers have declared to actuate us. Neither are humans reducible to the category of animals, for we are the *human* animals, a humanity which adds to being a dimension lacking in all other animals, creatures of immense and extraordinary educability, capable of being molded into virtually every and any desired shape and form. Humans are not born *tabulae rasae,* blank tablets, without any predispositions whatever. They are born with many predispositions, to talk, to think, to engage in sexual behavior, to love, to be aggressive, and the like, but they will achieve none of these behaviors unless they are exposed to the external stimuli necessary for the development of those potentialities into abilities. It takes many months to learn how to speak. It may take years to learn how to love or how to engage in sexual behavior. It may take much less time to learn to be aggressive.

At birth the human infant is endowed with a large number of potentialities, some of which, like crying and weeping (i.e., crying with tears), smiling, and laughing, it will not altogether need to learn, but for the development of most of its other potentialities it will be dependent upon very specific kinds of social stimulation. It may be taken as axiomatic that genes in different ways significantly influence the development of behavioral traits in every individual, and hence, that no two individuals will ever be alike in the expression of their behavioral traits. The power of genes in the development of behavior is not to be underestimated, but neither should the organizing power of the social environment be underrated, for it is the human-made part of the environment that fashions the raw material supplied by potentialities into behavioral abilities. The genes for potential behavior, the potentialities, the predispositions, or whatever other name we may choose to call the genetic potentialities, are all there at birth, but only as potentialities. How, and to what extent, and to what degree they will develop, will depend upon the kind of organizing experience to which they are exposed. The genetic constitution which enables humans to function as human beings has been fashioned by the human environment, *not* by the animal environment. It is not that man or society has superimposed a socially learned series of controls over man's animal nature, but that human nature is itself a product of the history of our social development. It is the *human* nature of human nature that is the outstanding characteristic of humans, a fact too little understood, and therefore misinterpreted by the innate aggressionists. In any event, however much a behavioral trait may be genetically influenced, since the expression of every gene is a function of the environment, genetic influences are to a certain extent amenable to human control. Genes do not determine behavioral traits; what they do is to influence the responses of the organism to the environment, and those responses will differ as the environments acting upon the organism differ. As we have seen, in social environments in which cooperation and amiability are encouraged and the expression of aggressive behavior is discouraged, such behavior is thoroughly under control. This fact makes it clear, beyond dispute, that whatever genetic potentials for aggressive behavior with which the individual is born, whatever the biologic tendencies, the social environment is capable of so conditioning the individual that he or she develops as a fundamentally unaggressive person—as, for example, among the Tasaday of Mindanao, the Ifaluk of the Pacific, the Pygmies of the Ituri Forest, or the Semang of Malaya, to mention only four peoples, among whom aggressive behavior is so rare that when it occurs it is either group sanctioned or considered a sign of abnormality. The genetic potentialities for aggressive behavior shared by all these peoples with the rest of humanity have received so few of those stimulations necessary for the development of aggression, and so strong have been the negative social sanctions applied against the expression of aggressive behavior, they have simply learned to be nonaggressive. This does not mean that their genetic potentialities for aggression have been abolished or even attenuated. What it does mean is that those potentialities have not been afforded adequate opportunities for development.

American Indians are well known for their emotional restraint; when moved by the loss of a loved one of any age, they do not weep. This is not because they have lost the capacity to do so. All the neural and other organic arrangements necessary for weeping are there, but they have learned to control, to inhibit, their functioning. Many males of Anglo-Saxon countries especially have similarly learned not to weep because it is considered "unmanly" to do so. Most of them have learned the lesson so well that they are unable to weep even when they would wish to do so. It is much the same with aggression. Clearly, it is possible to grow up, even in a violent society such as that of the United States, in a family in which the conditions of socialization are so favorable for the development of nonaggression that the children and adults who are the products of such families tend to be as nonaggressive as human beings can be. It is the overwhelming consensus of the behavioral sciences that the personal attitudes and relationships of an individual to others are formed primarily on the pattern of his or her relationships with parents in early infancy and childhood, and that destructive aggression is, in most cases, a response to the experience of rejection, frustration, or aggression in infancy and childhood.

No human being has ever been born with aggressive or hostile impulses, and no one becomes aggressive or hostile without learning to do so. Again, this does not for a moment deny the existence of potentialities for aggression and hostility based on neural arrangements which can be readily organized to function in aggressive behavior. What *is* denied is that without the added stimulation of those neural arrangements by the appropriate stimuli and their social or-

ganization into certain patterns of behavior, aggression will
not spontaneously make its appearance in any human being.

The explanation of aggressive human behavior is by no
means as simple as the innate aggressionists have made it out
to be. It is very much more complex than is suggested by
their simplistic and erroneous animal hydraulic models.
Simple solutions have an immediate appeal to those who
are looking for ready answers to complex problems, but
truth is not advanced by explanations based on false analogies with animal behavior, wild extrapolations from animals
to human beings, misinterpretations of the evidence both in
animals and in humans, neglect of the vitally important
verifiable facts of behavior in living nonaggressive human
societies, loose speculations and violent distortions of the
evidence relating to prehistoric humans, and the attribution
to them of traits as genetically determined which are, in
fact, for the most part culturally determined.

Selective Preference for Evidence

The range of variability among primate species is very great.
As Professor Annette Ehrlich has pointed out, because of
this diversity it is possible to find a "basis" for virtually any
social system by recourse to the primate literature. Families,
mixed sex groups, matriarchies, patriarchies, mixed dominance groups, all exist among primates. It is also possible, by
careful selection of the "evidence," to prove that almost any
kind of behavior, from the most altruistic to the most selfish
and destructive, constitutes a "basic" primate trait. Such
personal preferences for "evidence" help neither to establish
the truth nor contribute toward any reasonable understanding or solution of our problems. The truth is that it is difficult to make general statements about social organization

and behavior that will apply to all nonhuman primates, and it is even more difficult to generalize from them to humans. Nor can we cite the behavior of nonhuman primates to justify our own social arrangements or attempt to explain certain aspects of our social system by recourse to the old argument that they are part of some mythical 'primate heritage." The behavior of each species has to be understood in relation to its own environment. If we desire to resolve the specifically human problems such as war then we have to look specifically at such human environmental problems as the military-industrial complex, nationalism, education, racism, poverty, and the like. Perhaps the most important lesson to be learned from primate studies is that we belong to an order of animals whose social behavior and organization are not static, but change in response to the challenges of the environment. Primates are adaptable animals, and humans are so beyond all others. This is, possibly, the most hopeful lesson of all to be drawn from primate studies.

The Facts versus the Fantasies

The facts of human evolutionary history are far more interesting than the fallacies and fantasies of the innate aggressionists. Those facts afford a very different view of the nature of humanity from that which has been conjured up by these writers. Indeed, that picture is a very heartening one, one in which we may take justifiable pride, for as creative beings we constitute the only example of a species that has made itself. Evolving as the most educable of creatures, released from the constraints of a limited learning capacity into the freedom of an unlimited educability, humans have with that freedom created the vast orchestra of cultures that constitute their varied responses to the challenges of the environments with which they have been confronted. They have, until relatively recent times, acted their parts well.

Civilized humans, during the last few millennia, have increasingly abused their freedoms and taken advantage of their power to produce change, till that power has run away with them. Change throughout the whole of human history was evolutionary, not revolutionary—evolutionary change, however, that had revolutionary consequences. But the rate of change during the recent period of human history has greatly accelerated and immensely increased the problems with which people and societies are confronted. The first of these, upon which virtually all authorities agree, is the population problem. From the small gatherer-hunter populations of some twenty to thirty or so persons we have grown to populations in our cities running into millions. In these cities people in large numbers live in squalor, poverty, and hopelessness. Disease, crime, violence, alienation, are the usual products in such places where the disengagement of people from each other has become endemic. But even in the midst of such debasing conditions, such is the quality of the human spirit that one not uncommonly finds individuals who have somehow managed to retain their dignity as human beings. They have emerged, it seems, even more strongly tempered as a consequence of the ordeals through which they have passed. For others the pressures are too much, the frustrations beyond endurance, and the resort to violence a means of getting even with a cruel and heartless society. The irresponsible multiplication of people has resulted in the debasement of the larger part of humanity, for excess quantity makes it extremely difficult to develop, maintain, and control quality. The violence, the crime, and the corruption of our cities constitute but one evidence of a general breakdown of civilized humanity, evils which signal the loss of that humanity which once bound human beings together.

"Evil," as Erich Fromm has said, "is man's loss of himself in the tragic attempt to escape the burden of his humanity." That burden is involvement in other humans. Anarchic and destructive multiplication, growth for the sake of growth, is the ideology of the cancer cell, and like a cancer overpopulation, crowding and all the attendant evils that follow upon it have robbed humans of the ability to control that runaway overgrowth and its metastatic invasions of every aspect of life.

It is not innate depravity that has brought humanity to this sorry pass, but the simple failure to understand that no living organism, and especially such a vulnerable creature as *Homo sapiens,* can go on multiplying uncontrolledly without destroying its environment, and eventually itself. This is a vast subject, upon which innumerable books have been written, and if there is any one point on which their writers agree it is that unless the problem of overpopulation is solved we shall be able to solve few if any of the other social problems that beset us.

Robert Ardrey sees the juvenile delinquent of our modern cities as an almost glorious re-creation of those violent ancestors conjured up by his fertile imagination who wielded the first weapons. "This ingenious, normal adolescent creature has created a way of life in perfect image of his animal needs . . . creat[ing] directly from his instincts the animal institution of territory . . . the blood and loot of the predator. And . . . always the weapon, the gleaming switchblade. . . ."

This lurid picture of the nature of man in society, contemporary society, is understandable in one who was initiated into African anthropology, as Ardrey informs us he was, in the basement of his Sunday school. "A new member or two would be initiated," we are told, "and if seriously injured, helped home to his mother. There would be a short prayer and a shorter benediction. And we would turn out all the lights and in total darkness hit each other with chairs. It was my Sunday-school class in Chicago, I believe, that prepared me for African anthropology."

One of several possible comments on that curious confession is that there are, perhaps, less violent and more efficient ways of being prepared for the study of what Ardrey calls African anthropology. In any event, whatever Ardrey may think of the relation of australopithecines to the behavior of juvenile delinquents in *West Side Story* or the streets of New York, serious students of the causes of juvenile delinquency are of another opinion. Delinquency, like crime, is restricted to no one class. To the extent to which others have failed an individual, and bonds of attachment to them have been weakened, the probabilities of juvenile delinquency are increased. Émile Durkheim many years ago summed it all up when he wrote: "The more weakened the groups to which [the individual] belongs, the less he depends on them, the more he consequently depends on himself and recognizes no other rules of conduct than what are founded on his private interests." Juvenile delinquents make their appearance not as some kinds of atavistic throwbacks to the much maligned australopithecines, but as a consequence of a complex of social factors such as the weakening of family bonds, lack of attachment to others amounting often to rejection by them, lack of respect for conventional values picked up from the hypocritical lip-service to these values of the society as a whole, and the development of an alienated view of life which frees one from any obligation to others. We find no juvenile delinquents in "primitive" societies simply because the conditions for producing them are absent in such communities, whereas in civilized societies, especially in our large cities, those conditions abound. The juvenile delinquent is the product of a delinquent so-

ciety, in which parents, teachers, and the community have
forgotten, if they have ever known, what it is to be human
and what the needs of a growing human being are, the need,
especially, for love. No child who was ever adequately loved
ever became a delinquent or a murderer. Aggressive behavior is frequently the response to the frustration of the need
for love, as well as a means of compelling attention to that
need. Thus, aggression is often a signal, even at its most violent, of the need for love. But the varieties of aggression are
many, and not all of them, by any means, are to be interpreted as such signals. However, in human beings, children
in particular, aggressive behavior frequently constitutes such
a signal. More often than not it is either misunderstood or
ignored, or both, and the victim—for that is what he or she
is—feels more abandoned than ever. Under such conditions,
as a juvenile, the individual is likely to look for support to
those who, like himself, have also been failed in their need
for recognition, for love. In the cities especially, among the
impoverished such support is most likely to be found among
one's peers in the street gang.

As I have said, the birthright of every child is growth and
development free from physical and mental handicap. The
most important of the requirements for the achievement of
such growth and development is the satisfaction of the need
for love. Love frustrated leads to maldevelopment, an inability to love, and aggression. Love satisfied leads to healthy
development, the ability to love, and cooperativeness.

Love

We talk a great deal about love in the Western world, but
we do very little about it. We treat the Golden Rule as if it
were the exception rather than the rule. We pretend to a
creed in which most of us do not believe, reserving its ritual

celebration for those occasions when collectively we ostentatiously burn our particular brand of incense before our empty shrines. This is nihilism, it is hypocrisy; it represents the abdication from humanity which leads to dehumanization.

It is not sports or circuses that will provide the solution to the problems of human aggressiveness, but the restoration to that humanity which all humans possess as a potentiality, and through which alone one learns to become a humane being, through love. The only way one learns to love is by being loved. This is neither a fantasy nor a theory. It is a fact—a verifiable fact. Prophets, simmering with millennial ardor, have long preached the virtues of love, but few have themselves shown the way. Since the meaning of a word is the action it produces, love has assumed a ritual significance, but for the most part failed to spell out its real meaning as involvement in the sense of something that one does, something that is part of the conduct of one's everyday life. Let us always remember that humanity is not so much an inheritance as it is an achievement. Our true inheritance lies in our ability to make and shape ourselves, not the creatures but the creators of our destiny.

References

Page and Line

1. A Controversy

6 : 4-7   For some interesting works on this subject see Hannah
           Arendt, *On Violence*. New York: Harcourt Brace Jo-
           vanovich, 1970; Kurt Singer, *The Idea of Conflict*.
           Carlton: Melbourne University Press, 1949; Philip P.
           Wiener and John Fisher (eds.), *Violence and Aggression*.
           New Brunswick, N.J.: Rutgers University Press, 1974.

8 : 18   Konrad Lorenz, *On Aggression*. New York: Harcourt,
           Brace & World, 1966.

   : 18   Robert Ardrey, *African Genesis*. New York: Atheneum,
           1961; Robert Ardrey, *The Territorial Imperative*. New
           York: Atheneum, 1966; Robert Ardrey, *The Social Con-
           tract*. New York: Atheneum, 1970.

   : 18   Raymond Dart, *Adventures with the Missing Link*. New
           York: Harper & Row, 1959; and other works.

   : 18-19 Desmond Morris, *The Naked Ape*. New York: McGraw-
           Hill, 1967; Desmond Morris, *The Human Zoo*. New
           York: McGraw-Hill, 1969.

   : 19   Anthony Storr, *Human Aggression*. New York: Atheneum,
           1968; Anthony Storr, *Human Destructiveness*. New
           York: Basic Books, 1972.

   : 19   Niko Tinbergen, "On War and Peace in Animals and
           Man," *Science*, vol. 160, 1968, pp. 1411-18.

327

Page and Line

13 : 21–33   Erich Fromm, *The Anatomy of Human Destructiveness.*
              New York: Holt, Rinehart & Winston, 1973.

15 : 7–11   Kenneth E. Moyer, "Kinds of Aggression and Their Phys-
              iological Basis," *Communications in Behavioral Biology,*
              Part A, vol. 2, 1968, pp. 65–87; Kenneth E. Moyer, "A
              Preliminary Physiological Model of Aggressive Behav-
              ior." In *The Physiology of Aggression and Defeat,* B. E.
              Eleftheriou and J. P. Scott (eds.). New York: Plenum
              Press, 1971, 223–63.

  : 17–23   Roger N. Johnson, *Aggression in Man and Animals.* Phil-
              adelphia: W. B. Saunders & Co., 1972.

17 : 34 to   For a discussion of this subject by various authorities see
18 : 4   Ashley Montagu (ed.), *Race and IQ.* New York: Oxford
              University Press, 1975; Arthur Whimbey and Linda S.
              Whimbey, *Intelligence Can Be Taught.* New York: Dut-
              ton, 1975.

  : 6–9   Ashley Montagu (ed.), *Culture and Human Development.*
              Englewood Cliffs, N.J.: Prentice-Hall, 1974.

  : 9–22   Ashley Montagu, *Prenatal Influences.* Springfield, Ill.: C C
              Thomas, 1962; Ashley Montagu, *Life Before Birth.* New
              York: New American Library, 1966.

19 : 14–19   Grant Newton and Seymour Levine (eds.), *Early Experi-
              ence and Behavior.* Springfield, Ill.: C C Thomas, 1968;
              Urie Bronfenbrenner (ed.), *Influences on Human De-
              velopment.* Hinsdale, Ill.: Dryden Press, 1972; Yvonne
              Brackbill (ed.), *Infancy and Early Development.* New
              York: Free Press, 1967.

20 : 17–20   Sheldon and Eleanor Glueck, *Unraveling Juvenile Delin-
              quency.* Cambridge: Harvard University Press, 1950.

  : 20–24   L. B. Silver, C. C. Dublin, and R. S. Lourie, "Does Vio-
              lence Breed Violence? Contributions from a Study of
              the Child Abuse Syndrome," *American Journal of Psy-
              chiatry,* 1969, 126:404–7.

  : 27   Albert Bandura, "Relationship of Family Patterns to
              Child Behavior Disorders," Progress Report, 1960, Stan-
              ford University Project No. M-1734, United States Pub-
              lic Health Service.

  : 28   Albert Bandura and R. H. Walters, *Adolescent Aggres-
              sion.* New York: Ronald Press, 1959.

21 : 2–5   M. L. Hoffman, "Power Assertion by the Parent and Its
              Impact on the Child," *Child Development,* vol. 31, 1960,
              pp. 129–43.

2. *Man as Killer: An Acceptable Idea*

24 : 27–31   Konrad Lorenz, *On Aggression*. New York: Harcourt, Brace & World, 1966, p. 239.

25 : 16–27   Raymond Dart, "The Predatory Transition from Ape to Man," *International Anthropological and Linguistic Review*, vol. 1, 1954, pp. 207–8.

: 29–33   Robert Ardrey, *African Genesis*. New York: Atheneum, 1961, p. 29.

: 33 to 26 : 2   Ibid.

26 : 20–22   Lionel Tiger and Robin Fox, *The Imperial Animal*. New York: Holt, Rinehart & Winston, 1971.

: 24–26   Margaret Mead, Review of Konrad Lorenz's *On Aggression*. In *Redbook Magazine*, November 1966, pp. 24seq.

: 26–28   Roger D. Masters, "Modern Man's Ancient Instincts," *Saturday Review*, 17 September 1966, p. 34.

: 29–32   Marston Bates, "How Did We Get This Way?" *New York Times Book Review*, 19 June 1966.

: 32 to   Sherwood L. Washburn and David A. Hamburg, "Aggressive Behavior in Old World Monkeys and Apes." In
27 : 2   Phyllis C. Jay (ed.), *Primates*. New York: Holt, Rinehart & Winston, 1968, pp. 459–60, n. 2.

: 2–7   Howard E. Evans, "Biology: The New Salvation of Man," *Harper's Magazine*, September 1966, pp. 107–8.

: 18   William Golding, *Lord of the Flies*. London: Faber, 1954.

28 : 22–24   Mr. Bob Krauss interviewed at my request by Professor Floyd Matson. Communicated 7 October 1974.

29 : 11–13   Stanley Kubrick, in an interview with Craig McGregor, "Nice Boy from the Bronx," *New York Times*, 30 January 1972, p. D1.

: 13–16   Stanley Kubrick, "Now Kubrick Fights Back," *New York Times*, 27 February 1972, p. D1.

: 16–21   Ibid.

: 23–29   Tom Burke, "Malcolm McDowell: The Liberals They Hate 'Clockwork,'" *New York Times*, 30 January 1972, p. D13.

30 : 2–7   Aljean Armetz, "Man Was a Killer Long Before He Served a God," *New York Times*, 31 August 1969, p. D9.

31 : 1–6   For a source-book critical examination of the book by writers of many different backgrounds see William Nelson (ed.), *William Golding's Lord of the Flies: A Source Book*. New York: Odyssey Press, 1963.

Page and Line

35 : 33 to   Edward Glover, *The Roots of Crime*. London: Imago
36 : 10   Publishing Co., 1960, p. 8. Reprinted by International
                    Universities Press, New York, 1970.

37 : 19 to   Sigmund Freud, *Civilization and Its Discontents*. London:
38 : 3   Hogarth Press, 1930, p. 86.

   : 15–16   Charles Darwin, *On the Origin of Species*. London: John
                    Murray, 1859.

   : 16   Charles Darwin, *The Descent of Man*. London: John
                    Murray, 1871.

39 : 23–26   For references to their writings see Ashley Montagu, *Dar-
                    win, Competition and Cooperation*. New York: Henry
                    Schuman, 1952. Reprinted by Greenwood Publishers,
                    Westport, Conn., 1973.

            3. Social Darwinism: A Case History and a Cautionary Note

42 : 1–5   Charles Darwin, *On the Origin of Species by Means of
                    Natural Selection, Or the Preservation of Favoured Races
                    in the Struggle for Life*. London: John Murray, 1859,
                    p. 62.

   : 19–23   T. H. Huxley, "The Struggle for Existence: A Pro-
                    gramme," *Nineteenth Century*, vol. 23, 1888, pp. 161–
                    80.

43 : 24–28   Alfred Espinas, *Des Sociétés animales*. Paris: Ballière,
                    1878.

   : 28 to   Professor Kessler, "Mutual Aid as a Law of Nature and
44 : 3   the Chief Factor of Evolution," *Memoirs (Trudy) of the
                    St. Petersburg Society of Naturalists*, 9, 1880.

   : 16–24   Petr Kropotkin, *Mutual Aid: A Factor of Evolution*. Lon-
                    don: Heinemann, 1902.

47 : 17–32   John Rowan Wilson, Review of *The Territorial Impera-
                    tive*. In *The Spectator*, 7 April 1967, p. 398.

48 : 8–22   Antony Jay, *Corporation Man*. New York: Random House,
                    1971.

49 : 10–14   Cesare Lombroso, *L'Uomo Delinquente*. Turin: Bocca,
                    1876; published as *Criminal Man*, New York: Putnam's
                    Sons, 1911.

50 : 23–24   Arthur Keith, *The Place of Prejudice in Modern Civiliza-
                    tion*. New York: John Day, 1971.

53 : 4–5   David Pilbeam and Steven Jay Gould, "Size and Scaling
                    in Human Evolution," *Science*, vol. 186, 1974, pp. 892–
                    901.

4. Instinct and Adaptation

56 : 34 to   Konrad Lorenz, *On Aggression*. New York: Harcourt,
57 : 6   Brace & World, 1966, p. 225.

   : 13–18   Arthur Keith, *Essays on Human Evolution*. London:
Watts & Co., 1946.

   : 18–24   Robert Ardrey, *African Genesis*. New York: Atheneum,
1961, p. 172.

58 : 13–27   Richard J. Barnet, *The Roots of War*. Baltimore: Penguin Books, 1973.

59 : 1–3   Hannah Arendt, *On Violence*. New York: Harcourt, Brace
& World, 1970.

   : 3–4   Lionel Tiger and Robin Fox, *The Imperial Animal*. New
York: Holt, Rinehart & Winston, 1971.

   : 5–7   Julian Huxley, "War as a Biological Phenomenon." In his
On Living in a Revolution. London: Chatto & Windus,
1944, pp. 60–68.

60 : 19–29   Anatol Rapoport, "Approaches to Theories of Large Scale
Human Conflicts." In *Progress in Mental Health,* Hugh
Freeman (ed.). London: J. & A. Churchill, 1969, p. 41.

62 : 6–8   A. G. Karczmar and C. L. Scudder, "Aggression and Neurochemical Changes in Different Strains and Genera of
Mice." In S. Garattini and E. B. Sigg (eds.), *Aggressive
Behavior*. New York: Wiley, 1969, pp. 209–27; J. M.
Stewart and Howard M. Reid, "Effects of Genotype and
Social Experience on the Development of Aggressive
Behavior," *45th Annual Report, 1973–1974,* Jackson
Memorial Laboratory, Bar Harbor, Maine, 1974, p. 92.

   : 22–25   R. A. Hinde, *Biological Bases of Human Social Behavior*.
New York: McGraw-Hill, 1974, pp. 249–92.

   : 26–32   Ibid., p. 292.

65 : 8–15   William McDougall, *An Introduction to Social Psychology*. London: Methuen, 1908; 23rd ed., New York:
Barnes & Noble, 1960, p. 25.

   : 21–28   Niko Tinbergen, *The Study of Instinct*. Oxford: The
Clarendon Press, 1951, p. 112.

   : 28   For these see L. L. Bernard, *Instinct: A Study in Social
Psychology*. New York: Holt, 1924; Ronald Fletcher,
Instinct in Man. New York: International Universities
Press, 1957; Claire H. Schiller, *Instinctive Behavior:
The Development of a Modern Concept*. New York:
International Universities Press, 1957; Robert C. Bir-

Page and Line

ney and Richard C. Teevan (eds.), *Instinct.* Princeton:
D. Van Nostrand Co., 1961; S. A. Barnett, *Instinct and
Intelligence.* Englewood Cliffs, N.J.: Prentice-Hall, 1967.

66 : 10–18   Tinbergen, op. cit., p. 112.

: 34 to   Daniel S. Lehrman, "A Critique of Konrad Lorenz's
67 : 2   Theory of Instinctive Behavior," *Quarterly Review of
                 Biology,* vol. 28, 1953, pp. 337–63; see also Birney and
                 Teevan (eds.), *Instinct,* and John H. Crook (ed.), *Social
                 Behavior in Birds and Mammals.* New York: Academic
                 Press, 1970.

: 11–20   Peter H. Klopfer, "Instincts and Chromosomes: What Is
                 an 'Innate' Act?" *American Naturalist,* vol. 103, 1969,
                 pp. 556–60.

69 : 12–17   D. S. Lehrman, "Semantic and Conceptual Issues in the
                 Nature-Nurture Problem." In L. R. Aronson, E. To-
                 bach, D. S. Lehrman, and J. S. Rosenblatt (eds.), *Devel-
                 opment and Evolution of Behavior.* San Francisco:
                 W. H. Freeman, 1970, pp. 17–52.

: 22–25   Peter H. Klopfer, *On Behavior: Instinct Is a Cheshire Cat.*
                 Philadelphia: J. B. Lippincott, 1973, pp. 26–27.

70 : 14–29   Gilbert Gottlieb, *Development of Species Identification in
                 Birds: An Inquiry into the Determinants of Prenatal
                 Perception.* Chicago: University of Chicago Press, 1971.

: 30 to   Howard Moltz, "Contemporary Instinct Theory and the
71 : 2   Fixed Action Pattern," *Psychological Review,* vol. 72,
                 1965, pp. 27–47.

72 : 32 to   Joseph W. Howe, *Excessive Venery, Masturbation, and
73 : 2   Continence.* New York: Bermingham & Co., 1888, p. 18;
                 P. Semmens and W. M. Lamers, Jr., *Teen-Age Preg-
                 nancy.* Springfield, Ill.: C C Thomas, 1968; S. C. Reed,
                 Counseling in Medical Genetics. Philadelphia: W. B.
                 Saunders, 1955, pp. 36–37; D. E. R. Kelsey, "Phantasies
                 of Birth and Prenatal Experiences Recovered from Pa-
                 tients Undergoing Hypnoanalysis," *Journal of Mental
                 Science,* vol. 99, 1953, pp. 212–23; Clellan S. Ford and
                 Frank A. Beach, *Patterns of Sexual Behavior.* New
                 York: Harper & Bros., 1951.

74 : 5–9   Frank A. Beach, "The Descent of Instinct," *Psychology
                 Review,* vol. 62, 1955, pp. 401–10.

: 12–13   C. K. Ogden and I. A. Richards, *The Meaning of Mean-
                 ing.* 3rd ed. London: Kegan Paul, 1930.

: 12–19   S. A. Barnett, "Instinct," *Daedalus,* vol. 92, 1963, pp. 564–
                 80.

Page and Line

75 : 8–13   John Stuart Mill, *Principles of Political Economy*. 2 vols. London: Longmans, 1848.

76 : 23–28   T. C. Schneirla, "Instinct and Aggression," *Natural History*, December 1966, pp. 16seq.

: 29 to   See Daniel S. Lehrman, "A Critique of Konrad Lorenz's
77 : 1   Theory of Instinctive Behavior," *Quarterly Review of Biology*, vol. 28, 1953, pp. 337–63; W. H. Thorpe, *Learning and Instinct in Animals*. Cambridge: Harvard University Press, 1956; Adriaan Kortlandt, "Aspects and Prospects of the Concept of Instinct," *Archives Neerlandaises de Zoologie*, vol. 11, 1955, pp. 156–284; A. Kortlandt, "An Attempt at Clarifying Some Controversial Notions in Animal Psychology," *Archives Neerlandaises de Zoologie*, vol. 13, 1959, pp. 196–229; D. O. Hebb, "Heredity and Environment in Mammalian Behaviour," *British Journal of Animal Behaviour*, vol. 1, 1953, pp. 43–47; R. Aronson et al. (eds.), *Development and Evolution of Behavior*. San Francisco: W. H. Freeman, 1970; E. Tobach et al. (eds.), *The Biopsychology of Development*. New York: Academic Press, 1971; Robert A. Hinde, *Animal Behavior*. 2nd ed. New York: McGraw-Hill, 1970; Robert A. Hinde, *Biological Bases of Human Social Behaviour*. New York: McGraw-Hill, 1974.

: 5–12   Robert A. Hinde, *Animal Behaviour*.

78 : 9–26   Ashley Montagu (ed.), *Culture and the Evolution of Man*. New York: Oxford University Press, 1962; Ashley Montagu (ed.), *Culture: Man's Adaptive Dimension*. New York: Oxford University Press, 1968.

: 27 to   Clifford Geertz, "The Growth of Culture and the Evolu-
79 : 9   tion of Mind." In *Theories of the Mind*, Jordan M. Scher (ed.). New York: Free Press, 1962, pp. 713–40.

: 18–28   Ralph L. Holloway, Jr., "Cranial Capacity and the Evolution of the Human Brain." In *Culture: Man's Adaptive Dimension*, Ashley Montagu (ed.), pp. 170–96.

: 28–29   Ralph L. Holloway, Jr., "The Evolution of the Human Brain: Some Notes Toward a General Theory." *General Systems Yearbook*, vol. 12, 1967.

80 : 15–26   Ralph L. Holloway, Jr., "Cranial Capacity and the Evolution of the Human Brain." In *Culture: Man's Adaptive Dimension*, Ashley Montagu (ed.), p. 188.

81 : 1–9   Ernst Caspari, "Selective Forces in the Evolution of Man." In *Culture: Man's Adaptive Dimension*, Ashley Montagu (ed.), pp. 159–69; Theodosius Dobzhansky, *Mankind*

Page and Line

Evolving. New Haven: Yale University Press, 1962; Ashley Montagu, *The Human Revolution*. New York: Bantam Books, 1967.

82 : 24 to   J. B. S. Haldane, "The Argument from Animals to Men."
83 : 5   In *Culture and the Evolution of Man*, Ashley Montagu (ed.), pp. 65–83.

84 : 7–16   Ashley Montagu, "Unmaking a Scapegoat," *New York Times*, 10 July 1941, p. E7; William L. Straus, Jr., and A. J. E. Cave, "Pathology and Posture of Neanderthal Man," *Quarterly Review of Biology*, vol. 32, 1957, pp. 348–61.

: 18–24   Ralph S. Solecki, *Shanidar: The First Flower People*. New York: Knopf, 1971.

: 24–29   Ashley Montagu, "Some Anthropological Terms: A Study in the Systematics of Confusion," *American Anthropologist*, vol. 47, 1945, pp. 119–33; Ashley Montagu (ed.), *The Concept of the Primitive*. New York: Free Press, 1968, pp. 148–74.

85 : 23 to   V. C. Wynne-Edwards, "Ecology and the Evolution of So-
86 : 4   cial Ethics," In *Biology and the Human Sciences*, J. W. S. Pringle (ed.). Oxford: The Clarendon Press, 1972, p. 59.

: 13–18   A. Kortlandt, "Aspects and Prospects of the Concept of Instinct," p. 207.

: 18–23   J. L. Cloudsley-Thompson, *Animal Conflict and Adaptation*. London: G. T. Foulis & Co., 1965, p. 80.

: 23–25   Ueli Nagel and Hans Kummer, "Variation in Cercopithecoid Aggressive Behavior," In Ralph L. Holloway (ed.), *Primate Aggression, Territoriality, and Xenophobia*. New York: Academic Press, 1974, pp. 159–84.

: 33 to   Edward O. Wilson, *Sociobiology: The New Synthesis*.
87 : 5   Cambridge: Harvard University Press, 1975, pp. 248–50.

: 6–20   Irwin S. Bernstein and Thomas P. Gordon, "The Function of Aggression in Primate Societies," *American Scientist*, vol. 62, 1974, pp. 304–11.

88 : 9–12   Edward O. Wilson, op. cit., p. 247.

89 : 11–14   Konrad Lorenz, *On Aggression*. New York: Harcourt, Brace & World, 1966, p. 50.

: 17–24   Ibid., p. 51.

: 30 to   For an excellent discussion of this work see Irenäus Eibl-
90 : 4   Eibesfeldt, *Ethology: The Biology of Behavior*. New York: Holt, Rinehart & Winston, 1970, p. 43.

91 : 10–17   P. E. Van Hemel and J. S. Meyer, "Satiation of Mouse

            Killing in an Operant Situation," *Psychonomic Science,* vol. 21, 1970, pp. 229–30.

91 : 18–22   R. N. and L. D. Johnson, "Interspecific Aggression in Siamese Fighting Fish," quoted in Roger N. Johnson, *Aggression in Man and Animals.* Philadelphia: W. B. Saunders, 1972, p. 211.

: 28 to   For a collection of eighteen of these histories see Eric
92 : 3   Williams, *The Book of Famous Escapes.* New York: W. W. Norton, 1953.

: 3–6   P. P. Read, *Alive.* Philadelphia: Lippincott, 1974.

: 10–12   Erich Fromm, *The Anatomy of Human Destructiveness.* New York: Holt, Rinehart & Winston, 1973.

: 12–14   Gregory Rochlin, *Man's Aggression: The Defense of Self.* Boston: Gambit, 1973.

: 16–18   R. A. Hinde, "Energy Models of Motivation," *Symposia of the Society for Experimental Biology,* vol. 14, 1960, pp. 119–230.

: 23–28   Peter H. Klopfer, " 'Behavior,' " *Science,* vol. 165, 1969, p. 887.

93 : 3–8   J. P. Scott, "Comparative Psychology and Ethology," *Annual Review of Psychology,* vol. 18, 1967, pp. 65–86.

: 13–21   Konrad Lorenz, *On Aggression.* New York: Harcourt, Brace & World, 1966, p. 244.

: 27 to 94 : 16   Ibid., p. 244.

95 : 3–19   Omer C. Stewart, "Lorenz/Margolin on the Ute." In *Man and Aggression,* Ashley Montagu (ed.). 2nd ed. New York: Oxford University Press, 1973, pp. 221–28.

96 : 1–7   George B. Grinnell, "Coup and Scalp Among the Plains Indians," *American Anthropologist,* vol. 12, 1910, pp. 296–310.

: 9–18   John Beatty, "Taking Issue with Lorenz on the Ute." In *Man and Aggression,* Ashley Montagu (ed.), New York: Oxford University Press, 1968, pp. 111–15.

: 29 to   John Paul Scott, *Aggression.* Chicago: University of Chi-
97 : 5   cago Press, 1958, p. 62.

: 13–16   L. T. Hilliard and Brian H. Kirman, *Mental Deficiency.* 2nd ed. Boston: Little, Brown, 1965, p. 471.

: 16–18   Lorna Wing, *Autistic Children.* New York: Bruner-Mazel, Inc., 1972; "Aggression in Childhood," *The Lancet,* vol. 1, 1966, p. 722.

: 28–32   Hilliard and Kirman, op. cit.

98 : 1–8   Gerhard Bosch, *Infantile Autism.* New York: Springer, 1970, p. 99; see also E. A. Tinbergen and N. Tinbergen,

Early Childhood Autism: An Ethological Approach. Berlin and Hamburg: Verlag Paul Parey, 1972.

98 : 20–24   Charlotte Bühler, "Die Ersten Sozialen Verhaltungsweisen des Kindes." In *Soziologische und Psychologische Studien über das Erste Lebensjahre.* Jena: Fischer, 1927; Charlotte Bühler, "Spontaneous Reactions of Children in the First Two Years," *Proceedings and Papers of the 9th International Congress of Psychology,* 1919, pp. 99–100.

: 24–26   M. J. Muste and D. F. Sharpe, "Some Influential Factors in the Determination of Aggressive Behavior in Preschool Children," *Child Development,* vol. 18, 1947, pp. 11–28; K. Lewin, R. Lippitt, and R. K. White, "Patterns of Aggressive Behavior," *Journal of Social Psychology,* vol. 10, 1939, pp. 271–99; M. D. Fite, "Aggressive Behavior in Young Children," *Genetic Psychology Monographs,* vol. 22, 1940, pp. 151–319; R. R. Sears, J. W. M. Whiting, V. Nowlis, and P. S. Sears, "Some Children Rearing Antecedents of Aggression and Dependency in Young Children," *Genetic Psychology Monographs,* vol. 47, 1953, pp. 135–234.

: 26 to   Lauretta Bender, "The Genesis of Hostility in Children,"
99 : 6   *American Journal of Psychiatry,* vol. 105, 1948, pp. 241–45; Lauretta Bender, *Aggression, Hostility and Anxiety in Children.* Springfield, Ill.: C C Thomas, 1953.

: 14–24   Abraham Maslow, "Our Maligned Animal Nature," *Journal of Psychology,* vol. 28, 1949, pp. 273–78. Abraham Maslow, *Motivation and Personality,* 2nd ed. New York: Harper & Row, 1970.

: 25–31   Katherine M. Banham, "The Development of Affectionate Behavior in Infancy," *Journal of Genetic Psychology,* vol. 76, 1950, pp. 283–89.

: 32 to   Leonard Berkowitz, *Aggression: A Social Psychological*
100 : 8   *Analysis.* New York: McGraw-Hill, 1962; Leonard D. Eron, Leopold O. Walder, and Monroe M. Lefkowitz, *Learning of Aggression in Children.* Boston: Little, Brown, 1971; J. P. Scott, *Aggression.* Chicago: University of Chicago Press, 1958.

: 28 to   Frank J. Curran and Paul Schilder, "A Constructive Approach to the Problems of Childhood and Adolescence,"
101 : 6   *Journal of Clinical Psychopathology,* 2 October 1940, pp. 123–29.

: 10–13   Lauretta Bender, op. cit.; Ashley Montagu, *The Direction*

Page and Line

	of Human Development. Rev. ed. New York: Hawthorn Books, 1970.
101 : 15–26	"Aggression in Childhood," *The Lancet*, vol. 1, 1966, p. 722.
: 28 to 102 : 15	Nevitt Sanford and Craig Comstock, *Sanctions for Evil*. San Francisco: Jossey-Bass, 1971, pp. 312–13.
: 16–32	Lauretta Bender, "Hostile Aggression in Children." In *Aggressive Behavior*, S. Garattini and E. B. Sigg (eds.). New York: Wiley, 1969, pp. 322–25.
: 33 to 103 : 5	Jeffrey H. Goldstein, *Aggression and Crimes of Violence*. New York: Oxford University Press, 1974.
: 9–12	G. M. Carstairs, *This Island Now*. New York: Basic Books, 1962.
: 12 to 104 : 3	A Consultant Psychiatrist, "The Anxious Tiger," *The Listener*, 4 July 1963, pp. 3–5.
: 12–13	Sherwood L. Washburn and David A. Hamburg, "Aggressive Behavior in Old World Monkeys and Apes." In Phyllis C. Jay (ed.), *Primates*. New York: Holt, Rinehart & Winston, 1968, p. 460.
105 : 3–9	Sherwood L. Washburn and C. S. Lancaster, "The Evolution of Hunting." In *Man the Hunter*, Richard B. Lee and Irven DeVore (eds.). Chicago: Aldine, 1968, p. 299.
: 13–16	David A. Hamburg, "Emotions in the Perspective of Human Evolution." In *Expression of the Emotions in Man*, Peter H. Knapp (ed.). New York: International Universities Press, 1963, pp. 300–17.
106 : 15–21	Robert Claiborne, *God or Beast*. New York: W. W. Norton, 1974, pp. 205–11.

5. Cannibalism and Aggression

108 : 9–10	Robert Ardrey, *The Territorial Imperative*. New York: Atheneum, 1966, p. 263.
: 16–17	Eli Sagan, *Cannibalism: Human Aggression and Cultural Form*. New York: Harper & Row, 1974.
109 : 2–5	Ronald M. Berndt, *Excess and Restraint*. Chicago: University of Chicago Press, 1962.
: 22–26	Konrad Lorenz, *On Aggression*. New York: Harcourt, Brace & World, 1966, p. 239.
: 28–31	Franz Weidenreich, "Six Lectures on Sinanthropus," *Bulletin Geological Society of China*, vol. 19, 1939.
: 31 to 110 : 3	Kenneth P. Oakley, "On Man's Use of Fire, with Comments on Toolmaking, and Hunting." In *Social Life of*

Page and Line

Early Man, S. L. Washburn (ed.). New York: Viking
Fund Publications in Anthropology No. 31, 1961, pp.
176–93.

110 : 8–14   Aleš Hrdlička, *The Skeletal Remains of Early Man.* Washington, D.C.: Smithsonian Institution, 1930, pp. 202–29.

: 33 to   Piers Paul Read, *Alive: The Story of the Andes Survivors.*
111 : 6   Philadelphia: Lippincott, 1974, p. 338.

: 16–22   Klaus-Friedrich Koch, "Cannibalistic Revenge in Jalé Warfare," *Natural History,* vol. 79 (Feb.), 1970, pp. 40–51.

112 : 5–16   Hermann Helmuth, "Cannibalism in Palaeoanthropol-
ogy." In *Man and Aggression,* Ashley Montagu (ed.).
New York: Oxford University Press, 1973, pp. 229–53.

113 : 29–33   T. Jacob, "The Problem of Head-Hunting and Brain-
Eating Among Pleistocene Men in Indonesia," *Archaeol-
ogy & Physical Anthropology in Oceania,* vol. 7, 1972,
pp. 81–91.

116 : 1–8   Michael W. Young, *Fighting with Food.* Cambridge: Cambridge University Press, 1971.

: 9–14   Stanley M. Garn and Walter D. Block, "The Limited Nu-
tritional Value of Cannibalism," *American Anthropologist,* vol. 72, 1970, p. 106.

: 15–29   The best general discussion of cannibalism remains J. A.
MacCulloch's article "Cannibalism" in *Encyclopaedia of
Religion and Ethics,* James Hastings (ed.), vol. 3. New
York: Scribners, 1910, pp. 194–209.

117 : 7–26   F. M. Bergounioux, "Notes on the Mentality of Primitive
Man." In *Social Life of Early Man,* S. L. Washburn
(ed.). New York: Viking Fund Publications in Anthro-
pology, No. 31, 1961, p. 114; F. M. Bergounioux and
Joseph Goetz, *Primitive and Prehistoric Religions.* New
York: Hawthorn Books, 1966, p. 56.

118 : 26–31   Geza Teleki, *The Predatory Behavior of Wild Chimpanzees.* Lewisburg, Pa.: Bucknell University Press, 1973.

119 : 25–33   F. M. Bergounioux, "Notes on the Mentality of Primitive
Man." In *Social Life of Early Man,* S. L. Washburn
(ed.), p. 115.

120 : 1–15   Alberto C. Blanc, "Some Evidence for the Ideologies of
Early Man." In *Social Life of Early Man,* S. L. Washburn (ed.), p. 126.

: 16–21   For a further discussion of skull cults see Folke Henschen,
The Human Skull. New York: Praeger, 1966. For an
interesting discussion of cannibalism from a largely psy-

Page and Line

choanalytic viewpoint see the Eli Sagan work cited in
reference for p. 108:16–17.

6. Weapons or Leopards?

122 : 2   Raymond A. Dart with Dennis Craig, *Adventures with the Missing Link*. New York: Harper & Bros., 1959, pp. 106–13.

124 : 8–9   Mary D. Leakey, "Stone Artefacts from Swartkrans," *Nature*, vol. 225, 1970, pp. 1217–25.

: 30–33   Konrad Lorenz, *On Aggression*. New York: Harcourt, Brace & World, 1966, p. 239.

: 34 to   Raymond Dart, "The Predatory Transition from Ape to
125 : 5   Man," *International Anthropological and Linguistic Review*, vol. 1, 1953, pp. 201–18.

: 13–19   Robert Ardrey, *African Genesis*. New York: Atheneum, 1961, p. 29.

130 : 14–18   Raymond Dart, "The Predatory Implemental Technique of *Australopithecus*," *American Journal of Physical Anthropology*, vol. 7, 1949, pp. 1–16; Raymond Dart, "A Cleft Human Mandible and the Nine Other Lower Jaw Fragments from Makapansgat," *American Journal of Physical Anthropology*, vol. 20, 1962, pp. 267–86; Robert Ardrey, *African Genesis*, p. 299; L. S. B. Leakey, "Exploring 1,750,000 Years into Man's Past," *National Geographic*, October 1961, pp. 564–92.

: 21–23   Joseph Birdsell, "Discussion." In Carmine D. Clemente and Donald B. Lindsley (eds.), *Aggression and Defense*. Berkeley and Los Angeles: University of California Press, 1967, p. 14.

131 : 16–34   C. K. Brain, "An Attempt to Reconstruct the Behaviour of Australopithecines: The Evidence for Inter-Personal Violence," *Zoologica Africana*, vol. 7, 1972, pp. 379–401.

132 : 5–11   Joseph Birdsell, op. cit.

: 14–18   P. V. Tobias, *Olduvai Gorge: The Cranium of Australopithecus (Zinjanthropus) boisei*. Cambridge: Cambridge University Press, 1967.

: 19–22   Carl Weidenreich, "The Duration of Life of Fossil Man in China and the Pathological Lesions Found in His Skeleton," *Chinese Medical Journal*, vol. 55, 1939, pp. 34–44.

Page and Line

132 : 30 to   Marilyn Keyes Roper, "A Survey of the Evidence for In-
133 : 1   trahuman Killing in the Pleistocene," *Current Anthro-*
            pology, vol. 10, 1969, pp. 427–59.

   : 5–16   Adolph H. Schultz, "Comments on Mrs. Roper's 'Infrahu-
            man Killing,'" *Current Anthropology,* vol. 10, 1969, p.
            454.

   : 27–30   H. Zapfe, "Beiträge zur Erklärung der Entstehung von
            Knochenlägerstätten in Karstspalten und Höhlen," *Bei-*
            heft zur Zeitschrift Geologie, vol. 12, 1954, pp. 1–60.

   : 30–32   T. Mollison, "Die Verletzungen am Schädel und den
            Gliedmassenknochen des Rhodesiafundes," *Anthropolo-*
            gischer Anzeiger, vol. 14, 1937, pp. 229–34.

134 : 14–25   Robert Ardrey, *African Genesis,* p. 300.

   : 32 to   C. K. Brain, "New Finds at the Swartkrans Australopithe-
135 : 12   cine Site," *Nature,* vol. 225, pp. 1112–19.

7. *Cooperation*

143 : 19 to   George B. Schaller, *The Mountain Gorilla.* Chicago: Uni-
144 : 5   versity of Chicago Press, 1963, p. 308.

   : 5–7   Dian Fossey, "Making Friends with Mountain Gorillas,"
            National Geographic, January 1970, pp. 48–67; Dian
            Fossey, "More Years with Mountain Gorillas," *National*
            Geographic, October 1971, pp. 574–85.

   : 12–17   Carl Akeley, *In Brightest Africa.* Garden City, N.Y.: Gar-
            den City Publishing Co., 1923, p. 196.

   : 17–21   Ibid., p. 242.

   : 21–28   Ibid., p. 197.

145 : 1–5   Jane van Lawick-Goodall, *In the Shadow of Man.* Boston:
            Houghton Mifflin, 1971, p. 117.

   : 21–23   R. A. Butler, "Curiosity in Monkeys," *Scientific American,*
            February 1954.

   : 23–26   H. F. Harlow and G. Griffin, "Induced Mental and Social
            Deficits in Rhesus Monkeys." In S. F. Asler and R. E.
            Cooke (eds.), *The Biosocial Basis of Mental Retarda-*
            tion. Baltimore: The Johns Hopkins University Press,
            1965.

147 : 9–15   Geza Teleki, *The Predatory Behavior of Wild Chimpan-*
            zees. Lewisburg, Pa.: Bucknell University Press, 1973;
            Geza Teleki, "Primate Subsistence Patterns: Collector-
            Predators and Gatherer-Hunters," *Journal of Human*
            Evolution, vol. 4, 1975, pp. 125–84.

148 : 15–25   Syunzo Kawamura, "The Process of Sub-Culture Propaga-

Page and Line

tion Among Japanese Macaques," *Journal of Primatology*, vol. 2, 1959, pp. 43–60.

148 : 26–29   Irven DeVore and Sarel Eimerl, *The Primates*. New York: Time Inc., 1965, p. 89; Sherwood L. Washburn and David A. Hamburg, "The Study of Primate Behavior." In Irven DeVore (ed.), *Primate Behavior*. New York: Holt, Rinehart & Winston, 1965, pp. 3–4.

155 : 21–24   F. Kovács, "Biological Interpretation of the Nine Months Duration of Human Pregnancy," *Acta Biologicae, Tudom Academie,* vol. 10, 1960, p. 331.

159 : 7–14   R. Allen Gardner and Beatrice T. Gardner, "Teaching Sign Language to a Chimpanzee," *Science,* vol. 165, 1969, pp. 664–72.

: 14–17   David Premack, "Language in Chimpanzee?" *Science,* vol. 172, 1972, pp. 808–22. Ann James Premack and David Premack, "Teaching Language to an Ape," *Scientific American,* October 1972.

: 28–29   P. Lieberman, E. S. Crelin, and D. H. Klatt, "Phonetic Ability and Related Anatomy of the Newborn and Adult Human, Neanderthal Man, and the Chimpanzee," *American Anthropologist,* vol. 74, 1972, pp. 287–307.

160 : 9–18   Marjorie Le May, "The Language Capability of Neanderthal Man," *American Journal of Physical Anthropology,* vol. 42, 1975, pp. 9–14.

165 : 28 to   Paul Shepard, *The Tender Carnivore and the Sacred*
166 : 12   *Game*. New York: Scribners, 1973, pp. 139–40.

: 19–25   Kenneth MacLeish, "Stone Age Cavemen of Mindanao," *National Geographic,* August 1972, pp. 216–49.

167 : 3–8   John Nance, *The Gentle Tasaday*. New York: Harcourt Brace Jovanovich, 1975; see also Carlos A. Fernandez II and Frank Lynch, S.J., "The Tasaday: Cave-Dwelling Food Gatherers of South Cotabato, Mindanao," *Philippine Sociological Review,* vol. 20, 1972, pp. 275–330.

: 8–10   John Nance, "The Inheritors," *Sunday Times Magazine* (London), 8 October 1972, p. 48, p. 58.

168 : 3–14   Peggy Durdin, "From the Space Age to the Tasaday Age," *New York Times Magazine,* 8 October 1972.

: 21–26   Robert Thirkell, "Notes on the Aborigines of Tasmania," *Proceedings of the Royal Society of Tasmania for 1873,* 1874, p. 28. See also Ling Roth, *The Aborigines of Tasmania,* 2nd ed. Halifax (England): P. King & Sons, 1899, p. 45. Reprinted by Humanities Press, New York, 1971.

Page and Line

168 : 26–29   Clive Turnbull, *The Black War*. Melbourne: F. W. Chesh-
                   ire, 1948, p. 159.

169 : 4–19   Quoted in Turnbull, op. cit., pp. 2–3.

170 : 2–4   Elizabeth Marshall Thomas, *The Harmless People*. New
                   York: Knopf, 1959.

    : 4   For a critical examination of the view that life was and
                   is nasty, brutish, and short in primitive societies, see
                   Marshall Sahlins, *Stone Age Economics*. Chicago: Al-
                   dine-Atherton, Inc., 1972.

    : 7–11   Richard B. Lee, "The Intensification of Social Life
                   Among the !Kung Bushmen." In Brian Spooner (ed.),
                   Population Growth: Anthropological Implications.
                   Cambridge: Massachusetts Institute of Technology
                   Press, 1972, pp. 343–50; Patricia Draper, "Crowding
                   Among Hunter-Gatherers: The !Kung Bushmen," *Sci-
                   ence*, vol. 182, 1973, pp. 301–3; R. B. Lee and Irven
                   DeVore (eds.), *Kalahari Hunter-Gatherers*. Cambridge:
                   Harvard University Press. In Press.

    : 19–22   Elizabeth Marshall Thomas, *The Harmless People*. New
                   York: Knopf, 1959, p. 186; Richard B. Lee, op. cit.;
                   Richard B. Lee, "What Hunters Do for a Living, or,
                   How to Make Out on Scarce Resources." In Richard B.
                   Lee and Irven DeVore (eds.), *Man the Hunter*. Chicago:
                   Aldine, 1968, pp. 30–48.

    : 24 to 171 : 4 Personal communication.

171 : 5–9   Patricia Draper, "!Kung Women: Contrasts in Sexual
                   Egalitarianism in the Foraging and Sedentary Con-
                   texts." In Rayna Reiter (ed.), *Toward an Anthropology
                   of Women*. In Press.

    : 9–11   Patricia Draper, "Social and Economic Constraints on
                   !Kung Childhood." In R. B. Lee and Irven DeVore
                   (eds.), *Kalahari Hunter-Gatherers*. Cambridge: Harvard
                   University Press. In Press.

    : 12–23   Richard B. Lee, "!Kung Bushmen Violence." Paper pre-
                   sented at the annual meeting of the American Anthro-
                   pological Association, New Orleans, 1969.

173 : 13–20   Irenäus Eibl-Eibesfeldt, "The Myth of the Aggression-
                   Free Hunter and Gatherer Society." In Ralph L. Hol-
                   loway (ed.), *Primate Aggression, Territoriality, and
                   Xenophobia*. New York: Academic Press, 1974, pp. 435–
                   37; I. Eibl-Eibesfeldt, *Die !Ko Buschmann-Gesellschaft*.
                   Munich: Piper, 1972.

Page and Line

173 : 23–29   Robin Fox, *Encounter with Anthropology*. New York: Harcourt Brace Jovanovich, 1973, p. 164.

175 : 3–8   Richard B. Lee, "!Kung Bushmen Violence."

   : 16–18   Elizabeth Marshall Thomas, *The Harmless People*, p. 24.

176 : 4–23   Robert E. Peary, *To the North*. New York: Doubleday, 1910, pp. 46–48.

   : 25–30   Kaj Birket-Smith, *The Eskimos*. New York: Dutton, 1959, p. 55.

   : 33 to   Jean L. Briggs, *Never in Anger*. Cambridge: Harvard
177 : 4   University Press, 1970; Jean L. Briggs, "Aggression Among Two Canadian Eskimo Groups." In W. Muensterberger and A. H. Esman (eds.), *The Psychoanalytic Study of Society*, vol. 6. New York: International Universities Press, 1974, pp. 134–203.

   : 21–33   E. A. Hoebel, *The Law of Primitive Man*. Cambridge: Harvard University Press, 1954, p. 93.

178 : 12–19   Colin M. Turnbull, *The Forest People*. New York: Simon & Schuster, 1961, p. 124.

   : 19–25   Colin M. Turnbull, "Discussion." In *Man the Hunter*, Richard B. Lee and Irven DeVore (eds.), p. 341.

179 : 9–22   W. E. Harney, *Taboo*. Sydney: Australian Publishing Co., 1943, p. 200.

   : 23–29   Wilfred Hilliard, *The People in Between*. New York: Funk & Wagnalls, 1968, p. 127.

180 : 5–12   Baldwin Spencer and Frank J. Gillen, *The Arunta*, vol. 1. New York and London: Macmillan, 1927, p. 446.

   : 13–14   A. P. Elkin, *The Australian Aborigines*. New York: Anchor Books, 1964.

   : 15   Ronald M. Berndt and Catherine H. Berndt, *The World of the First Australians*. Chicago: University of Chicago Press, 1964.

   : 20–22   G. C. Wheeler, *The Tribe and Intertribal Relations in Australia*. London: John Murray, 1910; Nicolas Peterson, "Hunter-Gatherer Territoriality: The Perspective from Australia," *American Anthropologist*, vol. 77, 1975, pp. 53–68.

   : 23–25   C. E. C. Lefroy, "Australian Aborigines, a Noble-Hearted Race," *Contemporary Review* (London), vol. 135, 1919, pp. 222–23.

   : 30–33   A. H. Buss, *The Psychology of Aggression*. New York: Wiley, 1961.

181 : 19–24   Carleton S. Coon, *The Hunting Peoples*. Boston: Little, Brown, p. 51.

Page and Line

182 : 2–9   A. R. Radcliffe-Brown, *The Andaman Islanders*. Cambridge: Cambridge University Press, 1933, pp. 86–87.

: 32 to   John Paul Scott, *Aggression*. Chicago: University of Chi-
183 : 4   cago Press, 1958, p. 11.

: 31 to   In this connection see Colin M. Turnbull, *The Mountain*
184 : 4   *People*. New York: Simon & Schuster, 1972.

: 13–17   J. B. S. Haldane, *The Causes of Evolution*. London: Longmans, Green, 1932, p. 131.

: 24–28   Robert Bigelow, *The Dawn Warriors*. Boston: Little, Brown, p. 163.

: 28–30   Richard D. Alexander, "The Evolution of Social Behavior," *Annual Review of Ecology and Systematics*, vol. 5, 1974, pp. 325–83; Richard D. Alexander, "The Search for an Evolutionary Philosophy of Man," *Proceedings of the Royal Society of Victoria*, vol. 84, 1971, pp. 99–120; Richard D. Alexander, "The Search for a General Theory of Behavior," *Behavioral Science*, vol. 20, 1975, pp. 77–100.

: 31   Edward O. Wilson, *Sociobiology*. Cambridge: Harvard University Press, 1975.

: 34 to   Margaret Mead (ed.), *Cooperation and Competition*
185 : 13   *Among Primitive People*. New York: McGraw-Hill, 1937.

: 21–22   Charles Hose, *Natural Man: A Record from Borneo*. London: Macmillan, 1926.

: 22   W. R. Geddes, *Nine Dayak Nights*. New York: Oxford University Press, 1961.

: 22–23   Raymond Firth, *We, the Tikopia*. London: Allen & Unwin, 1957.

: 23–25   Raymond Firth, *Social Change in Tikopia*. New York: Macmillan, 1959.

: 25–29   Geoffrey Gorer, *Himalayan Village*. London: Michael Joseph, 1938.

: 31 to 186 : 1   Marston Bates, Personal communication, 30 October 1953.

186 : 1–5   Marston Bates and Donald Abbott, *Coral Island*. New York: Scribners, 1958, p. 66.

: 8–13   Ibid., p. 43.

187 : 9–15   Robert I. Levy, *Tahitians: Mind and Experience in the Society Islands*. Chicago: University of Chicago Press, 1973, pp. 276–84.

: 16   Sir Charles Bell, *The People of Tibet*. Oxford: The Clarendon Press, 1928.

Page and Line

187 : 17   M. G. Levin and L. P. Potapov, *The Peoples of Siberia*. Chicago: University of Chicago Press, 1964.

: 17   Roberto Bosi, *The Lapps*. New York: Praeger, 1960.

: 17   Walter W. Skeat and Charles O. Blagden, *Pagan Races of the Malay Peninsula*. 2 vols. New York: Barnes & Noble, 1966; Sir Richard Winstedt, *The Malays: A Cultural History*. New York: Philosophical Library, 1950.

: 18–19   Margaret Mead, *Sex and Temperament in Three Primitive Societies*. New York: Morrow, 1935, p. 25.

188 : 26   Colin M. Turnbull, *The Mountain People*.

189 : 3–7   Robert Ardrey, "Ignoble Savages," *Saturday Review*, 14 October 1972, pp. 72–75.

: 14 to   Colin M. Turnbull, Personal communication, 22 April
191 : 2   1975.

8. The Brain and Aggression

195 : 1–2   For a good discussion see Roger N. Johnson, *Aggression in Man and Animals*. Philadelphia: W. B. Saunders, 1972, pp. 66–85.

: 3–4   A. Brodal, *Neurological Anatomy*. 2nd ed. New York: Oxford University Press, 1969, pp. 538–39.

197 : 14–16   John D. Davies, *Phrenology: Fad and Science*. New Haven: Yale University Press, 1955.

: 29 to   R. L. Gregory, "The Brain as an Engineering Problem."
198 : 2   In W. H. Thorpe and O. L. Zangwill (eds.), *Current Problems in Animal Behaviour*. Cambridge and New York: Cambridge University Press, 1961, pp. 307–30.

199 : 1–5   For an excellent summary of these see Birger Kaada, "Brain Mechanisms Related to Aggressive Behavior." In *Aggression and Defense: Neural Mechanisms and Social Patterns*, Carmen D. Clemente and Donald B. Lindsley (eds.). Los Angeles and Berkeley: University of California Press, 1967, pp. 95–133; J. M. R. Delgado, *Physical Control of the Mind*. New York: Harper & Row, 1969; B. E. Eleftheriou and J. P. Scott (eds.), *The Physiology of Aggression and Defeat*. New York: Plenum Press, 1971; S. Garattini and E. B. Sigg (eds.), *Aggressive Behavior*. New York: Wiley, 1969; V. H. Mark and F. R. Ervin, *Violence and the Brain*. New York: Harper & Row, 1971; D. N. Daniels, M. F. Gilula, and F. M. Ochberg (eds.), *Violence and the Struggle for Existence*. Boston: Little, Brown, 1970; K. Akert, "Dien-

cephalon." In *Electrical Stimulation of the Brain*, D. E. Sheer (ed.). Austin: University of Texas Press, 1961; J. M. R. Delgado, "Free Behavior and Brain Stimulation," *International Review of Neurobiology*, vol. 6, 1964, pp. 349–449; W. R. Hess, *The Functional Organization of the Diencephalon*. New York: Grune & Stratton, 1957.

199 : 30–32   R. Plotnik, D. Mir, and J. M. R. Delgado, "Aggression, Noxiousness, and Brain Stimulation in Unrestrained Rhesus Monkeys." In *The Physiology of Aggression and Defeat*. B. E. Eleftheriou and J. P. Scott (eds.), pp. 143–221.

: 32 to   J. M. R. Delgado, "Social Rank and Radio-Stimulated
200 : 7   Aggressiveness in Monkeys," *Journal of Nervous and Mental Diseases*, vol. 144, 1967, pp. 383–90.

: 7–11   H. E. King, "Psychological Effects of Excitation in the Limbic System." In D. E. Sheer (ed.), *Electrical Stimulation of the Brain*. Austin: University of Texas Press, 1961, pp. 477–86.

: 21–25   Allan F. Mirsky and Nancy Harman, "On Aggressive Behavior and Brain Disease—Some Questions and Possible Relationships Derived from the Study of Men and Monkeys." In Richard E. Whalen (ed.), *The Neuropsychology of Aggression*. New York: Plenum Press, 1974, pp. 185–210; H. E. Rosvold, A. F. Mirsky, and K. H. Pribram, "Influence of Amygdalectomy on Social Behavior in Monkeys," *Journal of Comparative Physiology and Psychology*, vol. 47, 1954, pp. 173–78; Elliot S. Valenstein, *Brain Control*. New York: Wiley, 1973; Elliot S. Valenstein, "Brain Stimulation and the Origin of Violent Behavior," In W. L. Smith and A. Kling (eds.), *Issues in Brain Behavior Control*, New York: Spectrum Publications, 1975; Murray Goldstein, "Brain Research and Violent Behavior," *Archives of Neurology*, vol. 30, 1974, pp. 1–35.

201 : 24–29   B. Kaada, "Brain Mechanisms Related to Aggressive Behavior." In C. D. Clemente and D. B. Lindsley (eds.), *Aggression and Defense*, pp. 95–116.

: 29 to   P. Gloor, "Discussion of 'Brain Mechanisms Related to
202 : 5   Aggressive Behavior,' by B. Kaada." In C. D. Clemente and D. B. Lindsley (eds.), *Aggression and Defense*, pp. 116–27.

: 5–13   E. S. Valenstein, V. C. Cox, and J. W. Kakolewski, "Modi-

Page and Line

fication of Motivated Behavior Elicited by Electrical
Stimulation," *Science*, vol. 159, 1968, pp. 1119–21.

202 : 17–23   J. L. Brown and R. W. Hunsperger, "Neuroethology and
the Motivation of Agonistic Behavior," *Animal Behavior*, vol. 11, 1963, pp. 439–48.

203 : 3–11   Rod Plotnik, "Brain Stimulation and Aggression: Monkeys, Apes, and Humans." In Ralph L. Holloway (ed.),
Primate Aggression, Territoriality and Xenophobia.
New York: Academic Press, 1974, pp. 389–415.

204 : 8–9   V. H. Mark and F. R. Ervin, *Violence and the Brain*. New
York: Harper & Row, 1970.

: 9–10   R. G. Heath, R. R. Monroe, and W. A. Mickle, "Stimulation of the Amygdaloid Nucleus in a Schizophrenic Patient," *American Journal of Psychiatry*, vol. 73, 1955,
pp. 127–29.

: 13   J. M. R. Delgado, "Offensive-Defensive Behaviour in Free
Monkeys and Chimpanzees Induced by Radio Stimulation of the Brain." In S. Garattini and E. B. Sigg (eds.),
Aggressive Behaviour. New York: Wiley, 1969, pp. 109–
19.

: 13   See reference for page 199:30–32.

205 : 3–12   Jerry Hirsch (ed.), *Behavior-Genetic Analysis*. New York:
McGraw-Hill, 1969; David Rosenthal, *Genetic Theory
and Abnormal Behavior*. New York: McGraw-Hill,
1970; D. C. Glass (ed.), *Biology and Behavior: Genetics.*
New York: Rockefeller University Press, 1968; J. E.
Meade and A. S. Parkes (eds.), *Genetic and Environmental Factors in Human Ability*. New York: Plenum
Press, 1968.

: 17–24   R. W. Sperry, "How a Developing Brain Gets Itself Properly Wired for Adaptive Function." In *The Biopsychology of Development*, E. Tobach, L. R. Aronson, and
E. Shaw (eds.). New York: Academic Press, 1971, p. 32.

206 : 6–9   Ibid., p. 43.

: 16–20   Joseph Altman, "Postnatal Neurogenesis and the Problem of Neural Plasticity." In *Developmental Neurobiology*, W. A. Himwich (ed.), Springfield, Ill.: C C
Thomas, 1970, pp. 197–237; Anthony M. Adinolfi, "The
Postnatal Development of Synaptic Contacts in the
Cerebral Cortex." In *Brain Development and Behavior*,
M. B. Sterman, Dennis J. McGinty, and Anthony M.
Adinolfi (eds.). New York: Academic Press, 1971, pp.
73–89; R. J. Robinson (ed.), *Brain and Early Behaviour.*

Page and Line

                        New York: Academic Press, 1969; M. Jacobson, "De-
                        velopment of Specific Neuronal Connections," *Science,*
                        vol. 163, 1969, pp. 543–47.

206 : 32 to 207 : 9   Sperry, op. cit., p. 39.

207 : 17–31   Edward L. Bennett, Marian C. Diamond, David Krech,
                        and Mark R. Rosenzweig, "Chemical and Anatomical
                        Plasticity of the Brain," *Science,* vol. 146, 1964, pp. 610–
                        19; Mark R. Rosenzweig, "Effects of Environment on
                        Development of Brain and of Behavior." In *The Bio-
                        psychology of Development,* E. Tobach, L. R. Aronson,
                        and E. Shaw (eds.). New York: Academic Press, 1971,
                        pp. 303–41. For critical studies of this work see R. F.
                        Thompson, *Foundations of Physiological Psychology.*
                        New York: Harper & Row, 1967; and Barton Meyers,
                        "Early Experience and Problem-Solving Behavior." In
                        Howard Moltz (ed.), *The Ontogeny of Vertebrate Be-
                        havior.* New York: Academic Press, 1971, pp. 57–94.

      : 34 to   John A. Harvey, "Physiological and Pharmacological
208 : 2   Analysis of Behavior." In Richard E. Whalen (ed.), *The
                        Neuropsychology of Aggression.* New York: Academic
                        Press, 1974, pp. 125–47.

      : 2–4   Arthur Yuwiler, "Problems of Assessing Biochemical On-
                        togeny." In *Brain Development and Behavior,* M. B.
                        Sterman, D. J. McGinty, and A. M. Adinolfi (eds.), pp.
                        43–57; Steven Rose, *The Conscious Brain.* New York:
                        Knopf, 1973; C. U. M. Smith, *The Brain.* New York:
                        G. P. Putnam's Sons, 1970; Leonard A. Stevens, *Ex-
                        plorers of the Brain.* New York: Knopf, 1971; Nigel
                        Calder, *The Mind of Man.* New York: Viking, 1971.

      : 17–35   George Ellett Coghill, *Anatomy and the Problem of Be-
                        haviour.* Cambridge: Cambridge University Press, 1929,
                        pp. 109–10.

209 : 9–14   Paul D. MacLean, "Alternative Neural Pathways to Vio-
                        lence." In *Alternatives to Violence,* Larry Ng (ed.). New
                        York: Time-Life Books, 1968, p. 25.

      : 15–16   Vernon H. Mark and Frank R. Ervin, *Violence and the
                        Brain.* New York: Harper & Row, 1970.

      : 17–24   MacLean, op. cit., p. 28.

210 : 7–11   J. A. Stamps, "Social Behavior and Spacing Patterns in
                        Lizards." Manuscript.

211 : 6–11   E. Tobach, J. S. Rosenblatt, and D. S. Lehrman (eds.),
                        Selected Writings of T. C. Schneirla. San Francisco:
                        W. H. Freeman, 1972, p. 46.

Page and Line

211 : 30–33   H. B. Sarnat and M. G. Netsky, *Evolution of the Nervous System.* New York: Oxford University Press, 1974, p. 233.

: 34 to 212 : 2   MacLean, op. cit., p. 33.

212 : 12–14   Steven Rose, *The Conscious Brain.* New York: Knopf, 1973, p. 137.

: 25–33   T. C. Schneirla, op. cit., pp. 48–50, 914–17.

213 : 3 to   Orlando J. Andy and Heinz Stephan, "Comparative Pri-
214 : 3   mate Neuroanatomy of Structures Relating to Aggres-
sive Behavior." In Ralph L. Holloway (ed.), *Primate Aggression, Territoriality, and Xenophobia.* New York: Academic Press, 1974, pp. 305–30.

: 15–17   John A. King, "The Ecology of Aggressive Behavior," *Annals of Ecology and Systematics,* vol. 4, 1973, pp. 117–38.

: 28–31   Robert Ardrey, *The Social Contract.* New York: Atheneum, 1970, p. 353.

: 34 to   Brian Crozier, *A Theory of Conflict.* New York: Scribners,
215 : 10   1975, pp. xii–xiii.

: 11–19   Arthur Koestler, *The Ghost in the Machine.* London: Hutchinson, 1967, pp. 295–96.

216 : 1–8   J. L. Brown and R. L. Hunsperger, "Neuroethology and the Motivation of Agonistic Behavior," *Animal Behavior,* vol. 11, 1963, pp. 439–48.

: 8–14   Charles Boelkins and John H. Heiser, "Biological Bases of Aggression." In D. N. Daniels, M. F. Gilula, and F. M. Ochberg (eds.), *Violence and the Struggle for Existence.* Boston: Little, Brown, 1970, p. 28.

: 15–23   José M. R. Delgado, "The Neurological Basis of Violence." In *Understanding Aggression, International Social Sciences Journal,* vol. 23, 1971, pp. 27–35.

217 : 13 to   José M. R. Delgado, "Recent Advances in Neurophysiol-
218 : 3   ogy." In *The Present Status of Psychotropic Drugs.* Excerpta Medica International Congress Series, No. 180, New York, 1968, pp. 36–48.

: 6–7   B. E. Eleftheriou and J. F. Scott (eds.), *The Physiology of Aggression and Defeat.* New York: Plenum Press, 1971.

: 10–21   José M. R. Delgado, "Psychocivilized Direction of Behavior," *The Humanist,* March/April 1972, p. 15.

: 25 to   D. N. Daniels, M. F. Gilula, "Violence and the Struggle
219 : 10   for Existence." In *Violence and the Struggle for Existence,* D. N. Daniels, M. F. Gilula, and F. M. Ochberg (eds.). Boston: Little, Brown, 1970, p. 408.

: 19–21   Patricia A. Jacobs et al., "Aggressive Behaviour, Mental

Page and Line

                    Sub-Normality and the XYY Male," *Nature*, vol. 208,
                    1965, pp. 1351–52.

220 : 6–9   Ernest B. Hook, "Racial Differentials in the Prevalence
                    Rates of Male Sex Chromosome Abnormalities," *Ameri-
                    can Journal of Human Genetics*, vol. 26, 1974, pp. 504–
                    11.

    : 16–17   S. Kessler and H. S. Moos, "The XYY Karyotype and
                    Criminality: A Review," *Journal of Psychiatric Re-
                    search*, vol. 7, 1970, pp. 153–70; John L. Hamerton and
                    Park S. Gerald, "Studies Cast More Doubt on 'Criminal
                    Gene' Idea," *Journal of the American Medical Associ-
                    ation*, vol. 230, 1974, pp. 655–58.

    : 24–29   Ashley Montagu, "Chromosomes and Crime," *Psychology
                    Today*, vol. 2, 1968, pp. 42–49; see also the thorough-
                    going survey of the literature by W. Züblin, *Chromo-
                    somale Aberrationen und Psyche*. Basel: S. Karger, 1969.

    : 29 to   Ashley Montagu, "The Biologist Looks at Crime," *Annals
221 : 2   of the American Academy of Political and Social Sci-
                    ence*, vol. 217, 1941, pp. 46–57.

222 : 7–14   *New York Times*, 19 December 1972, p. 18.

228 : 20–32   Victor H. Dennenberg and M. X. Zarrow, "Rat Pax," *Psy-
                    chology Today*, vol. 3, 1970, pp. 47, 76.

228 : 32 to 229 : 7 Ibid., p. 67.

229 : 20–27   Ashley Montagu, *Darwin, Competition and Cooperation*.
                    New York: Henry Schuman, 1952.

              9. *The Philosophy of Real Estate and the*
                     Biologically Just Decision

231 : 3–5   Robert Ardrey, *The Territorial Imperative*. New York:
                    Atheneum, 1966, p 3.

233 : 14–29   Ashley Montagu (ed.), *Culture and the Evolution of Man*.
                    New York: Oxford University Press, 1962, p. ix.

    : 31–33   Ashley Montagu, *The Biosocial Nature of Man*. New
                    York: Grove Press, 1956.

234 : 4–12   J. B. Watson, *Psychology, From the Standpoint of a Be-
                    haviorist*. Philadelphia: Lippincott, 1919; J. B. Watson,
                    Behaviorism. New York: The People's Institute, 1925.

236 : 15–20   Noam Chomsky, *Language and Mind*. Enlarged edition.
                    New York: Harcourt Brace Jovanovich, 1972, p. 96.

237 : 6–8   Robert Ardrey, "Four-Dimensional Man," *Encounter*,
                    February 1972, p. 15.

Page and Line

237 : 25–30   François Bourlière, *The Natural History of Mammals.*
New York: Knopf, 1954, p. 100.

  : 32 to   J. L. Brown, "The Evolution of Diversity in Avian Terri-
238 : 2   torial Systems," *Wilson Bulletin*, vol. 76, 1964, pp. 160–
69.

  : 14–17   Thelma Rowell, *Social Behaviour of Monkeys.* Baltimore:
Penguin Books, 1972, p. 165.

239 : 9–17   Brian C. Bates, "Territorial Behavior: A Review of Recent Field Studies," *Primates*, vol. 11, 1970, pp. 271–84.

  : 22–25   Irven DeVore, "Comparative Ecology of Monkeys and
Apes." In *Classification and Human Evolution*, S. L.
Washburn (ed.). New York: Wenner-Gren Foundation,
1963, p. 306.

240 : 12–15   Robert Ardrey, *African Genesis.* New York: Atheneum,
1961, p. 77.

  : 15–24   Irven DeVore and K. R. L. Hall, "Baboon Ecology." In
Primate Behavior, Irven DeVore (ed.). New York: Holt,
Rinehart & Winston, 1965, p. 38.

  : 24–29   J. H. Crook, "Gelada Baboon Herd Structure and Movement." In *Play, Exploration and Territory in Mammals.* New York: Academic Press, 1966, pp. 237–58.

241 : 8–11   Geza Teleki, *The Predatory Behavior of Wild Chimpanzees.* Lewisburg, Pa.: Bucknell University Press, 1973,
pp. 119, 167.

  : 15–19   Hans Kummer, *Social Organization of Hamadryas Baboons: A Field Study.* Chicago: University of Chicago
Press, 1968.

  : 21–22   Eugene Marais, *My Friends, the Baboons.* New York:
Robert McBride, 1939.

  : 25–26   Eugene Marais, *The Soul of the Ape.* New York: Atheneum, 1969.

242 : 15–21   Dian Fossey, "More Years with Mountain Gorillas," *National Geographic*, October 1971, p. 585.

  : 22–26   J. T. Emlen, Jr., "Defended Area?—A Critique of the Territory Concept and of Conventional Thinking," *Ibis*,
vol. 99, 1958, p. 352.

  : 26–28   J. H. Kaufman, "Is Territoriality Definable?" In *Behavior and Environment: The Use of Space by Animals
and Men*, Aristide H. Esser (ed.). New York: Plenum
Press, 1971, pp. 38–40.

  : 28–31   Emlen, op. cit., p. 352.

  : 32 to   Peter H. Klopfer, *Habitats and Territories.* New York:

Page and Line

243 : 4   Basic Books, 1969, p. 102.

   : 5–9   Ibid., p. 105.

   :14–25   S. A. Barnett, "The Biology of Aggression," *The Lancet*,
                   vol. 2, 10 October 1964, pp. 803–7.

   : 30–31   Solly Zuckerman, *The Social Life of Monkeys and Apes.*
                   New York: Harcourt, Brace, 1932.

244 : 1–2   D. W. Chapman, "Food and Space as Regulators of Sal-
                   monid Populations in Streams," *American Naturalist*,
                   vol. 100, 1966, pp. 345–56; J. S. Gartlan and C. S. Brain,
                   "Ecology and Social Variability in *Cercopithecus aethi-
                   ops* and *C. mitis*." In P. C. Jay (ed.), *Primates*. New
                   York: Holt, Rinehart & Winston, 1968, 235–92.

   : 7 to   T. H. Langlois, "A Study of the Small-Mouth Bass, *Mi-
245 : 5   cropterus dolomieu* (Lacepede), in Rearing Ponds in
                   Ohio," *Ohio Biological Survey, Ohio State University
                   Studies*, Bulletin No. 33, vol. 6, 1936; T. H. Langlois,
                   "Sociological Succession," *Ecology*, vol. 18, 1937, pp.
                   458–61.

   : 6–9   P. K. Anderson, "Density, Social Structure and Non-Social
                   Environment in House-Mouse Populations and the Im-
                   plications for Regulations of Numbers," *Transactions
                   of the New York Academy of Sciences*, series II, no. 5,
                   1961, pp. 447–51.

   : 10–13   T. Struhsaker, "Auditory Communication Among Vervet
                   Monkeys." In *Social Communication Among Primates*,
                   Stuart A. Altmann (ed.). Chicago: University of Chicago
                   Press, 1967, pp. 281–324.

   : 15–17   J. S. Gartlan, "Ecology and Behaviour of the Vervet Mon-
                   key." Lolui Island, Lake Victoria, Uganda. Ph.D. dis-
                   sertation, Bristol University Library, 1966.

   : 17–23   Ueli Nagel and Hans Kummer, "Variation in Cercopithe-
                   coid Aggressive Behavior." In Ralph L. Holloway (ed.),
                   Primate Aggression, Territoriality, and Xenophobia.
                   New York: Academic Press, 1974, pp. 159–84.

   : 30–33   John H. Crook, "The Nature and Function of Territorial
                   Aggression." In *Man and Aggression*, Ashley Montagu
                   (ed.). 2nd ed. New York: Oxford University Press, 1973,
                   pp. 183–220; Peter H. Klopfer, *Habitats and Terri-
                   tories: A Discourse on the Spatial Distribution of Ani-
                   mals*. New York: Basic Books, 1969.

246 : 8–17   Wallace Craig, "Appetites and Aversions as Constituents
                   of Instincts," *Biological Bulletin*, vol. 34, 1918, pp. 91–

107; Wallace Craig, "Why Do Animals Fight?" *International Journal of Ethics*, vol. 31, 1928, pp. 246–78.

246 : 24–27   Crook, loc. cit., p. 198.

247 : 10–14   Charles H. Southwick, "Aggression Among Nonhuman Primates," Reading, Mass.: Addison-Wesley, Module No. 23, 1972, pp. 1–23.

248 : 3–7   C. R. Carpenter, "A Field Study in Siam of the Behavior and Social Relations of the Gibbon *(Hylobates lar),*" *Comparative Psychology Monographs*, vol. 16, no. 5, 1940, p. 158.

    : 11–15   C. R. Carpenter, "A Field Study of the Behavior and Social Relations of Howling Monkeys *(Alouatta palliata),*" *Comparative Psychology Monographs*, vol. 10, no. 2, 1934, p. 50.

    : 25–32   Robert Ardrey, *The Territorial Imperative*. New York: Atheneum, 1966, p. 3.

249 : 20   Desmond Morris, *The Naked Ape*. New York: McGraw-Hill, 1967, p. 176; Desmond Morris, *The Human Zoo*. New York: McGraw-Hill, 1969, pp. 125–26.

    : 20   Anthony Storr, *Human Aggression*. New York: Atheneum, 1968. Anthony Storr, *Human Destructiveness*. New York: Basic Books, 1972.

    : 20   Irenäus Eibl-Eibesfeldt, *Love and Hate: The Natural History of Behavior Patterns*. New York: Holt, Rinehart & Winston, 1972.

    : 27 to   Richard B. Lee, "Territorial Boundaries." In *Man the
250 : 2   Hunter*, Richard B. Lee and Irven DeVore (eds.). Chicago: Aldine, 1968, p. 157.

    : 2–8   Ibid., for a discussion of these and other hunting peoples.

    :15–17   T. G. H. Strehlow, "Culture, Social Structure, and Environment in Aboriginal Central Australia." In *Aboriginal Man in Australia*, R. M. Berndt and C. H. Berndt (eds.). Sydney: Angus & Robertson, 1965, p. 128.

    : 18–22   A. R. Radcliffe-Brown, "Patrilineal and Matrilineal Succession," *The Iowa Law Review*, vol. 20, no. 2, 1935. Reprinted in A. R. Radcliffe-Brown, *Structure and Function in Primitive Society*. New York: Free Press, 1952, p. 33.

    : 24–28   L. R. Hiatt, "Ownership and Use of Land Among the Australian Aborigines." In *Man the Hunter*, Richard B. Lee and Irven DeVore (eds.), p. 100.

    : 28–34   Ibid. See also Nicolas Peterson, "Hunter-Gatherer Terri-

Page and Line

          toriality," *American Anthropologist*, vol. 77, 1975, pp. 53–68.

250 : 34 to 251 : 2   For an account of this see T. G. H. Strehlow, op. cit.

251 : 4–8   James N. Anderson, "Analysis of Group Composition." In *Man the Hunter*, p. 154.

     : 10–16   Julian H. Steward, "Causal Factors and Processes in the Evolution of Pre-Farming Societies." In *Man the Hunter*, p. 334.

253 : 6–8   Robert Ardrey, "Why Is Man So Different?" *Time*, 22 May 1972, p. 69.

     : 16–18   Geza Teleki, *The Predatory Behavior of Wild Chimpanzees.* Lewisburg. Pa.: Bucknell University Press, 1973, p. 173.

254 : 6–10   Konrad Lorenz, *On Aggression.* New York: Harcourt, Brace & World, 1966, p. 270.

     : 34 to   Robert Ardrey, *The Territorial Imperative.* New York:
255 : 1   Atheneum, 1966, p. 103.

     : 15–17   H. von Albrecht, "Freiwasser Beobachtungen an Tilapien (Pisces, Cichlidae) in Ostafrika," *Zeitschrift für Tierpsychologie*, vol. 25, 1968, pp. 377–94.

     : 17–18   Peter Marler, "On Aggression in Birds." In *Topics in Animal Behavior*, V. G. Dethier (ed.). New York: Harper & Row, 1971.

     : 18–19   P. H. Klopfer, *Habitats and Territories.* New York: Basic Books, 1969.

256 : 21–24   Robert Ardrey, *The Territorial Imperative*, p. 266.

257 : 20–24   J. B. Birdsell, "Some Environmental and Cultural Factors Influencing the Structure of Australian Aboriginal Populations," *American Naturalist Supplement*, vol. 87, 1953, pp. 169–207.

     : 24–29   P. H. Klopfer, *Behavioral Aspects of Ecology.* 2nd ed. Englewood Cliffs, N.J.: Prentice-Hall, 1973, p. 143.

10. War and Violence

258 : 1–5   Konrad Lorenz, *On Aggression.* New York: Harcourt, Brace & World, 1966, pp. 284–85.

     : 6–11   Robert Ardrey, *African Genesis.* New York: Atheneum, 1961, p. 172.

     : 11–14   Ibid., p. 173.

     : 15–17   Robert Ardrey, *The Territorial Imperative.* New York: Atheneum, 1966, p. 236.

Page and Line

259 : 1–5   See Erich Fromm's discussion of Hitler in his *The Anatomy of Human Destructiveness*. New York: Holt, Rine-
hart & Winston, 1973.

: 6–9   Edmund Leach, "Don't Say 'Boo' to a Goose." In *Man and
Aggression*, Ashley Montagu (ed.). 2nd ed. New York:
Oxford University Press, 1973, p. 158.

: 15 to   Niko Tinbergen, "On War and Peace in Animals and
260 : 6   Man," *Science*, vol. 160, 1968, pp. 1411–18.

: 9–18   Desmond Morris, *The Naked Ape*. New York: McGraw-
Hill, 1967, p. 176.

: 30–34   Anthony Storr, *Human Aggression*. New York: Atheneum,
1968, p. xi.

263 : 34 to   Claude Lévi-Strauss, *Tristes Tropiques*. New York: Athe-
264 : 5   neum, 1974, p. 282.

265 : 5–22   E. F. M. Durbin and John Bowlby, *Personal Aggressiveness and War*. New York: Columbia University Press,
1939; Seymour L. Halleck, *Psychiatry and the Dilem-
mas of Crime*. New York: Harper & Row, 1967; David
Abrahamsen, *The Psychology of Crime*. New York: Columbia University Press, 1960; William McCord and
Joan McCord, *Origins of Crime*. New York: Columbia
University Press, 1960; Nigel Walker, *Crime and Punishment in Britain*. Edinburgh: at the University Press,
1965; John H. Cassity, *The Quality of Murder*. New
York: Julian Press, 1958; George Godwin, *Criminal
Man*. New York: George Braziller, 1957; Donald R.
Taft and Ralph W. England, Jr., *Criminology*. New
York: Macmillan, 1956; H. J. Eysenck, *Crime and Per-
sonality*. Boston: Houghton Mifflin, 1964; Austin L. Por-
terfield, *Cultures of Violence*. Fort Worth: Texas Chris-
tian University, 1965; S. Palmer, *A Study of Murder*.
New York: Thomas Y. Crowell, 1960; Ashley Montagu,
The Direction of Human Development. Rev. ed. New
York: Hawthorn Books, 1970.

: 24–28   Stanislav Andreski, *Military Organization and Society*.
Berkeley: University of California Press, 1968; Stanislav
Andreski, *The Uses of Comparative Sociology*. Berkeley:
University of California Press, 1965.

: 30 to   Richard G. van Gelder, "An Instinct for War?" *New York
266 : 3   Times Magazine*, 1 October 1967.

: 11–17   Storr, op. cit., p. 36.

: 30 to   Ralph Beals and Harry Hoijer, *An Introduction to An-
267 : 4   thropology*. 4th ed. New York: Macmillan, 1971, p. 408.

Page and Line

267 : 11–19   Robert H. Lowie, *Indians of the Plains.* New York:
                   McGraw-Hill, 1954.

    : 20–24   Harold E. Driver, *Indians of North America.* Chicago:
                   University of Chicago Press, 1971, p. 355.

    : 29–32   Sigmund Freud, "Why War?" *Collected Papers,* vol. 5.
                   New York: Basic Books, 1959.

268 : 9–16   Keith F. Otterbein, "The Anthropology of War." In
                   Handbook of Social and Cultural Anthropology, John
                   J. Honigmann (ed.). Chicago: Rand McNally, 1973, pp.
                   923–58.

    : 17 to   Verrier Elwin, *The Tribal World of Verrier Elwin: An
269 : 6   Autobiography.* New York: Oxford University Press,
                   1964, pp. 121–22; Verrier Elwin, *The Baiga.* London:
                   John Murray, 1939.

    : 13–16   W. H. R. Rivers, *The Todas.* London: Macmillan, 1906.

    : 25–34   L. T. Hobhouse, G. C. Wheeler, and M. Ginsberg, *The
                   Material Culture and Social Institutions of the Simpler
                   Peoples.* London: Chapman & Hall, 1915, p. 288. See
                   also Regnar Numelin, *The Beginnings of Diplomacy.*
                   New York: Philosophical Library, 1950.

270 : 6–8   Roberto Bosi, *The Lapps.* New York: Praeger, 1960; Frank
                   H. Butler, *Through Lapland with Skis and Reindeer.*
                   London: T. Fisher Unwin, 1917.

    : 21–23   M. G. Levin and L. P. Potapov (eds.), *The Peoples of Si-
                   beria.* Chicago: University of Chicago Press, 1964; M. A.
                   Czaplicka, *Aboriginal Siberia.* New York: Oxford Uni-
                   versity Press, 1914, reprinted 1969.

    : 25–27   Keith F. Otterbein, *The Evolution of War: A Cross-
                   Cultural Study.* New Haven: Human Relations Area
                   File Press, 1970.

272 : 2–8   On this subject see Hannah Arendt, *On Violence.* New
                   York: Harcourt, Brace & World, 1970.

    : 9–22   Karl E. Scheibe, "Legitimized Aggression and the Assign-
                   ment of Evil," *The American Scholar,* vol. 43, 1974, pp.
                   576–92.

    : 23–26   Jean Rostand, "A Gentle, Rumpled French Biologist Says,"
                   The New York Times, 30 May 1972, p. 2.

    : 27 to   Bernard Brodie, "Theories on the Causes of War." In
273 : 4   *War and the Human Race,* Maurice N. Walsh (ed.).
                   New York: Elsevier, 1971, p. 18.

    : 27 to   Friedrich von Bernhardi, *Germany and the Next War.*
274 : 5   New York: Longmans, Green, 1912.

276 : 11–13   Konrad Lorenz, *On Aggression.* New York: Harcourt,
                   Brace & World, 1966, p. 178.

References

357

Page and Line

276 : 30 to
277 : 1 — Anthony Storr, *Human Aggression*. New York: Atheneum, 1968, pp. 117–18.

: 17–21 — Richard D. Sipes, "War, Sports and Aggression: An Empirical Test of Two Rival Theories," *American Anthropologist*, vol. 75, 1973, pp. 64–86.

280 : 3–7 — John H. Crook, *The Nature and Function of Territorial Aggression*. 2nd ed. Ashley Montagu (ed.), New York: Oxford University Press, 1973, pp. 215–16.

: 16–23 — Roger N. Johnson, *Aggression in Man and Animals*. Philadelphia: W. B. Saunders & Co., 1972; Leonard Berkowitz, *Aggression: A Social Psychological Analysis*. New York: McGraw-Hill, 1962; A. H. Buss, *The Psychology of Aggression*. New York: Wiley, 1961.

: 26–29 — William Menninger, "Recreation and Mental Health," *Recreation*, vol. 42, 1948, pp. 340–46. See also his brother's work, Karl Menninger, *Love Against Hate*. New York: Harcourt, Brace, 1942.

: 31–33 — Leonard Berkowitz, *Control of Aggression*. 1971. (Unpublished.)

: 33–34 — Warren R. Johnson, "Aggression," *Psychology Today*, October 1970, pp. 70–73.

281 : 1–4 — *National Commission on the Causes and Prevention of Violence*. Washington, D.C.: Government Printing Office, 1968.

: 4–7 — Albert Bandura, *Aggression: A Social Learning Analysis*. Englewood Cliffs, N.J.: Prentice-Hall, 1973, pp. 148ff.

: 20–23 — Konrad Lorenz, "Lorenz Warns: 'Man Must Know That the Horse He Is Riding May Be Wild and Should Be Bridled,' " *Psychology Today*, November 1974, p. 93.

11. Ideological Consequences

284 : 22–23 — Aljean Harmetz, "Man Was a Killer Long Before He Served a God," *New York Times*, 31 August 1969, p. D9.

287 : 22 to
288 : 2 — S. C. McRae, "Inheritance of the Earth," *Journal of the American Medical Association*, 26 April 1971, p. 679.

289 : 21–29 — Konrad Lorenz, *On Aggression*. New York: Harcourt, Brace & World, 1966, p. 253.

290 : 4–8 — Patrick Bateson, "Naked Apes and Corporation Men," *The Listener* (London), 14 September 1972, pp. 332–35.

291 : 2–5 — Ashley Montagu, *Darwin, Competition, and Cooperation*. New York: Henry Schuman, 1952.

Page and Line

291 : 22–32   Roderick Nash, *Wilderness and the American Mind*. New Haven: Yale University Press, 1973, pp. viii, x.

292 : 7–8   Joseph Jastrow (ed.), *The Story of Human Error*. New York: Appleton Century, 1936.

: 21–30   Robert Ardrey, *The Social Contract*. New York: Atheneum, 1970, pp. 13–14.

: 31 to   Review of *The Social Contract*. In *The New Republic*, 31
293 : 1   October 1970, pp. 31–32.

: 3–10   Robert Ardrey, op. cit., p. 12.

: 13–14   Ibid., p. 23.

: 31 to   Vincent R. Ruggiero, "When Description Becomes Crea-
294 : 3   tion," *Karamu* (Eastern Illinois University), vol. 2, April 1969, pp. 3–7.

: 7–9   Konrad Lorenz, *On Aggression*, p. 253.

: 30 to   Patrick Bateson, "Naked Apes and Corporation Men,"
295 : 3   p. 335.

: 31 to   John H. Crook, "Introduction." In J. H. Crook (ed.), *So-
296 : 3   cial Behaviour in Birds and Mammals*. New York: Academic Press, p. xxiii.

: 7–9   Robert Ardrey, *The Social Contract;* Frédéric de Towarnicki, "A Talk with Konrad Lorenz," *New York Times Magazine*, 5 July 1970, pp. 4seq.

: 9–13   Ardrey, op. cit., p. 63.

: 15–26   Theodosius Dobzhansky and Ashley Montagu, "Natural Selection and the Mental Capacities of Mankind," *Science*, vol. 105, 1947, pp. 587–90.

: 26 to   George Gaylord Simpson, *Biology and Man*. New York:
297 : 2   Harcourt, Brace & World, 1969, pp. 104–5.

: 11–12   Reference for 296:7–9, interview with Frédéric de Towarnicki.

12. Conclusions

303 : 9–14   Ashley Montagu, *Darwin, Competition and Cooperation*. New York: Henry Schuman, 1952; W. C. Allee, *Cooperation Among Animals*. New York: Henry Schuman, 1951; Ashley Montagu, *The Direction of Human Development*. Rev. ed. New York: Hawthorn Books, 1970; Petr Kropotkin, *Mutual Aid*. London: Heinemann, 1902; T. A. Goudge, *The Ascent of Life*. London: Allen & Unwin, 1961; J. H. Crook, "Introduction." In *Social Behaviour in Birds and Animals*, John H. Crook (ed.). New

York: Academic Books, 1970, pp. xxv–xxx; John H. Crook, "Sources of Cooperation in Animals and Man." In J. F. Eisenberg and Wilton S. Dillon (eds.), *Man and Beast.* Washington, D.C.: Smithsonian Institution Press, 1971, pp. 235–60; Paul Shepard, *The Tender Carnivore and the Sacred Game.* New York: Scribners, 1973.

303 : 24–25   Michael W. Fox, *Behaviour of Wolves, Dogs and Related Canids.* New York: Harper & Row, 1971.

305 : 1–7   Roger N. Johnson, *Aggression in Man and Animals.* Philadelphia: W. B. Saunders, 1972, p. 211.

: 7–14   J. P. Scott, "That Old Time Aggression," *The Nation,* 9 January 1967, pp. 53–54.

: 14–19   Erich Fromm, *The Anatomy of Human Destructiveness.* New York: Holt, Rinehart & Winston, 1973, p. 20.

: 25–31   Dennis Chitty, "Crowding Together," *Science,* vol. 173, 1971, p. 42.

306 : 25–27   J. H. Crook, "The Nature and Function of Territorial Aggression." In *Man and Aggression,* Ashley Montagu (ed.). 2nd ed. New York: Oxford University Press, 1973, p. 217.

307 : 18–20   Colin M. Turnbull, *The Mountain People.* New York: Simon & Schuster, 1972.

: 21–26   Robert Ardrey, in an advertisement in the *New York Times,* 8 January 1973, p. L37. See also his review of Turnbull's book, *Saturday Review,* 14 October 1972, pp. 73–75.

310 : 29–31   Ashley Montagu, *Man's Most Dangerous Myth: The Fallacy of Race.* 5th ed. New York: Oxford University Press, 1974; Ashley Montagu, *Statement on Race.* 3rd ed. New York: Oxford University Press, 1972; George Gaylord Simpson, *Biology and Man.* New York: Harcourt, Brace & World, 1969, p. 104; Margaret Mead, Ethel Tobach, and Robert E. Light (eds.), *Science and the Concept of Race.* New York: Columbia University Press, 1970; Theodosius Dobzhansky, *Genetic Diversity and Human Dignity.* New York: Basic Books, 1973; James C. King, *The Biology of Race.* New York: Harcourt Brace Jovanovich, 1971; Unesco, *Race and Science.* New York: Columbia University Press, 1961. Ashley Montagu (ed.), *Race and IQ.* New York: Oxford University Press, 1974; Milton Kamin, *The Science and Politics of IQ.* Hillsdale, N.J.: Lawrence Erlbaum Associates, 1974.

360   *References*

Page and Line

310 : 32 to   Paul E. Simonds, *The Social Primates.* New York: Harper
311 : 2   & Row, 1974, p. 3.

  : 9–13   Ludwik Krzywicki, *Primitive Society and Its Vital Statis-
                   tics.* New York: Macmillan, 1934; Richard B. Lee and
                   Irven DeVore (eds.), *Man the Hunter.* Chicago: Aldine,
                   1968; Richard B. Lee, "Population Growth and the Be-
                   ginnings of Sedentary Life Among the !Kung Bush-
                   men." In *Population Growth: Anthropological Implica-
                   tions,* Brian Spooner (ed.). Cambridge: Massachusetts
                   Institute of Technology Press, 1972, pp. 329–42.

  : 31 to   W. D. Hambly, *Origins of Education Among Primitive
312 : 3   Peoples.* London: Macmillan, 1926; Nathan Miller, *The
                   Child in Primitive Society.* New York: Brentano, 1928;
                   John Middleton (ed.), *From Child to Adult.* Garden
                   City, N.Y.: Natural History Press, 1970.

  : 31   Marshall Sahlins, *Stone Age Economics.* Chicago: Aldine-
                   Atherton, 1972; Erich Neumann, *The Great Mother.*
                   New York: Pantheon, 1955.

313 : 23 to   Paul Radin, *The World of Primitive Man.* New York:
314 : 1   Grove Press, 1953, p. 11.

  : 2–6   Ibid., p. 340.

  : 7–11   For an excellent discussion of this see Stanley Diamond,
                   "The Uses of the Primitive." In *Primitive Views of the
                   World,* Stanley Diamond (ed.). New York: Columbia
                   University Press, 1964, pp. v, xxix; see also Joseph B.
                   Casagrande (ed.), *In the Company of Man.* New York:
                   Harper & Bros., 1960.

315 : 30   Weston La Barre, *The Human Animal.* Chicago: Univer-
                   sity of Chicago Press, 1954.

318 : 18–25   Lydia Jackson, *Aggression and Its Interpretation.* London:
                   Methuen, 1954; Ian Suttie, *The Origins of Love and
                   Hate.* New York: Julian Press, 1966; Ashley Montagu,
                   The Direction of Human Development. Rev. ed. New
                   York: Hawthorn Books, 1970; A. H. Buss, *The Psychol-
                   ogy of Aggression.* New York: Wiley, 1961; R. R. Sears,
                   "Relation of Early Socialization Experiences to Aggres-
                   sion in Middle Childhood," *Journal of Abnormal and
                   Social Psychology,* vol. 63, 1971, pp. 466–92; E. F. M.
                   Durbin and John Bowlby, *Personal Aggressiveness and
                   War.* New York: Columbia University Press, 1939; Lau-
                   retta Bender, *Aggression, Hostility and Anxiety in Chil-
                   dren.* Springfield, Ill.: C C Thomas, 1953; Leonard D.
                   Aron, Leopold O. Walder, and Monroe M. Lefkowitz,

Learning of Aggression in Children. Boston: Little, Brown, 1971; Leonard Berkowitz, *Aggression: A Social Psychological Analysis.* New York: McGraw-Hill, 1961; John Paul Scott, *Aggression.* Chicago: University of Chicago Press, 1958; Seymour Feschbach, "Aggression." In *Carmichael's Manual of Child Psychology,* Paul H. Mussen (ed.), vol. 2. New York: McGraw-Hill, 1970, pp. 159–259; Ernest Becker, *Angel in Armor.* New York: George Braziller, 1969; Austin L. Porterfield, *Cultures of Violence.* Fort Worth: Texas Christian University, 1965; Erich Fromm, *The Anatomy of Human Destructiveness.* New York: Holt, Rinehart & Winston, 1973; Albert Bandura, *Aggression: A Social Learning Analysis.* Englewood Cliffs, N.J.: Prentice-Hall, Inc., 1973; Jerome L. Singer (ed.), *The Control of Aggression and Violence.* New York: Academic Press, 1971; Jan de Wit and Willard W. Hartup (eds.), *Determinants and Origins of Aggressive Behavior.* The Hague: Mouton, 1975.

321 : 19–25   For a novelistic treatment of this theme for the Asiatic Indian scene see Kamala Markandaya's beautiful novel, *Nectar in a Sieve.* New York: John Day, 1964; for the American Black there are many books, but see especially Claude Brown's *Manchild in the Promised Land.* New York: Macmillan, 1965; for South Africa see Naboth Mokgatle, *The Autobiography of an Unknown South African.* Berkeley: University of California Press, 1971; for Jews see Erich Kahler, *The Jews Among the Nations.* New York: Frederick Ungar, 1967; Abram Leon Sachar, *A History of the Jews.* 5th ed. New York: Knopf, 1967; for nonliterate peoples see Joseph Casagrande (ed.). *In the Company of Man.* New York: Harper & Bros., 1960.

322 : 1–2   Erich Fromm, *The Heart of Man.* New York: Harper & Row, 1971, p. 192. See also Herbert Selg (ed.), *The Making of Human Aggression.* New York: St. Martin's Press, 1976, p. 57.

   : 23–28   Robert Ardrey, *African Genesis.* New York: Atheneum, 1961, p. 333.

   : 32 to 323 : 4   Ibid., pp. 21–22.

323 : 11–12   Milton R. Barron, *The Juvenile Delinquent Society.* New York: Knopf, 1954; William C. Kvaraceus et al., *Delinquent Behavior.* Washington, D.C.: National Education Association, 1959; Juan B. Cortés with Florence M.

Page and Line

Gatti, *Delinquency and Crime*. New York: Seminar Press, 1965; Ashley Weeks, *Youthful Offenders at Highfields*. Ann Arbor: University of Michigan Press, 1963; Seymour Rubenfeld, *Family of Outcasts*. New York: Free Press, 1965; Travis Hirschi, *Causes of Delinquency*. Berkeley: University of California Press, 1969; Jeffrey H. Goldstein, *Aggression and Crimes of Violence*. New York: Oxford University Press, 1975.

323 : 16–21   Émile Durkheim, *Suicide*. New York: Free Press, 1951, p. 209.

324 : 13–15   Ian Suttie, *The Origins of Love and Hate*. New York: Julian Press, 1966; John Bowlby, *Attachment and Loss*. 2 vols. New York: Basic Books, 1969–73; Ashley Montagu, *The Direction of Human Development*. Rev. ed. New York: Hawthorn Books, 1970.

Index